OUTWARD
LEG

TRISTAN JONES

OUTWARD LEG

QUILL
WILLIAM MORROW
New York

Originally published by the Bodley Head, Ltd, England,
in 1985 under the title *A Star to Steer Her By*

It is the policy of William Morrow and Company, Inc., and its imprints and
affiliates, recognizing the importance of preserving what has been written, to print
the books we publish on acid-free paper, and we exert our best efforts to that
end.

Library of Congress Cataloging-in-Publication Data

Jones, Tristan, 1924–
    [A star to steer her by]
    Outward Leg / Tristan Jones—1st Quill ed.
      p.   cm.
    Previously published as: A star to steer her by. 1985.
    ISBN 0-688-08255-6 (pbk.)
    I. Jones Tristan, 1924–   . 2. Outward Leg (Yacht) 3. Voyages
and travels—1951–1980.   I. Title.
G470.J642   1988
910.4'5—dc19   88-11426
                                                                     CIP

Printed in the United States of America

First Quill Edition

    2 3 4 5 6 7 8 9 10

BOOK DESIGN BY PATRICE FODERO

*To the meek, who shall inherit what's left of the earth,
and to Ivan Buenza González, of San Sebastián, Spain,
for his intense loyalty in difficult times*

Foreword

I have written most of this book either as the events described in the recent past were going on, or shortly afterward.

It is the story of how I met with disaster in the midst of triumph, and how I struggled to overcome it. It is the tale of how I returned to sea despite almost unimaginable obstacles placed in my way by the fates. It is the account of how I turned a desperate situation into an opportunity to serve others. It is also the tale of how I incidentally sailed fourteen thousand miles on my way around the world.

If what I write here brings some hope to people who might have lost it, or might never have known it, then all my struggle, all my suffering and all my hard labors over the past three years will not have been in vain. Nothing is of value unless it is shared.

I believe now that a true state of grace can only be reached through suffering. I have not yet reached that state of grace, but I do not despair over the suffering ahead of me, because I know that when I at last have grace, the prize will have been well earned, and worth all the long, long days and nights of agony.

To other handicapped people, and especially to the young, I say do not ever forget, for one minute, that you can be of use to someone else who, in some way, is less fortunate than you. Go and find that someone, somehow. Do not give up. Do not despair. The gift of life in you is too precious. Fight; stand your ground and fight; move and fight. The strength you will expend will be strength gained. Fight for others, too, and you will be fighting for yourself. Find something you can do well, and try to do it better than anyone else.

Never despair. Without hope there can be no faith; without faith in the world and in yourself there can be no true love, no real compassion, and without compassion there can be no future. You are part of the future. Therefore: fight for yourself; stay the course!

Bahía Concha, Colombia,
St. Kruis Bai, Curaçao, and
St. Katherine's Dock, London
Onboard Outward Leg
February–September 1984

Contents

Foreword   7

PART ONE: CONCHITA

1   A Tale of Two Cities   15
2   The Crunch   24
3   The Kept Promise   32
4   Outward Leg   40
5   The Crucible   46
6   Of Shoes and Ships and Sealing Wax . . .   54
7   . . . and Cabbages and Kings   60
8   Ready . . .   68
9   . . . Go!   75
10 Naked Under the Stars   85
11 Mexican Encounters   93
12 The Rich Coast   102
13 A Nest of Thieves   111
14 Old Haunts   120
15 Old Friends   128
16 The Springboard   136
17 The Spanish Main   145
18 Out in the Blue   154
19 The Chase   162
20 The Pirate Coast   170
21 Smugglers   179
22 Escape   188
23 Into the Lion's Den . . . and Out   197

PART TWO: TO LONDON

24	*The Treasure Coast*	209
25	*A Sailor's Heaven*	218
26	*Raves and Caves*	228
27	*Another Bloody Revolt*	237
28	*The Big Apple*	245
29	*Across the Western Ocean*	253
30	*Old Friends, New Faces*	262
31	*Home—and Dry*	272
	Epilogue	283
	Acknowledgments	285

"Nid a bwyall y mae canu crwth"
("A violin is not played with an axe")
—WELSH PROVERB

"A tree is not felled with a bow"
—TRISTAN JONES

PART ONE

Conchita

I must down to the seas again, to the
  lonely sea and the sky,
And all I ask is a tall ship and a star
  to steer her by,
And the wheel's kick and the wind's
  song and the white sail's shaking,
And the grey mist on the sea's face
  and a grey dawn breaking.

I must down to the seas again, for the
  call of the running tide
Is a wild call and a clear call that may
  not be denied;
And all I ask is a windy day with the
  white clouds flying,
And the flung spray and the blown
  spume, and the sea-gulls crying.

I must down to the seas again, to the
  vagrant gypsy life,
To the gull's way and the whale's way
  where the wind's like a whetted
  knife;
And all I ask is a merry yarn from a
  laughing fellow-rover,
And quiet sleep and a sweet dream
  when the long trick's over.

"Sea-Fever," by John Masefield

1

A Tale of Two Cities

As I rolled down old South Street, a fair maid I did meet,
Who asked me then to see her home, she lived on Fountain Street.

Chorus:
And away, you Johnny, my dear honey,
Oh! you New York gals, you love us for our money!

Says I, "My dear young lady, I'm a stranger here in town,
I left my ship only yesterday, to Lisbon I am bound."

"Now come with me, my dearie, and I will stand you treat,
I'll buy you rum and brandy, dear, and tabnabs for to eat."

When we got down to Fourteenth Street, we stopped at Number Four,
Her mother and her sister came to meet us at the door.

And when we got inside the house, the drinks were handed round,
The likker was so awful strong my head went round and round.

Before we all sat down to eat we had another drink,
The likker was so very strong, deep sleep came in a wink.

When I awoke next morning I had an aching head,
And there was I, Jack all-alone, stark naked on the bed.

My gold watch and my pocket book and lady friend were gone,
And there was I with not a stitch and left there all alone.

On looking all around the room, oh nothing did I see,
But a lady's shift and pantaloons not worth a damn to me.

With a flour barrel for a suit I wished I'd never been born,
A boarding master then I met who shipped me 'round the Horn.

Now all you bully sailormen take warning when ashore,
Or else you'll meet some charming gal who's nothing but a whore.

Your hard earned cash will disappear, your rig and boots as well,
For Yankee gals are tougher than the other side of Hell!

"New York Gals," a bowline shanty from the heyday of sail in the
latter half of the nineteenth century

Some of the great cities of the world are sailors' cities, built by peoples
of the sea for the sea peoples—Bristol, Liverpool, Copenhagen, Amsterdam, Lisbon, Venice, Hong Kong, Singapore, Sydney, San Francisco, and although she does not on the surface care to show it too
flagrantly, New York.

Of all these, the most obvious sailors' city is Amsterdam; the least,
New York or, as she was once known, New Amsterdam, but anyone
who really knows these cities and is not affectionate toward both of them
cannot, I think, be counted as a sailor who knows his roots.

Amsterdam preserves her sea heritage carefully. Some parts of the
city reek of the sea and of distant voyages—as indeed they should, for
the three greatest capes in the world all have Dutch names—Horn,
Leeuwin and Good Hope—and the city was in the main founded upon
treasure wrested from lands at the very ends of the earth.

New York, apart from a valiant attempt at the South Street Seaport, does her best to ignore the sea—to treat it as though it does not
exist. For her the sea is somewhere that taxi drivers go to with their
families on holidays, somewhere to splash in, at places like Fire Island
or Coney Island. To New York the sea is something that generations of
immigrants crossed in often squalid conditions, to reach the promised
land; it is something to be remembered with a coy horror, something to
turn one's back on so as to face the golden prairies and a land flowing
with milk and honey. That, it seems, is how the vast majority of New
Yorkers view the sea; but there are communities in the city, tiny and
scattered, that yet live by the sea and on the sea. Often, surprisingly,
walking down some busy traffic-laden street in Lower Manhattan or
Brooklyn, a sailor sees some magic remembrance of the sea and sailors
of the past. It might be some odd line in the structure of a building, a
door lintel, a window in Greenwich Village, a beam in a bar. Somehow
a sailor knows that it was put there by a sailor, and a warm feeling, rare
in Babylon, stirs his soul. Sometimes I see a face in a hundred thousand, perhaps a young face, perhaps an old face, and I know that he or
his forebears were of the sea. It might be an Irish face, Portuguese,
Danish, African or Dutch, but I know by the stance and the set that
the sea has worked her will on his people for centuries, and he stands

out clearly to me among the millions of landsmen.

When I walked down the West Side Highway—when I could walk down it—as I did most mornings, the rushing traffic was blurred, and so were the ramshackle, decrepit, rotting warehouses and piers too, and I saw in my mind's eye the lofty ships of the last century—sleek hulls and spars of astounding grace, crowding the Hudson River shore; or the svelte, monster liners of sixty years ago—the *Mauretania, Berengaria, Queen Mary, Normandie, Queen Elizabeth, Andrea Doria*—waiting to perform yet again their transit of excellence between the New World and the Old.

The sea is New York's, and New York is of the sea. The finest sea trip, and the cheapest, in all the Americas, aboard public transport, is from Battery Park to Staten Island. Battery Park itself, off which the Dutch ships lay to their moorings in the days of Peter Stuyvesant, lies like an anchor to the high towers of Wall Street, to the bows of the huge ship of Manhattan Island. Farther along the shore on the port side of Manhattan, the old three-master *Peking* lies disdainfully off South Street. On the starboard side of Manhattan, in the West Village, warehouses where Melville labored as a Custom's inspector still show their red-brick faces to the sometimes sweating, sometimes freezing streets. Farther amidships the incredible, man-built cliffs of Midtown are piled up—but always, under them, lies the sailors' town. Below them are Broadway and the Bowery—celebrated in a hundred shanties even now sung from the English Channel to the South China Sea.

I lived in Manhattan for six years on and off, to sing my songs of the sea and sailors. When sailors have asked me how I could live there, so far from the sea and things of the sea, I did not tell them that I thought New York was the world capital of the oceans and that every time I walked down any street anywhere in that sprawling hubbub I was continually reminded of the sea and of things of the sea and of peoples of the sea, for how would they have believed me? But how else could it be for a city whose main river is named after one of the greatest and bravest sea navigators of all time, Henry Hudson?

Now I write in a lonely bay on the northern shore of Colombia. My view is one of blue sea and jungle-clad hills rising over a golden beach to the snowy peaks of the Sierra Nevada de Santa Marta. The sun-dappled house at Conchita, in which I write, is set over a tiny beach only a hundred yards away from the leaping seas of the Equatorial Current as it charges westerly to the north, on the other side of a headland. Yet I think I was closer to the sea in West Greenwich Village. Closer to the true sea, the toil and delights of all the centuries of seafaring, and to the honest songs of the ocean, and the hearts of the sea people of whom Melville and Conrad wrote so perceptively. There, in my scruffy rooms in the Village, I did my best to do what I had promised myself I would do—tell the world that sail and sailing and sailors are not dead and gone, and that the spirit that peopled a continent, that overcame unimaginable difficulties, is still alive and well, and again coming into its own. For my pains, I was called everything from "the last of his kind" to "a poet of the unendurable." Now, after bashing and slashing my way through the Pacific Ocean waters from San Diego to Panama, and then beating and smashing against the reinforced winter-season trades of the southern Caribbean—one of the most difficult sail passages anywhere—I smile to myself as I try to imagine those people who wrote their epithets at their desks, working out the week's expense account, while I sit here above the beach of Conchita, with the sound of the surf in my ears and shining fresh fish for breakfast. It is I who will scramble up the bluff beside the bay this afternoon, to watch the sun go down over Cabo de la Aguja: surely one of the finest views in all the Caribbean. While my critics pack the remains of their lunchtime sandwiches into their briefcases and head for the subway, to go home and pay the mortgage, I sit on the stone seat atop the bluff and reckon with the ghosts of Waal, Drake and Morgan, and see the pale galleons ride by in the gloaming under a blanket of clear stars, and feel the sand beneath my foot as I scramble down the bluff under the rising moon.

In Manhattan I learned the true meaning of solitude, I who had probably been more truly alone than anyone else on earth—for fifteen months during my Arctic voyage in *Cresswell* twenty and more years ago. It was in New York that I encountered the very real solitude of the writer, and how he must, like Prometheus chained to his rock, feed the public on his own bleeding guts. I learned real profligacy, which is an artist's defense, nature's balance against the headiness of having been, for but a fleeting moment, of the kingdom of heaven. I learned how to lose myself—and for that New York is an ideal place. I suppose that only writers can really lose themselves, unless other people do it by falling in love. But a writer is already in love with everyone—how else could he suffer the hell on earth of creativity? I learned that the only thing that could save me was the very thing that was destroying me— work, work and more work. In New York I learned to care about what I should care about—and nothing else. I learned that I care about people and the world in which they live. I learned that they are the only people we have, and that this world is the only world we have. I learned that to care for the world and the people in it—all the people—is the only way to true art; and so art must be for and of and by the people and to hell with all the critics and experts and dilettantes, except as they, too, are people, although with some of them that is hard to believe.

In New York I learned, too, that true loneliness and boredom are only possible in a crowd. Loneliness because I am me, and boredom because I was boring myself; because I could never be part of the crowd. I learned that solitude—not loneliness—is a wonderful thing, the mainstay of freedom. There is no freedom within a group. Each one is chained to the others. It is only in solitude that we can go into a dream and stay there as long as we like. The only harm that solitude might do is to isolate us from those who might understand us. But if you are reading this, then that is discounted. Whether you understand me or not is an entirely different matter. That is for you to decide. And there is the crux of something else I learned in New York: You only understand what you want to understand.

Everyone makes two journeys in life. The outer journey, known to all who know him, and the inner journey. In my outer life I have traveled far, mostly in arduous circumstances. But in my inner life I traveled farther in New York than anywhere else. New York gave my mind and my soul and my spirit nine-league boots, but it crippled me physically. I reckon the exchange was fair.

On the practical side of being alone in a great city, I learned that it is easier to be courageous when you are alone than when you are with a group. It is easier because you never apologize to yourself for your own courage—and not to have to apologize is the hallmark of achievement. This is quite a discovery, and it is important to anyone who is afraid of being alone for any length of time.

In Manhattan, too, I learned how desperately the poor longed for the material possessions of the rich, who live among their riches so thinly, so poorly. I learned how the realization of the dream of possession transforms the wonderful into the commonplace, magic into mundane. The acquisitive impulse is a beast alive in New York; it is the predominating obsession in the city; evil and misery are everywhere present, except in a few corners where they know that it is useless to try to put out a fire by heaping straw upon it. You cannot kill a lion by feeding it meat.

Once a year in New York City I dumped everything I owned that

was not of me or the sea into the street—a sort of annual cultural revolution. It is the only way to beat the beast in New York. It is the only
way to avoid sacrificing bits of yourself to dead things. As soon as it
starts to own you, dump it.

There is little wrong with poverty, except that it prevents you from
being generous with material things. But it does not prevent you from
being generous with yourself—and that is far more important. As long
as there is enough warmth for your body and food for your stomach, you
do not need to sell yourself to the beast. And if there is not, then make
sure that what you sell is of the tiniest quantity and the worst quality
that is within you; drive a hard bargain—the hardest you can.

The two most powerful groups of people in New York are those who
have everything and those who have nothing at all. But the first group's
power derives from fear, while the second's derives from the pure strength
of having nothing to lose. The most powerful people in the second group
are those who wish to gain nothing, and I was privileged indeed to know
some of them, on the Bowery and in Lower Manhattan, and among
them were some of the most remarkable people I have ever met in a
lifetime of wandering the earth. They taught me not to apologize, that
circumstances will apologize for themselves. They also confirmed what
I had already guessed—that the only true riches are to be found between your ears. That the only thing you should regret is what you did
not do, not what you did. Reputation means nothing in New York—it
is the most animallike city, and at the same time the most incurious,
on the face of the earth.

But becoming old in New York, to be crippled and not able to run,
to have to depend on anyone else in New York, must be like becoming
impotent before a dominant but still beautiful lover, helpless to give
one's love, and too weak for the burden of trying. Here, at Conchita,
someone fitted mosquito screens a few years back on the window of my
room. Now the screens, of green plastic material, are in shreds and tat-
ters, with only a few ragged remnants of the edges, fluttering in the breeze.

Two woodpeckerlike birds called *carpinteros* inhabit the tree outside the
window. They are black-and-white, with long, curious beaks, evidently
very sharp, and early every morning, I hear their chucklelike chopping.
The male bird has a red topknot and a blue tail, and a gallant air about
him. His mate is not much less colorful and more subdued. In the day,
when the sun is on the tree, they disappear into their green nests high
in the branches—made of plastic fibers. Everlasting nests: what a very
good idea! A justifiable use for plastic waste at last! I have no doubt

that sooner or later some sea creature will find a way to use to advantage the millions of plastic bottles that we have so unthinkingly cast into the oceans. Only I hope to be alive to see what strange construction they make of them. Life will find a way. The sight of that plastic bird's nest makes me feel very good indeed, and I hobble out of the house each morning especially to stand and stare up at it and wonder at the miracle of life.

So far as I know, the two woodpeckers are the only birds around Conchita, except for a very few seabirds who stray in from their hungry hunt under the easterly trades in the fish-sparse Caribbean. . . .

Chi-chi is fifteen years old. He is from a poor barrio on the outskirts of Santa Marta. His father is dead—early death is the lot of the poor in Colombia. His mother is alive but he doesn't know where. Chi-chi helps the fishermen in the next baylet. He is engaged to watch our boat at night, to sleep on deck, and to fish for us in the day. He will do this for $2.50 per twenty-four hours. This, with his food, is good pay here for a lad of fifteen. As with all young people brought up in hunger, his extremities are too big for him, his legs too long and his belly protrudes. But he has a golden-brown skin, regular features and a happy smile, so we will see what he makes of life among the sailors . . . *los veleros gringos*, as we have come to be known.

Few tourists would go to Amsterdam in February. The weather there should be miserable, but for me, in 1982, it was like April, and I wallowed in the fleshpots of the sailors' quarter like a good 'un. I always had a hankering for more and more Heineken beer, and when I crossed over the Leiderplein Straat that February morning I was quite happy, humming to myself "The Man Who Broke the Bank at Monte Carlo." The jolt in my hip, like a hundred thousand kilowatts of electricity, almost killed me with the shock of it. I went down right in front of a streetcar and only the driver's alertness saved me from being chopped to mincemeat.

I was dragged to the side of the road and managed to stand, but in intense pain. The main problem with pain is that it prevents logical calculation and thought. I dragged myself to the nearest bar and drank a deep whiskey. With the first drink I cursed the thing that drives anyone who writes to drink, to sharpen his senses at the same time as seeking oblivion from his sensitivities. With the second whiskey I cursed the frailty of the human frame. With the third I cursed my own weakness and sought a pharmacist.

I found myself back in the seamen's quarter, in the waiting room of a free medical service for the denizens of the district. I was surrounded by the women of the night; I was the only male waiting, the subject of five dozen female eyes all seeking to recognize me from—two or three nights before?

When I eventually entered the doctor's office, I found an Indonesian gentleman, tall and thin and bronzed, intellectual-looking and about thirty—perhaps all Indonesians are thirty? His English was almost as bad as my Dutch.

"Where you from?"

So as not to complicate matters, "England, Doctor."

"Hmm—you seaman?"

"Sort of—yes." Useless to tell him I'd been researching the background of a novel, set partly in Amsterdam.

"You drink der beer? Whiskey?"

"Yes."

"Hmm." Long silence. "You got the English disease."

Consternation on my part. The doctor grinned.

"Wait minute I look—" He reached up to his library shelf for an English-Dutch medical dictionary, flicked through it, then suddenly looked up and beamed. My left leg and foot were burning.

"Ja, here it is—gout!"

I felt intense relief. Now I could stop boozing and eat sensible food.

"You keep your foot up on a chair. You drink no more beer, whiskey, and you not eat spicy food, eh?"

"Right, Doctor. Thank you. God bless you."

I went back to my hotel and sat on the bed and suffered for three days and nights, promising myself that if only this pain would go away, I would live the life of a saint for ever and ever, amen.

But it didn't, and neither did I.

When you are down there is, it is said, only one way to go—up. But there is another way, too—sideways. I decided to go sideways—to make leeway as we sailors say. For me that meant a return to sea. And that's why I am in Conchita, Colombia, telling you this tale.

The true enemy of intelligence is not fear—it is pain. The true hallmark of mankind's progress is its steady defeat of pain. It is not death that is the most fearsome prospect—it is unbearable pain. To defeat pain is the most difficult task known to man. It is the ultimate challenge. In telling my story I declare war—hard, bloody and eternal—on physical pain. Anything I can do to defeat it in myself and in others I will do, until the last dying breath of my body.

Pain is stupid. It must be, or it would not be so indiscriminate in its choice of victims. But perhaps the gods chose me. If that is so, they must have had their reasons, and where there is reason, then more than one can play the game. I will play the game right down to the limits.

Can there be life without pain? I don't know. It seems doubtful—at least mental pain may be with us for eons to come—but physical pain, that is another story. Pain cannot be conquered—only controlled.

Consider this—we are more than our mere bodies; if this were not so, I would have died in Amsterdam two years ago.

2

The Crunch

I wished I had ten thousand pounds,
I'd steer my ship for miles around.

I'd load her up with grub and gin,
And stay in port where we was in.

I'd stand you drinks three times a day,
And feed you well and raise your pay.

With a bully ship and a bully crew,
And a bucko skipper for to kick her
     through.

Oh, I wished I was in London town,
With those London Judies to dance around.

Wake up, you bitch, and let us,
Wake up, you bitch, we want some gin.

From the shanty "Dollar and Half a Day,"
mid-nineteenth century

The night guard here in Conchita, while Wally is away, is Cotes, the caretaker, Chi-chi and José. José is sixteen years old and reminds me of a younger Muhammad Ali. He is thick-set and will be a fine strong man when he joins the Colombian navy in four years' time, which he says is his ambition. José is a friend of Chi-chi, from the same starvation-barrio, and he joined my crew only yesterday. His duties are to share the night guard with Chi-chi and Cotes, and to take messages over the hills along the beach and along the "highway," a dirt road that leads to Santa Marta. A road of sinister name, *el camino de los muertos*—the road of death. Murders take place there frequently. Some say the police kill criminals there; some say the criminals kill each other. In the daytime there is not so much danger. However, José must make sure to be back in Conchita before dark.

Hence our main concern at night is thieves. An American yacht full of goodies sitting at anchor must be a sore temptation to a man whose family is starving, whose yearly income might, if he is lucky, come to five hundred dollars. But we have other concerns, too. One is the marine police patrol, *la patrulla antinarcótica*, which creeps around the coast at night searching for drug-smuggling craft. We can only hope that the port authorities in Santa Marta have alerted the patrol that we are here in Conchita. This is a small hope, and the patrol have itchy trigger fingers.

Our other concern is the drug mafia themselves. Their main area of activity is farther east along the coast from here for about 150 miles, as far as the Guajira peninsula; there might be one or two boatloads of desperados around here. We have no means of knowing. It is for this reason that I must employ José as a foot messenger. I dare not use the boat's radio, for fear of alerting the *drogueros* that we are in Conchita.

José says his father died eleven years ago. He has four siblings all younger than he, and they exist, somehow, with his mother in the Barrio María Cristina; a fertile breeding ground for crime of all kinds, and practically every other pestilence known to man.

Wally is a stocky young man of twenty-four, of German extraction. When I reached San Diego and the vessel that was to become *Outward Leg*, even before any work had been started in her, the wheels were turning to get Wally to me, through mutual friends. He was at that time instructing in a rock-climbing school in the mountains of Wyoming. For a navigator with one leg, the direst need is for someone who can clamber to the top of the mast whenever it is needed. Who better than a rock climber? Wally can get up there, in an emergency, all forty-two feet, in no time at all, with no aid but his bare hands and feet. Besides being a rock climber, Wally had another very important asset, as far as experience goes. He had lived and cruised on board his father's trimaran—he had even helped to build her—since he was ten years old, mainly around Baja California, Mexico. That brings about more assets—Wally speaks some Spanish, he is accustomed to the peculiarities of multihulls and, unlike the vast majority of his generation of Americans, he expects no more than the essentials in life: food in his belly, a bed when he is exhausted and something worthwhile to do. His German blood dictates to him that everything he does must be done properly and to the best of his ability; everything except domestic chores.

At first I was amazed how German attributes can be discerned in someone whose family has been in America for generations, but they were there, sure enough, the good and the bad, through and through. An inclination to nitpick over semantics (and God knows English-English and American-English are two separate languages); a rigid adherence to the known rules (ah, the flexibility of the Welsh mind!) and a sometimes callous-seeming indifference to the finer points of an argument. But at the same time Wally has the almost holy Teutonic respect for any poetry—verbal, visual or of any other sensibility. His taste in music, unfortunately, does not follow the dictates of his genes. Beethoven means little to him; he goes in for rock and roll . . . and this, together with lip service to justice and fairness, and equal treatment of all we encounter, makes him an American per se. His German-American inheritance makes Wally the potential Mister Fixit of all time. If something does not work he will maybe make it work, and often when he makes it work, it *works*. Although it probably wouldn't be so in the U.S.A., here in Colombia Wally would, if he were promiscuous, be in great demand among the ladies, with his fair hair and blue eyes and his sturdy build. The women pretend to melt at the sight of him, and when Latin women seem melted, they stay melted, at least all the time that Wally is around.

Often, when we sit in the pavement cafés on the Avenida Bastida, the seafront of Santa Marta, passing women reach out and touch his fair hair, and laugh as they walk on, while their escorts glare with Latin darkness at the *gringo rubio* and his laughing gnome's blue eyes, straight out of the Nibelungs. He has red-rosy cheeks, and reminds me often of a very young Santa Claus in ragged T-shirt and shorts.

Now Wally is away from *Outward Leg*, helping to outfit *Amorua*, a Boston-built sixty-four-year-old schooner, the darling of Jesús Montoya, a Colombian businessman and fellow sailor, who is at the moment our patron, the owner of Conchita. The locals call him Don Jesús, and so shall I.

Thus the reason for sending young José into Santa Marta with scrawled notes for Wally.

José, Cotes and Chi-chi set out a net last night in the bay. There was a fine catch of seven large red snappers this morning. We shall dine well today. A safe boat—reasonably safe if God wills it—and a good meal under the stars; what more could anyone wish?

Pain has another aspect. It can destroy self-respect. When I crawled into the outpatients' department of St. Vincent's Hospital in Greenwich

Village, New York, after my fall in Amsterdam, I must have looked like a Bowery bum. Three weeks of excruciating agony had deprived me of the right to stay clean or tidy. I had doped myself on painkillers all the way back from Amsterdam, and across London in a wheelchair, hardly aware that I was in my native land and too stupid to realize that I was only a few miles from the Greenwich Seaman's Hospital, where I could have had the finest medical treatment in Britain—for no cost at all.

It took the American doctor in New York only a couple of hours to tell me that if my left leg was not removed I would certainly die very soon. An occlusion, he called it. I called it a bloody bastard and many other names besides and "Take the bugger off, doctor—just rid me of this pain," I begged him. And so they did. . . .

I can't recall the name of the drug they gave me. I woke up with a feeling of ecstasy. For the first time in weeks I felt no pain, only that I was alive and comfortable for once. I was in a bed, and there were other people around, but apart from that—nothing, just peace.

The next time I woke someone was giving me an injection in my arse.

A nurse walked in, beautiful and very Irish, with golden hair and the blue-green eyes of County Mayo. She smiled at me, then looked at my chart at the bottom of the bed. She read my name and that I was British. Her face clouded, then cleared again, and she spoke sweetly to me, as the Irish do when they are taunting:

"Ah, Mr. Jones, good morning!" says she, in a voice that would bring the birds flying from the Twelve Mountains of Connemara to the grave of sweet Rhyddiach. "I've good news for you today."

"Good morning, nurse," says I, "and what might that be?"

"The Argentines invaded the Falkland Islands last night and have taken over from the English, bless them."

"The bloody bastards," says I. "They waited until I was in here, then?"

There was silence for a minute while the Connemara lass took this in, then she added, "And more good news, Mr. Jones."

"?" I looked at her. Dylan Thomas died quite nearby, I was told later.

"We've had to take your left leg off at the thigh; they tried a below-the-knee amputation—twice—but it didn't work."

"The whole leg?" I could feel nothing. I still, surely, had two legs?

"The whole leg, it is. You have about four inches left. The rest is gone." She smiled twice as sweetly for Ireland—she thought. For the Ireland that she thought she knew, not for the Ireland that I know.

"The whole leg," she repeated, gloatingly. She jerked her shoulders, flounced and steamed out of the room.

I fell asleep again, grinning. Was I not a son of the Cymry, from the hunting grounds of the Hounds of the King of Hell? . . .

When a Welshman has nothing else to dream of, or to hope for, or to think about, what else would he dream of but Wales and the land of the comrades, so far away across the looking-glass sea, and himself crippled like the King of Claerddion, one foot in the gutter and the other in its own grave? To dream and to see the Cliff of Gloomy Caves and the mountain of Eyrery.

I once anchored in the dusk off Staten Island—not the one in New York but at the southern tip of all the Americas, and listened to the tribal chant of the penguins (Welsh word, that, lads); a mysterious chant under the setting sun, evocative and compelling, like the sound of thousands of earthy country folk at a fair, well dined. Penguins are not at all like English butlers. More they are like well-fed farmers gathered at a market in a merry town, with wenches squealing, bursts of drunken song and old men reminiscing in the bar of a well-kept pub.

Young sharks, when newly born, swim into their mother's mouth if they are frightened, and she swallows them. After the danger is past, she spews them out again. They hide in her warm stomach, just as I hid in that painkilling warmth all about me. I was back again in my mother's womb. It was the only place to be. Everywhere else there was only pain and death. I am not afraid of death, but I was curious, in a tiny corner of my soul, to know just how the hell I was ever going to get out of that bloody mess I was in and if I was to go to the Feasting Halls of the Men of Harlech, I would have liked one more tale to tell them, so that they would know that I am truly one of the Sons of Merioneth, from the Nine Islands of the Mighty.

I woke in agony and screamed until someone stuck something in me; then I returned to the mountains of Ffestiniog and the burbling streams of Clwyd and the moon in the night of Wales. . . .

And days and nights passed in dreams, and in between the dreams there was pain. But for the dreams I would have bargained with Hell itself: The heather brushed my cheek, and the trees—oak and ash, lime, larch, elder, chestnut, willow and thorn, I saw every leaf as plain as the pages of a Bible, every line as clear as the words of Christ himself, "Suffer the little children to come unto me" . . . and the lucerne and mayapple, clover, chervil, watercress and sweet-water, coriander and cowpea and the deadly, deadly nightshade—encrusted dust on the air conditioner . . .

"How the heck are you going to get out of this hole?" exclaimed my agent Cursive Curtis.

"What hole?" said I and in a flash I was back behind that bloody iceberg and the black Arctic night and cold all around me. "Call this a hole? I've seen better ones," said I.

Cursive looked sad. "Well, what are you going to do, Tristan?" he asked.

"Survive, for the time being," I replied. "Stay alive. Then we'll see . . . *And finish singing my song in Amsterdam, by the blood of Christ!*"

Cotes has been at Conchita for twenty years. He is of mixed Negro, Indian and white blood, as are most Colombians of the coast. His age is indefinable; I would say a comfortable forty or so. He lives on a minute income from caretaking for Don Jesús here, and from fishing. He fishes with hooks and nets and is resigned about the dynamiters of the cooperative union in Tacanga, who come to blow the fish, and everything else alive, out of the water. Cotes never wears a shirt. I am not even sure that he has one. He has honest eyes, open and straightforward, and the body of a youth of nineteen. He has a son, about eleven or so, who is much darker than he, and who makes his living, somehow, washing taxis in Santa Marta. The coastal people here are known as *costeños;* according to the high and mighty they are undependable, tend to violence, and lazy. Of course they are, by other standards, but people are the product of the climate they live in. The weather here is undependable and sometimes lazy and sometimes violent, but usually the sun shines, just as the *costeños* love music, and laugh and smile most of the time. Good God, since when has the worth of a man been measured only by his willingness to put his nose to someone else's grindstone?

For such a tough-looking *hombre*, Cotes is of a surprisingly tender disposition. Yesterday, as I wrote in my cabin, he came and placed a small white sea shell (a *conchita* in Spanish) on my windowsill. For that I love him more. It is, perhaps unconsciously, a symbolic gesture, to let me know that he will protect me. Words are sometimes quite unnecessary. A gesture can carry the world.

It took me almost a month to leave my bed in St. Vincent's Hospital, to leave the fantasies and dreams and to return to the world of so-called reality. What I found there was almost as hard to bear as any pain. The patients sat around staring morbidly into the inanity of TV contests, or crying inwardly in the depths of utter despair and hopelessness. I talked some of them into a wheelchair race and after that was forbidden to leave my bed for two more days for my efforts. There were men of youngish aspect who had lost their feet, having fallen down drunk on the frozen Bowery. One face of courage, though, was worn by a Cherokee Indian, who had slipped on an icy girder a hundred feet above the street, bounced off another, and fallen to the sidewalk below. Every bone in his body was shattered, but somehow I know he is now either back at work, or living on his compensation in the woods. But the youngsters, lads and lasses, were there by the dozen, usually victims of car crashes with amputated arms and legs, and the vast majority wallowing in despair. I wandered among them, not talking much but listening and looking, and I knew then what I had to do: get my arse moving. Make them say to themselves, "Well, if this old guy can do it at close on sixty, then so can I!" I must get back to sea, sometime soon. But first I must survive, somehow.

In one of my more lucid moments, I took one look at the account for hospital services, $22,000, and discharged myself an hour afterward. I was pushed into the street on a borrowed wheelchair by the Ghost of Hamlet, Hans Anderson, a budding chess champion; he pushed me over the sidewalk edge foot first and spilled me in front of a taxi . . . which barely halted inches away from my helpless soul. A ghost pushed by a ghost.

Somehow, God only knows how, I had put together, in the crowded hospital room, a book, *One Hand for the Ship and One for Yourself.* Never, I suppose, has such an unlikely book been written and pieced together in such unlikely surroundings. But I did it, and when I got home to my little apartment I set to on a full translation of the Welsh *Mabinogion,* just as I had remembered it in my dreams in St. Vincent's. It poured out of me, word for word, as it was told to me forty-five years before by Blind Sioni ap Rhyssiart by the gray roadside in Merioneth.

There's a problem with an amputation though, at least for men of my age. There's a phenomenon (though I called it many other names and still do whenever it grips me, vicelike) called "phantom pains." The pain you felt before the limb was removed is so deeply engraved in the corridors of the mind, so firmly etched, that it takes years—for me it seems the rest of my life—to be rid of it. It demands a continual act of will, an eternal struggle against self-pity, an adamant refusal to submit. But it also makes sitting down for any length of time extremely uncomfortable. I found myself having to stand up every five minutes, yet not able to stand for longer than that. So the translation, entitled *Echoes of*

Distant Thunder, was written half standing and half sitting, with me cursing the frailty of my frame. But I did it. The book has not yet seen the light of public day, but it will in England, soon. I can only hope that I shall live long enough to see it in the hands of the children of the storm, so that they will know that the whirlwind is very ancient and, indeed, becoming tired and mild compared to what it was when the world was young.

Then, absolutely broke and grubbing for money to pay for a false leg, I went into the sail-sculpture-mobile business. I sold quite a few to some blessed people all over the world—and while I was doing that I wrote, still half standing and half sitting, a sister book to *Saga of a Wayward Sailor*, half in jest, half serious, but all in love, entitled *Seagulls in My Soup*.

Within nine months of my amputation I wrote, as a gesture to the gods, three books, while I subsisted on what I could earn from my sail mobiles. This I say under the watching stars, my witnesses.

The next task was to give up writing for a while and go and meet my readers. Most of them are involved, in some way or other, in boating. The obvious way to meet them was to go to as many boat shows as I could, and this I did, from Newport to Annapolis. The other way to meet them was to give talks, and this I did—from Amsterdam to Anchorage, Alaska—dragging and hobbling my way through one airport after another.

And thereby hang a couple of tales. I wouldn't be a Welshman if I didn't tell them to you, would I?

3

The Kept Promise

I am the ghost of Benjamin Binns,
I was cut right down in the midst of my sins.
Whisky-O, Johnny-O!
Rise me up from down below, oh-oh-oh!
Rise me up from down below, boys,
Rise me up from down below!

I'm just up from the world below,
That is where the cocks do crow.

I'll tell you, boys, 'tis hot in hell,
An' I should know the place damn well.

An' now the bleedin' sail is set,
Back to me hole I'll have to get.

"Rise Me Up from Down Below," the only
"stamp and go" shanty known. It was sung
to start and haul a line fast along the deck.
It was sung very fast, except for "Whisky-O,
Johnny-O," which was shouted loud, and to
which two strong pulls of the line were
given, to get it started.

Chi-chi is a silent iconoclast. He looks, I think, like James Baldwin
must have looked when he was fifteen, and he probably thinks like
Baldwin did, too. He is very thin, and still weak, but a couple of weeks
on our food should set him straight and start to bring him to Wally's
standard of how a youth should be. He has a very strong spirit though,
and when he sidles into company, silently, I am somehow aware of his
presence, listening to everything and watching quietly, continually
learning. He has an infectious grin, which is poison to any pomposity.
I started to show him the alphabet the other evening, but Chi-chi could

not stop grinning. I will try again later, when he has become more accustomed to our habits of sustained effort. Now he is like a wild colt, and must first be enticed into merely being with us, before anything can be imposed upon him. At the moment all that matters to him is fishing with Cotes, a cigarette once in a while, and local music over the radio, to which he taps his feet, and closes his eyes as he listens, enraptured, to the repetitious clamor of a Cumba or a Salsa. When he returns from fishing, salt-sprayed, he looks as if he had been rolling about in a flour mill. The salt encrusts around his long eyelashes and his lips, and makes me think of the reverse of a "black minstrel" of years ago. A little black boy playing at being white, but Chi-chi, of course, is not playing; catching a couple of fish has been to him a matter of eating or starving.

Cotes's youngest son, Mario, is a deaf-mute aged seven. He plays by himself on the beach most of the time. He is very shy, but is becoming slowly more friendly. For some reason the dogs—there are six of them, all sly, miserable-looking tropical dogs of puzzling ancestry—avoid Mario although they scamper around the others, and it is as if they and Mario live in two separate worlds.

All the while, *Outward Leg* swings to three anchors and two lines secured to cypress trees on the foreshore. The holding ground here, hard sand, is not very good, and there is an almost continual onshore breeze. This, with the steady sound of the surf on the beach, and the threat of piracy or banditry, keeps me awake for hours at night, and keeps one half of my mind on the boat during the day. But we are reasonably safe here, as long as we are vigilant, and the cost of the berth in money is nothing, so it is a fair exchange.

The leg I left St. Vincent's Hospital with was what is known as a "pylon." This was an aluminum tube with a plaster-of-Paris cast at the upper end, in which my stump sat, with my hipbone sitting on top of the whole and a rough "foot" on the other end, on which was laced a shoe. It had to be an odd shoe because the foot on the pylon was bigger than my own right foot, but it served the purpose, which was for me to practice walking indoors, using a pair of crutches. Fourteen painful steps either way, back and forth, in between half lying on my recliner (kindly lent by friends) and weaning myself off painkilling tablets. It was three weeks before I could manage to make more than four passes of the room at a time. By then the April sun was beckoning outside, and it was time to take a stroll down to the River Hudson, four blocks along the street. The salt air was calling.

I made it down the slight incline of West Tenth Street with some alarums crossing the roads—and even across the West Side Highway and back again. But when I tried the uphill incline, the paster-of-Paris cup broke away from the aluminum pole. I had to sit on a step and surreptitiously take off the leg. By that time it was getting dark. I slung the leg around my neck and started crutching my way home on one leg in a slight drizzle. Two dark figures overtook me, knocked me sideways into a doorway, bowled me over, rifled my pockets and disappeared—all in a moment. Twenty dollars in cash and my credit cards . . . Some people will say they were suffering from "inner-city deprivation": I say they were vicious little bastards.

Somehow I managed to right myself—and the starboard crutch collapsed on me, its middle bolt having come loose and dropped out. So with my pylon leg draped around my neck and with the broken crutch trailing behind the good one, supporting myself with one hand and the good crutch, I crawled back over Hudson Street. Not one stranger out of the dozens that saw me offered a hand. I blamed myself as much as anyone—I had been warned by a therapist not to attempt to go outside for a while but my adventurous spirit had not heeded him. I had to be in the salt air of the Hudson River. I made up my mind to leave New York as soon as I could. It is no place for the elderly or the crippled. I needed to be somewhere safe and *flat,* where I could write the book *Heart of Oak.*

The removal of a leg in New York costs around $32,000, and a respectable prosthesis (how I hate that word), a good false leg, costs around $3,000. A couple of weeks later I had earned enough to be able to be fitted for a "latest state-of-the-art" prosthesis. The best false-limb maker in New York (and so probably the best on earth) is in Spanish Harlem. All his staff are Latins. At first they were offhand with me, even cursory, until I spoke Spanish—and then they almost fell over themselves to make me comfortable and to speed my way through the labyrinth of measurements and fittings. I'm still wearing that leg.

It took three weeks for the new leg to be ready to wear, and once I got it home I started limping with a walking stick. Within a week I was walking daily around the block, up West Tenth Street, along Bleeker, down Christopher, and so back along Hudson, rain or shine. In two weeks I was going both ways around the block twice every day. And in between, writing, writing, still half standing and half sitting.

In May I gave my first lecture since my amputation. That was at a school of dyslexic boys in upstate New York while I was still wearing the pylon. The boys' eyes, as I hobbled in on my aluminum structure, were like so many oysters, but they seemed to love the yarn I told them.

The next lecture was in Newport, Rhode Island, in July. On the way to Newport from New York—I suppose over two hundred miles—I noticed that apart from a few dogs locked up in the back of speeding cars on the highway, I did not see one live animal. When we came to the Budweiser depot in northeastern Connecticut there were two model horses—cart horses—made of fiberglass, standing in a field. This struck me as so funny that I had to have my picture taken astride one of them. But when I had clambered up the damned thing fell over, and I decided that horse riding was not for me, and I had better stick to sailing after all. Luckily the horse fell to the side of my good leg, and so there was little damage but a bruise or two.

The big turnout at Newport was encouraging. It was the first time I had been purposely to a yachting center to "expose myself," and I found that I was famous or notorious—it is not easy for me to know which. I could not hobble two yards down America's Cup Avenue without someone grabbing my hand. I have no false modesty about it—that did me more good than all the therapist's chat. It was the first time I realized that my words were getting through to the modern sailors and that they were taking notice of what I had been writing so painfully for so long, that they needed me. But what pleased me most was that I realized that I was still the same old me, and bugger the begrudgers.

And all the time I wrestled at a return to sea. By now I had realized that the "normal"-type boat, monohulled, with its heeling moment, would not do. I cannot manage slopes of more than twenty degrees. The solution was obvious. It would have to be a multihull. But how? Not to mention where, which and with what? A fifty-thousand-dollar debt is a sticky starting point after all. But the why was perfectly clear: to set an example. One example is worth a thousand sermons. I could not get out of my mind those people, and especially the young ones, I had encountered in St. Vincent's Hospital. Now I began to consider how many millions of them there are, all over the world. So was born the idea of Operation Star.

It was good—it was to me triumphant—to be back in dear old London. I'd been invited over by the BBC to take part in a television talk show about travel, along with Sir Laurens van der Post and Paddy Leigh Fermor—an honor indeed. One is a world-renowned travel writer, the other a brilliant raconteur.

I made my hobbly way through the confusion of a strikebound Heathrow Airport, and to the studios. The welcome there was almost overpowering. Van der Post and Leigh Fermor had each spent at least fifteen minutes going into all kinds of esoteric explanations on how they felt about travel. When it was time for me to answer the question "What does travel do for you?," all I could think of saying was "Gets me from A to B." I don't recall much more about it, except that for a few minutes the studio audience was in a state of uproar.

My London editor, Euan Cameron of The Bodley Head, was there at the studios.

"Where do you go from here, Tristan?" he asked.

"To Amsterdam and St. Petersburg in Florida—I've to attend a boatshow there," I replied.

"And Amsterdam?"

"I want to finish singing a song there."

"A song?"

"Yes—'The Man Who Broke the Bank at Monte Carlo.' "

Euan is a Scotsman and so, although his eyes lit up, he said no more, at least about going to Amsterdam to finish singing a song. Of course that was not the whole reason for going to Amsterdam. I also had an appointment to meet the curator of the National Maritime Museum—one of the finest in the world—and Dirk van Scheltema, the cheese-warehouseman, my first meeting with whom is described in *Saga of a Wayward Sailor*. Incidentally, I suppose that was the only time in the history of seafaring when an oceangoing vessel was sunk by two tons of Edam cheese.

One thing can be said for the BBC—they are never stingy with booze for guests and staff. That may be why their talk shows are so scintillating and witty, at least to British ears. By the time I left the studios I was as happy as a lark. My recent woes were all forgotten, all breezed away in the sunshine of Scotland and Johnny Walker Black Label. Nothing but the best for the BBC. They have it made—no advertisers to answer to, and every television set in the land paying them a license fee each year. They can afford to lay it out.

My plane for Amsterdam was leaving very early in the morning; I had to catch the last subway to Heathrow. I slid out of the studios and took a cab. We hared down to Leicester Square subway station and I swung across the deserted station foyer like a soldier of the line. I travel light—toothbrush and change of undercloths in a shoulder bag, which is all I can manage on one leg anyway. I grabbed a ticket and headed for the stairs, only they turned out to be an escalator, and down I went, arse over tit, down, down, bangity-bump, bumpity-bang, all the way down. Fortunately my shoulder bag slid around and protected my head and shoulders to a degree, but at the bottom of the escalator I was a mess, with blood everywhere and me trying my best to scramble up on to my leg.

As I struggled to support myself on my walking stick, up strolled a bobby—a very young-looking bobby; he looked almost a child, which shows you how old I'm getting. Of course, I was swearing and cursing, more at myself than at anything or anyone else.

"Good evening, sir," the bobby greeted me. Always polite, the good old British bobby. There was down on his cheek.

"Bloody fucking shit . . ." I gasped.

He smiled. "Do you realize that the escalator you just fell down is the longest in the world?" he said.

I was staggered. My cursing stopped at once. I must have tried to grin at him. "Well, I didn't," I gasped, "but I certainly do now!"

He grabbed my arm to help me right myself. "Come along, sir," he murmured. "I'd better help you along to the Middlesex Hospital; you look in a bad way. . . ."

"You'll do no such thing, officer," I exclaimed. "I'm on my way to Amsterdam and St. Petersburg, and the last train leaves very shortly. . . ."

"To where, sir?" the bobby asked in a hushed tone.

"Amsterdam and St. Petersburg."

The bobby held me for a moment at arm's length and looked me, seriously, in the eye.

"My God, you must be ancient!" he exclaimed. "Surely you mean *Leningrad*, don't you?"

The plane landed at Schiphol about six A.M. and I crawled to the first taxi I could find. "Take me to the Leiderplein Straat, please."

Then, at about seven o'clock in the morning, in the rain, still with my shoulder bag bloody from the previous night's encounter with the escalator, I limped across the Leiderplein Straat amid hundreds of workers cycling to their labors. Most of them turned to stare at me as though I was stark raving bonkers, as I sang to myself and to the world.

> As he strolls along the Bois de Boulogne,
> With an independent air,

You can hear the girls declare,
He must be a millionaire!

You can see them sigh,
And wish to die,
And see them wink the other eye,
At . . . the man who broke the bank at Monte Carlo!

Two streetcars missed me by a hairbreadth, and any number of cars, but I made it and staggered to the canal railings on the far side of the square and laughed into the murky waters. Above me a seagull joined in. I had kept my promise to myself. That's the thing. Then I had to sit down, even in the rain, and coddle a severe attack of phantom pains. They really *are* persistent. Little victories are the sweetest.

Dirk was supposed to meet me alone at the Maritime Museum, but as it turned out he brought half the male population of Volendam, his hometown, with him, and each one had, of course, a bottle of schnapps in his pocket. You may imagine the state we were in by late afternoon. I hazily recall having to raise a full-scale search in the museum for my leg, which I had misplaced in the toilet, but I remember little else.

I have had to fire José. When I sent him into Santa Marta with a note to Wally, I enclosed a five-hundred-peso note for purchases. That is about six dollars. When Wally opened the envelope there were only three hundred pesos in it. It is not the money loss that I mind so much as the breach of trust, although we can ill afford to lose anything right now. Also I could not endure José's steadfast lie that he had not opened the letter. No sociologist can tell me that the values of the barrio are not those of *Outward Leg*. José knew he had stolen, and he knew he was lying when he denied it, and he knew he had betrayed a trust. In most other places I could probably overlook the breach on the first occasion but here I dare not, and if I tell José that I know about it and yet forgive him, I shall be looked upon as a fool, and on every opportunity I shall be subjected to more pilferage. It seems that you cannot trust those who have never been trusted. In such circumstances as ours, in a land like Colombia, to accept a lie is to walk over a hole, and you can break your neck doing that. Now I am taking a risk, because José will talk in his barrio, and temptation may overcome certain wild spirits there. We shall have to be doubly zealous at our night guard. The fiesta season is almost upon us, and just before the fiestas is the high time for crime here in Colombia; money has to be found to spend at the fiestas.

Wally returned from Santa Marta yesterday. He can do little more on board *Amorua* until Don Jesús returns from New York. He tells me that two people were shot dead on the town beach on Wednesday. He was sitting in the Café Rápido Rico at eight in the evening, along with his lady friend Anna Ruth. Suddenly shots sounded. Wally did not wait around; he grabbed Anna Ruth and they headed for the town center, away from the beach. Supposedly the police had sighted five *guerilleros* on the beach and opened up on them. Three got clean away, from what we know. I think of the words of Erwin Rommel, the best of the German generals: "Mortal danger is the best antidote for fixed ideas. . . ."

Wally returned exasperated. He will learn about Latin-American ways here; about the incessant probes for personal advantage, the lack of co-ordination whenever more than two people are involved in any activity; the difficulty of expressing ideas—not words, *ideas*—in another language than your own. It is difficult enough for an English-speaking sailor to express sea ideas to a landsman in English, but when it is a matter of trying to convey those ideas to a landsman in another language, it is almost an impossibility; you find yourself waiting for some inevitable failure, or even disaster, to convince them that what you have been saying is true and logical. But it amazes me how Wally manages to convey his meaning in his Spanish, which is very basic indeed. He seems to be developing a third language, a sort of mixture of American-English and Spanish, let's call it *Spamerish,* and somehow the Colombians, in the main, seem to understand him. But in reality, language is not a thing for professors and academicians, nor for pedants. Real live people can spin a web of language as they need it, without any regard at all for the precepts of pedants: *"Tire eso goddam cuerda, fercrissake!"*

Here on the coast of Colombia, communication with the locals is doubly difficult because their Spanish is badly pronounced. They cut off the ends of their words, and run them all into each other. They seem to eat their vowels, too. *Costeño* is not the Spanish of Madrid, that's for sure.

4

Outward Leg

Hvert land av godt og ondt har sit,

Chorus:
Ota Hayti! Ota Hayti!
Jeg holder nu paa Norge mit,
In the Ota Hayti, ho!

Blow boys, blow, for Californi-oh!
There's plenty of gold, so I've been told,
On the banks of Sacramento!

"Each country has its good and its shit . . .
On Norway I will always bet . . ."

Norwegian version of the capstan shanty
"Sacramento," late nineteenth century

In the months that followed my leaving New York, I wrote *Heart of Oak,* and then traveled the length and breadth of North America, lecturing to earn my way. I visited every state on the eastern seaboard, and as far west as Anchorage, Alaska. All this I did alone and unaided.

My visit to Alaska was short—a mere three days. I have the impressions of snow-covered mountains all around Anchorage, drunken Eskimos downtown, supermarkets warm and full of treasure the same as if they were in Pennsylvania or Kansas—and this is not derogatory—and a moose waking me up by rubbing its huge nose against my frosty bedroom window, friendly yatties and warm hospitality.

California was—California. I did a lecture tour that would have paid for itself if the woman who organized it—the owner of a well-known bookstore in Ventura—had not part-paid me in a check that later bounced. Many and many a time since, the money she owes me would have made my life that much easier. But she not only bilked me, she also almost sold my intense respect for her land of origin, and I might have fallen for that trap, too, if I did not know better—that any land is capable of producing people who break their word and betray the trust placed in them. But she has to live with herself.

In Santa Barbara I lived for a week in the Hotel California, renowned in song. There, on the pier just down the road and across the avenue, a year after my amputation, still fighting phantom pains, I walked my first full mile. There, in the harbor, I set my mind on a multihull—a trimaran. But those I saw in Santa Barbara did not impress me too much. They were mostly rather clumsy—even ugly-looking—and at sea if it doesn't look right it usually isn't. There is always the problem of possible capsize to think about. It was on the pier at Santa Barbara, too, that Operation Star was nurtured. The Star is the star of hope. "A star to steer her by . . ." To show, by personal example, that it is possible for severely handicapped people to help themselves, to act for themselves, to drag themselves by their boottop(s) out of the rut of uselessness. I dreamed of independent groups of handicapped youngsters forming the world over, to act in all kinds of ways, all kinds of activities, useful not only to themselves but also to others.

I went back to the Hotel California and scribbled on a piece of paper—I think it was a torn-off piece of newspaper—"Operation Star—whichever way you turn me I shall stand." I don't know what made me think of this. It is the age-old slogan of Manaan, the one-legged king of the Isle of Man in Celtic legend, the first conqueror of Ireland, which he wrested from the evil Firbolgs. He was the king who rode the white horses of the wind across the Irish Sea. It was also, I thought, the ideal slogan for a trimaran, which might—or might not—*capsize.*

Here in Conchita it's interesting to reflect on Florida. There's a strong connection between Colombia and Florida. Florida is where many of the drugs exported from here enter the United States, via the Bahamas. To be specific, via Carlos Lehder (El Muchacho) who owns Norman Cay and who operates with the aid of God only knows who in the Florida corridors of power. . . . Of course there are many other drop-off points for drugs in the Bahamas, and the yachtsmen—everyone—should know where they are—Bimini, Gorda Key, Black Rock, Staniel Key, Derby Island, Georgetown, Hawks Nest Creek, and Andros Island. Approach any of these places at your grave peril. These are main switches on the sewer system of those who are busy making money at killing everything that the Western world means. These are the ratholes of those who are murdering the minds of children. The U.S. invaded Grenada to avoid a far less grave danger to its future. If the U.S. Drug Enforcement Agency really means business it should move in on those places I have mentioned as soon as possible. There is no human court on earth that, knowing the bastard end of drug consumption, could possibly condemn such a move. It is a far graver danger to the world than is the threat of nuclear war—simply because, unlike nuclear war, it is actually going on right now.

Failing action by the DEA or the Bahamian government, it is up to the ordinary man and woman to avoid all the Bahamas—to stop spending money there for any reason whatever until the flow of tons of drugs per day through the islands stops. The tourists take as much money into the islands, probably, as do the drug dealers. That money should stop. Dead. Now.

The British government should warn the Bahamas that continuation of this vile trade will mean expulsion from the Commonwealth and the end of British protection—and that means far more than it appears to on the surface.

I don't give a damn about bringing criminals to justice, but I do care about minds being murdered and about children starving, and I hope that this is getting through. I am writing this in the very heart of the matter—in Colombia. I am not sitting in some plush apartment in Washington, nor blabbing over a pub table in Bloomsbury. Some of the Colombian government officials seem to be doing their best to staunch the flow of drugs from this country. Only this week *two tons* of cocaine was discovered and destroyed in Medellin. But as long as selfish instant-nirvana pursuers insist on demanding these drugs so long will the destruction of lives and the hunger of children persist. So long will the worst crime against humanity of this century—not excluding the holocaust in Nazi Germany or the massacres of Joseph Stalin's Russia—persist. So long will the advancement of millions of lives be impeded. If there is a God in heaven, then there must be a special kind of hell awaiting these ladies and gentlemen who run the drug trade. Cold turkey for eternity. And if it is to be my fate to go down there too, by the living God, I'll have a word or two in old Nick's ear and demand to stoke the fires. . . .

The return to Key West from California was as flat as the island itself. I was never too eager to return to New York when I was away from that city, but once I was back I was always happy to be there. Not so in Key West. I was a fish out of water. But I flapped my tail and finished *Heart of Oak*—the tale of my wartime years. Then it was time to go back on the road, to earn money to pay off outstanding debts.

I had only one lecturing appointment, in mid-1983, in San Diego. Normally I would not have crossed the continent for one engagement—the expenses are only just covered. But this time something told me that I ought to go. I had warm memories of my previous visit in 1977. I recalled its good, dry, warm climate and its friendly people, among other things. Besides, it was another port, a place to look for a trimaran. By that time I'd already been to some ports in the eastern states, but had seen no multihull that impressed me as being what I thought she should be. The agent in San Diego arranged for a telephoned radio interview the week before I went there, and in it I mentioned my intention to make a voyage, as an example, for Operation Star, and that I was on the lookout for a suitable trimaran. I had about a thousand dollars at the time, but when destiny decrees, then money is of least importance—the will's the thing.

I had been in correspondence with Eric Le Rouge, one of France's leading multihull designers, for some months. Eric had told me that he could probably find sponsors for me to build a trimaran for the Star voyage—but it would take a year or two. Now a year or two at twenty or thirty or forty years of age is a fairly short time, but when you are approaching sixty years of age, it is a very long time indeed—it is perhaps a quarter of your remaining lifetime. Nevertheless, if no other solution to my problem of finding a suitable craft turned up, then I would wait the two years or so. But another solution did turn up—and I had a strange feeling, as I flew across America yet again, that synchronistic destiny was at work, bringing unknown strands together into the weft and warp of a certain design. . . .

She was at anchor off a golf clubhouse. She was low, and fast-looking, and of the right sort of line; there was an indefinable air of longing about her and when my eyes fell upon her, all the other yachts around her dissolved into a blur. As I drew near her in a borrowed dinghy, she seemed to me to be imbued with the spirit of a song, a carefree, never-ending rhythm that was part of the rhythm of the sea, perhaps of the universe itself. She was, as I stepped, stumbled and clawed my one-legged way up her stern, an engine, pure and unadorned. A sailing engine and a hard nut if I ever saw one. My whole being was overcome by the feeling: This one's for me. On board, it was no longer "I" but "we."

I sensed her lines, their round practicality, and I knew that she was "just right." Even though she was bare of all gadgets like winches or guardrails, I could see them all in place, as she could be—as she would be.

She was not a makeshift craft, as most of the multihulls I had looked at had seemed to be. A makeshift craft will not do for any kind of serious voyaging. Skippers and crews are influenced above all by the temperament of the vessel they sail, and they adjust themselves to her living spirit. That a yacht can be but a machinelike convenience for sailing to distant lands is an illusion. She must be more. She must live, and she must be made to live. She must have the character, the turn of temperament, the high spirit, to dwell in salt water—with the flow of the wave, with something of the wind captured in her very bones. Perhaps all things touching the elements so completely must have this conforming character, this flame, in order to exist. The sea can make or break the spirit of any venture by making or breaking the spirit of the craft and, in turn, that of the crew.

The craft herself must also be an adventurer in the real sense—a living spirit. And the spirit is vital, not vague, in a good voyaging craft, emanating directly from the integral spirit of her designer; a symbol revealing his science and, more important, his art; and even before these, his ideals, loyalties, faiths. There was nothing mystical here for me, as I looked her over in San Diego, merely a hint that she was approved by my heart as well as my head, and that she had been designed by someone who went beyond the feel of ships, someone who was striving to find Truth in his creation; someone who was not only a scientist, and surely someone who was not a layman, for never have such sweet lines in a vessel been designed by a layman, and never yet has a happy amateur-designed vessel sailed the seas. The name on her side was *Osprey*, but to me she was already *Outward Leg*, and a symbol of far greater things than design only. . . . *And someone wanted to meet me and discuss fitting her out for the Star voyage.*

There is an interesting collection of insects here at Conchita. The ubiquitous housefly in squadrons, ordinary ants in legions, and beetles by the score. At first they are unsettling, particularly an extraordinary beetle, about an inch long, gray and powder-fluffy, as if it is covered in flour. But nature always maintains a balance, and so we have plenty of lizards but unfortunately not many spiders. The flies have special times for their activities on human bodies: early morning just after the sun rises, and late afternoon just before it sets. I have already nobbled at least two dozen houseflies with the rubber end of my walking stick, and this, together with preserving my fluency in good old Anglo-Saxon swearwords, keeps my sanity intact at the going down of the sun and in the morning. As for the gray fluffy beetles, they are active at any time and delight in crawling over me. Fortunately their footstep is very feathery, and so if I don't purposely look for them I don't feel them.

The dogs here have given up, if they ever tried, getting rid of the flies that crawl over them. They merely lie there, their eyes covered with the pests. The only time the dogs ever show any sign of intelligence, or indeed any sign that they are much more than alive, is when food is ready and on the table—then they stare piteously at the middle distance between us and them, and when someone approaches our baylet they howl and whine. Their noises would not discourage any self-respecting burglar or pirate.

Here we have no protection but our own strength, such as it is, a set of bow and arrows, and a flare pistol—together with a Scotland Yard police whistle, a hammer, an ax, and a couple of Molotov cocktails all made up and ready to throw. We have made no secret of our prowess with the bow and arrows, and we have made sure that anyone who comes by sees us practicing. Wally is accurate now at a hundred paces.

At night at Conchita the house is closed up like a fortress, and through my barred window I command a view of the whole bay. There, after the light generator is switched off at nine P.M. I sit for three hours, whistle at hand to give the alarm, until Wally starts his guard watch at midnight from on board. The boat is within bowshot of my windows, and anyone clambering on board would risk getting one right through the gizzard.

Not for one minute of the day or the night is there not a friendly eye on *Outward Leg*. She is probably the best-watched boat in the whole of the Caribbean.

5

The Crucible

As I was rolling down the Strand,
Hoo-dah, hoo-dah,
I met two fairies hand in hand,
Hoo-dah, hoo-dah day!
Blow, boys, blow!
For Califor-neye-O.
There's plenty of grass to wipe your ass,
On the banks of Sacramento!

This was one British version of "Cali-
forni-O," a capstan shanty sung in sailing ships of most seafaring nations in
the nineteenth century

False dawn here at Conchita is a mere sly hint of the splendors to come. The velvety blackness of the night suddenly trembles like a shivering veil; then the purples creep all around and the colorless grays and the trillion shades of blue on the sea in the bay, while gradually the hills and mountains in the distance take on their shades of emerald and topaz, and the beach across the bay turns from dead silver to lively gold, all in the space of twenty-five minutes. The boat herself changes from a sleeping gray ghost under the moon into her daytime splendor of turquoise decks and cool-gray hull.

The trade wind eases off during the wee small hours, as regularly as a clock, and stays civilized until local noon, when the sun is directly overhead. Then it rises again to its full strength. It is so regular, this rise, that if you knew the time of local noon you could set your watch by it. Then it blows in steady and frequent gusts right around the headland and so into our little bay, where it cools down the house but keeps me despondently alert. No right-minded sailor can rest easy while his boat is anchored in an onshore procession of strong gusts. But here we have the consolation of knowing that the strong gusts make it difficult for thieves or pirates to approach the boat too slyly. We are moored well, too, with three anchors out astern and two strong lines to trees on the shore.

Now Wally tells me that much of the stores of fresh food he sent from Santa Marta was never delivered by José. Potatoes and milk and sugar are missing from the consignment. Anywhere else this would not be too serious—perhaps ten dollars' worth of food; but we are so isolated it is not an easy thing to get into the town, and so we must draw from our stocks on board—our sea stocks of dried food and prepackaged meals. I fired José yesterday and he slunk away, but Chi-chi still hangs around, even though he must know we are convinced he had a hand in the stealing of the food, or at least knew that José was doing it.

Wally, after a week in the *mañana*-land of Santa Marta, is taking delight in getting things done without having interminable discussions and lengthy waits. Right now he is dismantling the winches and greasing them.

Ivan (pronounced Ee-van) is Spanish, from San Sebastián in northern Spain, the Basque country, although he himself is not Basque but a true son of Castile. He has been with us since November, when we reached Costa Rica, where he was crewing on board a Swiss yacht. He is twenty-three, and has served in the Spanish army—a prime requisite, it would seem, for any good, loyal deckhand. He has the real Spanish dignity, which is sometimes mistaken by others as a standoffishness, and at times can be infuriatingly cold in company, but he has the saving grace of Spain—a tremendous sense of the ridiculous, truly Quixotic. When he joined us his strength was far less than Wally's, but now he hauls lines and shoots arrows straight and true along with the best of us. I met Ivan in the "club" at Puntarenas—and I wanted to see the Spanish Main through Spanish eyes. Also it would be advantageous to have on board someone whose Spanish is flawless. He is to be the first— or one of the first—of Spain's modern ocean sailors from the lower classes—real sailors. Up to now there are very few of them, if there are any at all. This is my tribute to the people of modern, democratic Spain for all the hospitality they showed me during the years of their misery under Franco, and my years of penury. A sailor for Spain. Right now Ivan is putting finishing touches to paintwork down below, which we were not able to do before we left San Diego in such a hurry. Unlike Wally, Ivan can chat a woman up faster than anyone I have observed in recent years, and once he starts they fall for him like ninepins. When

Ivan talks to a young woman he uses everything he has, his body as well as his smile and his words. And yet he is strangely moral, and has an almost religious respect for what he calls *"una mujer de familia buena"*— a well-born woman. Ivan has an almost superstitious respect for me as his captain and as a writer, and he hovers about me like a bodyguard, so much so that I have to tell him to clear off at times. It is mainly through Ivan that I know what is being said here by the *costeños*, for I can understand hardly a word of their rapid, murdered Spanish.

But still, as the sailors say, Ivan gets the name, but Wally gets the game, bless 'em.

"There are no free lunches" in the United States. The people who financed most of the fitting out of *Outward Leg*, although they expressed sentimental (in the best sense of the word) reasons for doing so—to get me back to sea and sail and writing about it—also had other reasons. They had, as I had myself, visions of a *cruising* trimaran design for the future; safe, long-distance voyaging multihulls. They, as did I—and as I still do—thought that the Osprey-class trimaran was the most promising of all for this purpose. They wanted me in one of their craft, in the prototype, and they wanted me to test her out to the limits, and to promote the class. You know, as you read, what *Outward Leg* means to me. I have no need to go into any long rigmarole about the merits of the Osprey class over other classes of multihulls. That is not the purpose of this book, and yet it weaves right through this account of pain and difficulties overcome. But it is not forced—it is an integral part of the tale, and not written at anyone's behest or expectation. Multihulls do have disadvantages. The greatest of these, the tendency to capsize sooner than monohulls, I believe I have overcome—more about that later—but there are still other disadvantages that must be overcome before the trimaran can be said to be at last a true-blue voyaging vessel. In this book I will merely touch on technical aspects of multihull voyaging. This is to be the subject of another book at the completion of this voyage. I can only write about what I know, and I shall not know enough about it until the voyage is over.

H. & S. Bluewater Multihulls was formed to build multihull vessels to the designs of a brilliant young Australian, Leo Surtees. The two partners of H. & S. Bluewater Multihulls and I, Leo Surtees and Wally, were the five elements that synchronistic destiny brought together in 1983. I was offered a free hand in the rig and accommodation design of *Outward Leg*, and a charter for three years at a very favorable rate, renewable on option at the end of that period. Of course I jumped at the opportunity. Who, in my position, would not have? The understanding was that I would sail *Outward Leg* around the world by any route I chose and would be supported en route. It was heady, sitting in the patio at West Coast Yachts, scheming and dreaming of the possibilities. But all the while I knew that serendipity is the key to a really interesting voyage. It is the real reason for exploration. It is easy to write that now, but how very difficult it might have been to get that idea over in San Diego. You can never explain the improbable before it occurs. It does not make logical sense—until it happens.

The charter agreement, however, left open the way to serendipitous opportunity in the most generous manner, so that I would not be tied down to any particular track, or be forced to act for any particular person's benefit, and yet still be constrained to guard the vessel—as if I needed such constraint!

In Conchita, Cotes's deaf-and-dumb son, Mario, makes the most distressing whimpering noises outside as I write. My cheap Japanese typewriter, the only nonelectric model I could find in San Diego, is playing a cat-and-mouse game with me, sometimes writing, sometimes not, and I am feeling exasperated. Beyond the beach in the distance, burning trees, with smoke pouring from them, indicate that something is afoot. I shall go over there in the dugout this afternoon, and see what it is.

We sometimes bribe Mario into silence with candies, but we are running out. I must save what I have for my more poetic moments, or for writing about the technicalities of preventing capsize in trimarans. I wish I knew deaf-and-dumb sign language, so I could teach it to Mario in the afternoons. As it is, he uses his own signs, like some piteous mummer, and the locals laugh at his efforts to communicate while my heart bleeds for him. Later, when I know him better, I may try to teach him to read—but I shall have to work out a way to transmit sound to him. Ivan thinks I'm crazy for planning this. As always with the poor in Third-World lands, Mario is looked upon as one of the blessed-by-God, and there is a superstitious objection to interfering with the way God made him. But God also made the alphabet. Thank you, Lord . . .

I couldn't stand Mario's whimpering anymore. I drew him a cat, and alongside it I wrote GATO. He is delighted, and is copying down GATO time and again. I may be able to teach him a few words and their meanings before I leave. That's a start. He has no voice box, so it's hopeless for me to try to teach him to speak, but at least I may be able to get the idea of abstracts over to him. The sound is not as important as the idea behind the letters and words. Sounds might be of vital importance to a poet, but to a deaf-and-dumb fisherman's son in Colombia, what matters, it seems to me, is that he may stumble on some simple form of communication. Cotes will not live forever. Then Mario will be alone in a silent, inexpressible world. Truly alone—and I know what that means. I must help him.

Later, Ivan showed Mario a picture of a cat all alone, with no word, and we are triumphant; Mario wrote GATO alongside it! It is probably the first time in his seven years he has ever expressed anything without piteous moans and groans. To express himself is the first thing, to absorb the next. He is intelligent and bright, and until now has been an absolute prisoner of inability to communicate except in the most primitive way. Pray God we can help him and open up this wonderful world to him, apart from what he can see with his own eyes and feel through his own experience. Without the eyes and experience of others we are as nothing. God grant that one day he may read Cervantes and Lorca and Pablo Neruda. What a tragedy, to be of the Spanish world and yet not. . . .

The breeze blows midday fresh, the crickets sing, the surf sounds on the pebbly beach and the *carpintero* birds chatter away. Mario hears none of this—yet, and probably never will—but he will know of it, and his world will grow to something like the one we know and love because *Outward Leg* has been here in Conchita, and if it were only for that, all the work and worry of getting the voyage under way would have been well worth it, and more. . . .

After lunch yesterday Ivan and I clambered into Cotes's dugout and headed for the beach at the root of the bay. This was the first time I had left Conchita for ten days. It is always good to see your own little world from outside, now and again. Once past the headland on the northern side of our baylet, I was astonished to see that the part of the beach it hides was crowded with people. It turned out that it was Sunday; Cotes reminded me, otherwise it would not have occurred to me. It's a good sign that you are content and busy, when you forget which day it is.

There is a ruined jetty, and five half-demolished beach villas among which the *costeño* families frisk about and drink bottled beer, their radios blaring at full pitch. I am told that the houses were sacked by *marijuanistas*, who now use the jetty for loading small craft, which head out to supply, in turn, bigger ships at sea.

At night the beach is very dangerous, as trigger-happy police roam around, ostensibly to counter the marijuana traffic—but in reality to discourage anyone, to shoot anyone, who might see what is going on.

We landed on the beach in front of a bar-kiosk crowded with families on their Sunday outings from Santa Marta. I felt like a visitor from another world among these families. There are few signs of hungry children, like there are in Santa Marta. This beach is too remote, and too dangerous for them if they should be stranded here at night. The men are mostly hairy, fat and misshapen, obviously small businessmen or shopkeepers, while the women in the main are showing the effects of being treated the way they are—as breeding machines. The children of a family can be of all shades of coloring, from ebony blue-eyed blond to ebony black, and if you look carefully you almost always see one who has some severe form of physical defect, or whose body is misshapen. In Columbia there is not the symmetry of Spanish families, and Ivan wholeheartedly agreed with me.

A line of jeeps and Toyota cars glared behind the beach, and into a couple of them piled "fishermen" from along the bay. I couldn't help wondering how, in a birdless bay—birdless because there are very few fish anywhere along this coast now—a fisherman whose vessel is a dugout canoe can afford to own a jeep. But these things I must keep to myself. To express them aloud to a local would be a direct invitation for someone to blow my head off.

The house that H. & S. chose as Operation Star headquarters in San Diego was—original. It had been built as a sort of off-street retreat by two men. Before its conversion it had been a shelter for homeless people. Now it was resplendent inside, in the new fangled, French-invented "industrial" style, with a huge open-plan living-room-cum-vestibule just inside the street door. Also open to the amphitheater of a living room were two bed spaces aloft. To one side there were two bedrooms and a bathroom, which had two toilets facing one another, and mirrors all over the place. The outside of the building was painted a garish, rosy pink. The contrast between the dusty, noisy street outside (Sunset Cliffs Boulevard—how the Californians romanticize the impossibly unromantic!) and the quiet coolness of the house was dramatic. The first thing we did was set up an office for Leo, who was away at the time in Australia; this was where he and I would wrangle and argue until the small hours of the morning about the finer points of the rigging and design of *Outward Leg*. This was to be the crucible, the conception bed and the killing ground of thousands of ideas.

But first we had to take the boat on sailing trials, to be certain that she was, in a seaway, the sweet thing that she seemed at anchor. Off California, it seems, the only place to find conditions suitable, most of the time, for sea trials—that is, a good wind and a fair to heavy sea— is off Point Conception, north of Santa Barbara. With some borrowed sails, and with the boat almost bare of anything except her original engine and what was needed to sail her, we set off. Apart from a cheap Taiwanese turn buckle breaking off the Californian Channel Islands, all went well. I thought that the renting of expensive hotel suites in Santa Barbara, and the hiring of a film cameraman and a helicopter to film the trials was an extravagance. I thought then that the money spent at that time would have been better devoted to the actual voyage—which would, after all, be the true trial of the vessel. But when in Rome it is best to keep quiet about how the Romans spend their gains. All that mattered was that the boat should be ocean-worthy and safe. And in California, to speak up against "public relations" is utter heresy. The image is the thing, there. Look after the outside and the inside will take care of itself, they seem to think.

At Santa Barbara, after the trials and the filming were done—they were, of course, a complete success—I went alone to the town pier and rewalked the mile of planks just as I had done the previous year. I had come in the boat to where the dream of Operation Star had been formed. It was a start. The rest was simple—to get the boat outfitted for a world voyage in three months flat, and to undertake the voyage—all sixty thousand miles of it.

On the way back to San Diego I gave heavy and deep thought to the capsize problem. Until then it had been the most serious drawback to safe multihull voyaging. Trimarans do not, in the main, have keels. They had no ballast at all. In fact ballast was hitherto directly against the concept of multihull sailing, where the credo is "Keep down the weight." Less weight, more speed. Now this is all well and good in a racing craft in sheltered waters, or on short trips where not much food, water and stores need to be carried; but in long-distance voyaging it will not serve. We need fresh water and food for our bellies, and we need stores so as to maintain the vessel in a seaworthy state at all times during the voyage. In my case I wanted also a steadier sailing platform than could be afforded me by a monohull heeled over. Speed was to me way down on my list of priorities. It certainly came after 1. steadiness, 2. rig safety, 3. hull safety, 4. endurance, 5. ease of handling. Give me those and I will cross an ocean at one knot quite happily.

From these considerations sprang the thought, What a pity that this trimaran cannot carry two tons or so of ballast on her keel, so as to give her a downward thrust whenever a sea threatens to lift her over an angle of more than twenty degrees. That night, off the islands, as we made our way south under a waning moon, I sat in the then wide cockpit and stared and stared at the moonlit sea—and stared—and then it came to me—what I was staring at *was* our ballast. The threat was the remedy. We could use seawater for ballast! Seawater in seawater weighs nothing. Seawater outside of seawater weighs whatever it weighs.

It became clearer and clearer. I sketched a rough drawing in the light of the cockpit hand lamp. If seawater were hung from the keel—captured in some way—and if the boat started to heel over beyond twenty degrees, balanced on one ama (outrigger), then the weight of the seawater would not only be what it is outside of its own element, but *it would be multiplied by its distance from the capsize fulcrum,* the keel of the lee ama.

A hundred pounds of water hanging on to a center keel twelve feet from the keel of the leeward ama, in fact gives a downward thrust of *twelve hundred pounds* once it leaves the sea. To get a downward thrust of *two thousand pounds* on the main keel all we had to do was stick the right amount of seawater on the bottom of the keel. Then we would have two tons of ballast, which would weigh absolutely nothing until the keel rose out of the sea.

What we would do was: reduce the incidence of capsize in a trimaran to that of a monohull of the same length. What we would do was: *make a trimaran safer than any monohull with a ballast keel.*

Monohulls with ballast keels sink. *Trimarans don't.*

What happened off Santa Cruz Island was that the long-distance cruising vessel of the next century was conceived, and *Outward Leg* is the very first of them: tough, fast, easy and *safe.*

I called the discovery the "cool-tubes."

Leo Surtees almost flipped his lid when I revealed it to him.

It cost next to nothing to install. It had no moving parts, and its effect on the boat's speed is minuscule.

6

Of Shoes and Ships and Sealing Wax . . .

A wind's in the heart of me, a fire's in my heels,
I am tired of brick and stone and rumbling wagon-wheels;
I hunger for the sea's edge, the limits of the land,
Where the wild old Atlantic is shouting on the sand.

Oh I'll be going, leaving the noises of the street,
To where a lifting foresail-foot is yanking at the sheet;
To a windy, tossing anchorage where yawls and ketches ride,
Oh I'll be going, going, until I meet the tide.

And first I'll hear the sea-wind, the mewing of the gulls,
The clucking, sucking of the sea about the rusty hulls,
The songs at the capstan in the hooker warping out,
And then the heart of me'll know I'm there or thereabout.

Oh I am tired of brick and stone, the heart of me is sick,
For windy green, unquiet sea, the realm of Moby Dick;
And I'll be going, going, from the roaring of the wheels,
For the wind's in the heart of me, a fire's in my heels.

"A Wanderer's Song," by John Masefield

The trees here on the foreshore at Conchita are old and gnarled, beautiful and surely brave. How else could they live so strongly in this almost rainless climate? I am thinking to myself how little I have noticed trees in my lifetime of seafaring, no more than to give them a passing glance, or to seek their shade on hot sunny days ashore. Today I sat and stared at them for an hour, and realized how soothing and friendly trees are. I doubt if any tree has ever intentionally harmed a human being. They do have a presence, though. They must surely feel. Getting to know trees is like getting to know quiet, sturdy people. Whoever plants a tree must love life—and others whom he will perhaps never see. There is a small tree at the side of the house—I do not know its name but it looks like a cypress—which has somehow been badly burned. Perhaps it was struck by lightning. All its branches are mere stumps, but at the tip of one there is a sprouting leaf stem. The tree refuses to die. I feel very much in communion with that tree, and every morning I tap its trunk gently with my stick, to let it know that I feel that way, too, and the tree seems to nod as I hobble past. Now we are like old friends, that little tree and me.

All around us, except to seaward, there are trees. Some are all strained up to heaven from the dry earth, as if in prayer for rain; some rise at first only to swoop down again as if their leaves were seeking water in the hot, dry earth; there are some that are all a-twist, and seem to be in an agony of contortion, sometimes writhing toward the earth and sometimes toward the sky, sometimes inward, sometimes outward; seeming to me to lead tortured, uncertain lives, at the same time full of dread and full of beauty. All trees are beautiful; that's why the birds of God sing and nest in them.

My favorite tree is a large, overhanging *trupillo* in front of the house. I can never stand under it for more than a few moments before some large and wonderful thought comes into my head. I am certain that the tree has something to do with this. Whenever I look at it, it nods its head wisely in the breeze, and admonishes me for leaving its shade.

It is no wonder to me, now, that many savage and primitive cultures worshiped trees. They were probably, apart from dogs, the only *friendly* beings that the people ever knew. My forefathers, in the old Celtic culture, worshiped trees as representing *life*. No wonder at all. I cannot imagine nowadays living long ashore without trees around me.

The only trees I don't like are palm trees in the mass. They look to me somehow hostile and alien. All the rest I love, from the northern pine to the banyan tree. Sailors ought to make a ritual of planting a tree somewhere after every time they have enjoyed a sea venture. Or plant a tree and give it the boat's name. From now on, after Conchita's trees have so welcomed me, I shall try to do that, wherever I am.

My other main nature interest here in Conchita is a colony of ants. I never cease to wonder at their industry, and stare at them fascinated, so that my crew thinks I am going a bit daft. Their nest is under one of the stones in the courtyard, and into it disappears every tiny scrap of food that falls off the dining table and is not swept up. Some of the carriers miss the nest entrance, and wander about beyond it aimlessly until a watchkeeper from the door hurries out and nudges them back on track. So it must be with writers; what we carry must be for *all.* It is wrong to think that an author should write only to please himself. That is like pouring seawater into a bottomless bucket. It is like voyaging for the mere experience, and with no aim in mind. It is selfish; and anything that is selfish is worthless.

This afternoon both little Mario and I are elated. Twenty-four hours after I showed him the drawing of a cat and the word for it, I again drew a picture of a cat on a blank piece of paper and handed it to him. Alongside the drawing he carefully scrawled GATO. I was so pleased I went to lift him up into the air, but I stumbled on my false leg and almost fell and Mario went into a giggling fit. Now he is practicing the words for *house, dog, man* and *boat.* Without sound spoken or heard we are finding out first how he can learn to relate words to objects; then we will go into abstracts. That will be difficult, but Mario is bright and I have high hopes that by the time we leave he will be able to communicate in writing on at least a basic level, which will be a thousand percent better than he was doing when we arrived.

Wally also found on board our second bow. He and Ivan are now breaking it in on the "archery range." It was a last-minute gift from Leo Surtees, and will be employed by the night watch on board. Anyone attempting to board at night without permission will get an arrow well placed in him, with forty pounds of thrust behind it. We can have no second thoughts about this.

The total cost of outfitting *Outward Leg* was, I think, much more than it need have been if circumstances had been different—if tighter control could have been held over the painting contractors, for instance. There alone, thousands of dollars went into making the topsides and deck look pretty, which might better have been invested in safety gear. In the end I had to provide that myself out of money that should have been held in reserve for the first half of the voyage.

I do not know what the eventual total cost of the outfit was. H. & S. Bluewater Multihulls put a great deal into the venture; I put everything I had. During the period when the outfitting took place, my income was close to $23,000. This included advances on future earnings. This was all spent on costs of outfitting and living expenses. When *Outward Leg* left San Diego I had in hand, on board, almost $800 and debts of $32,000 still to be paid off. These were mainly medical debts. My investment in the boat was in the region of $12,000 with donors contributing something in the region of $10,000 worth of equipment, including four months' food supplies.

If would-be voyagers wait until everything is exactly in place and sufficient money available for the whole voyage, the chances are that the vessel will never leave her home port. The boat must be integral, not dependent on any particular port or base, and the people in her must be confident that they can make their way, somehow, even when cut off from their usual sources of income. There can be no half measures or faint hearts in this. The endeavor is either integral or it isn't, and if it isn't, then the voyage is best abandoned before it begins. I was determined that the Star voyage would not be abandoned. I forced the outfitting through as fast, yet as well, as possible.

Outward Leg returned from pre-outfitting sea trials on the fourth of August. Her outfitting was finished on the sixteenth of October 1983. The boat was hauled at Coronado on the tenth of August and was re-launched on the fourteenth of September.

We started off by planning all sorts of gadgets to enable me to get around the boat easily both at sea and at anchor. A dolly cart in stainless steel to get me to the bow and aft; an elevator hatchway to the after cabin; a "bosun's cage" to haul me up and down the mast—but the exigencies of the circumstances led to the abandonment or avoidance of such projects. But there is yet time for them to be taken up again, developed and tested, before the voyage of *Outward Leg* is over, if God wills it.

As it was, I decided that after certain structural changes had been made—for instance, a smaller cockpit, and thus a walk-through from the after part of the boat to the fore part—then we should concentrate on making the vessel fit for all occasions of the sea, and I would have to adapt myself to the boat from there on. I would have to learn to get around the decks myself, without any extra help.

I was fitted with a new leg, which was a failure as it turned out, and I made out a new will. Let's hope that neither will need to be used before this voyage is completed.

For the leading lights of H. & S. Bluewater Multihulls, it must have been very difficult to work with such a human complexity as sailors and their boat. One partner must have undergone inordinate strains to leave the hothouse ambience of a computer programming center, where everything is based on utter logic, and join us in our illogical love for an inanimate object not yet alive. The other, who had worked wonders in Singapore expediting equipment running into billions of dollars' worth from all accounts, must have found it hard to accept that the Japanese *kanban* (take delivery at the last minute) system simply will not work with a prototype, one-of-a-kind sailing boat, with her equipment ordered from all over the world. There is no such thing as "just on time" in this case. The gear must be on hand. If it is not, something will crop up that demands its presence in place. Practically everything in a boat, all the hundreds of different bits and pieces, is dependent in some way or another on each of the others, and they must be fitted together like the myriad pieces of a jigsaw puzzle. The way the puzzle is fitted together can later very well be a matter of life and death, or at least of the success or failure of the voyage and the avoidance of unforeseen hazards. There is no stopping a boat in midocean to order parts from a store up the road. Leaving things until the last minute, and not only things but ideas and solutions, aims and resolutions, simply will not do.

Considering these differences of interests, occupations, experience and philosophy, we five—the two partners at H. & S., Leo Surtees, Wally and I—did very well, I think, to have had the vessel at least a viable oceangoing entity by the second week of October.

We learned a lot—one hell of a lesson. Let's hope it did us all good. The final cost of *Outward Leg*, when she left San Diego, was probably a good one-third more than it should have been.

In those days the aim of the trip was, apart from being the example-to-handicapped Operation Star, to make a voyage around the world either west-about, across the Pacific to Australia and so on, or east-about. Setting records is of very secondary importance to Operation Star, but there already hovered the idea, too, of tackling the Equatorial Current in the southern Caribbean. *Nautical Quarterly* came up with help in the shape of an advance for a story. Joe Gribbins, bless him, said he would take the story whichever way I went, and told me not to be a damned fool, but to tackle only what I was fairly sure I could achieve. That advance kept Operation Star going for weeks.

The sails for *Outward Leg*, and the rigging, were designed and fitted with the help of Fritz Richardson, who himself tried to make a passage west-about around the Horn only weeks afterward, in *Cystic Fibrosis Crusader*, which failed. The vessel broke up off the Horn. But Fritz, brilliant and industrious as he is, is still only young enough to try for *sail*. I am trying for *people*. I do not want, I do not need, to prove what I myself can do. I want to find out, I want to show, what *other* people in my physical state can do. What I have done on this voyage to date they can *all* do. They cannot all sail around the Horn, and neither will

I attempt to show that they can—at least not yet. Never ask others to do, or suggest that they can do, what you yourself are not able and willing to do. That is the first rule of a good skipper.

Many people helped in the outfitting of *Outward Leg*—and a few of them put in great effort for no recompense at all except the satisfaction of knowing that their effort is not forgotten and that it will not stop.

A therapist, Glen Elia from Philadelphia, flew to San Diego to help and advise me for a week. He was astonished at my hopping about so well and at my determination to push the thing through; so much so that by the second day we had forgotten all about my leg, and he was helping to square away the boat and her gear. Now that's true therapy, when the patient gets the therapist working on something entirely different, when nothing matters but the aim of the effort.

Of course there were reports in the local yachting press—mostly vastly inaccurate, and I did nothing to disillusion them. Who am I to spoil their dreams? God knows they need romance in Southern California; the reality is too dreadful. As long as some progress had been made on the boat, it mattered to me not one whit how many gross inaccuracies or outright untruths were published about me or about the voyage. Let them wallow in their own errors.

Wally arrived on the twenty-second of August, and I woke to hear him at the door and to learn that Operation Star was now a mite more certain.

7

. . . and Cabbages
and Kings

Oh, a bulgine once was a-heaving,
Run, let the bulgine run!
Oh, high-ya, Oh, high-ya!
Run, let the bulgine run!
She's lovely up aloft and she's lovely down below,
She's a dandy flier and a sticker, too,
With a dandy skipper and a bully crew,
Oh, we'll run all night 'til the morning,
Oh, we'll rock and roll her over,
Oh, drive her, captain, drive her,
Oh, captain make her old nose blood,
Oh, we'll run her off the map to old Saccarap.

"Run, Let the Bulgine Run!" Capstan halyard,
nineteenth century. It probably is of black American origin. *Bulgine* was American slang for a
railroad engine.

Apart from my own special needs as a one-legged cripple for a boat that
heels over only slightly, what should we all aim for in a long-distance
voyaging vessel?

Security. No boat is ever built that is not lively in a seaway. The
sea is very rarely calm. To imagine otherwise is a foolish daydream. People
on board a boat must be secure against falling, or being washed, overboard. That means there must be good, solid guardrails, plenty of hand-
holds, and a cockpit just large enough to do the job it is meant to do
and no more. It also means that the right gear must be available to suc-
cor people who fall overboard: safety harnesses, signal pole, life jackets,
life belt, trailing line. It also means that there must be some easy way

of boarding the vessel from the sea. It amazes me to see how many oceangoing vessels do not have all of these simple provisions against personal disaster and death.

Included in security is **unsinkability.** Here is where the multihull has the edge on the monohull. Even if the trimaran is swamped she will not sink, for her hull is lighter than seawater. That means then that good hull pumps are a must, and they should be capable of pumping her out completely in a matter of an hour or two. It also means that a self-righting system must be included in the boat's gear. In *Outward Leg* this is provided for by pumps, a water-transference piping system, an A-frame, which can be rigged on the upside-down vessel, and a big rubber bag, into which seawater can be pumped and which provides the righting moment, once the seas have lessened.

Secondary to the self-righting system are the means for the crew to remain secure and reasonably fed and *dry* while the vessel is upside down. This means well-packaged food, some means of cooking it, and hammocks to sling above water level.

Unsinkability means that the vessel herself is her own life raft.

Uncapsizability is the aim of the cool-tubes. They work, and *Outward Leg* is, in fact, the most secure vessel under forty feet overall sailing the seas at this moment. With her specific gravity less than seawater, there is no way, short of being piled on rocks or reef, or being run over, that she can sink. Her endurance is limited only by that of her crew. Thus she is the cruising vessel par excellence.

Such vessels as *Outward Leg* will be indomitable. The survival factor is in direct proportion to the strength designed into her, and here Leo Surtees has done a superlative job. The hammering she can sustain, beating hard to windward for days on end, never ceases to amaze me. Apart from little *Sea Dart*, she is the only boat I ever sailed that is perhaps tougher in spirit than I am myself. It would take a very determined lunatic to destroy her. With the practically indestructible materials of which she is built, there is no reason why *Outward Leg* could not still be sailing a hundred, even two hundred, years from now.

The main danger with vessels like *Outward Leg* is one of their greatest joys: The elation that is felt at speed, and especially when running before the wind and the sea, may be so great as to overcome the seamanlike caution the ocean demands. You may probe this joy, this incautious elation, time and again and get away with it, but sooner or later, unless you are careful, the sea will catch up with you—so beware. Reef down much sooner, especially while running, than you would in a monohull. Remember, there is not the heeling moment to add extra warning to your senses of hearing, seeing and feeling. As for *Outward Leg* and me, speed I can have if I want it—probably well over twenty knots running—but I am cautious; if I can make a circumnavigation with an average speed of nine knots I shall be content, thank you very much. It is much more seamanlike to arrive in a fair time and in good order than to arrive quickly with a shattered vessel, or not to arrive at all.

Little Mario is not whining nearly so much now. He is using the pen I gave him more every day. He is learning what all boat outfitters know—that a blunt pencil is better than a bad memory.

Now, in the early morning haze, *Outward Leg* sleeps to her anchor, her furled sails like closed eyes. She has the look about her of a sleeping tiger—rather, a swan waiting for the music to commence. I flatter her, in my heart, every time I look beyond my window. In her livery of turquoise and light gray, morning light, she rides buoyantly, as though she were made of fragile porcelain—how very deceptive she is!

A plate, a spoon, a fork, a knife and a cup are missing from the kitchen—and so is Chi-chi. Ah, Colombia!

I shall try not to let my command of the finest voyaging vessel afloat lull me into a false belief in my own strength, my own luck. After all, it depends on her, as she depended on the people who brought her into the world. . . .

In the rushing, troubled ambience of Star-base in San Diego, it would have been impossible for me to convey what was in one half of my mind the whole time—that the sea knows nothing of money or power. To bring that up at one of our interminable meetings would have been an exercise in futility. The sea knows nothing of money or power. She knows only loyalty and audacity and determination and courage and, by God, she knows an unthinking, unseeing fool when she encounters one. She knows awareness, she knows patience, she knows staunchness, she knows foresight, yet she knows nothing of man's longing for riches or fame or even of his efforts to overcome or thwart her. She gives an illusion of freedom, but in reality she demands restraint, caution, self-discipline, and a deep belief in the grace of God. If we have none of these precious attributes when we join her, we shall have when we have known her for any length of time—or we will be defeated or dead.

Was I right? Did the others in San Diego see only the glittering crown, and not the difficult dead ore, not the dusty dreary road to the mine?

I can never love the sea, any more than I can love the air, or the stars in space. I can love only what I think about them. How can I love something that isolates me from all the things that I truly love? Good company, intricate conversation, live music, the welter of art, and people, people, people—and all their ways of wonder—and children, and the dream of the future. What does the sea know of them?

I know full well what it is that I love—that I think I love about the sea. It is the illusion of mastery, the pride of skill; and the seafaring life itself. But the sea herself—never. And even the mastery is an illusion, as is all mastery. We gain one eighth of an inch in a lifetime of struggle on the million-mile-long road to the stars and we think we are the lords of life. It's nonsense. I love an illusion, but I know that because I love it so well and truly, someday, somewhere, someone else will be yet another eighth of an inch along that arduous trail—and, after all, it really boils down to that first beer after a hard beat to windward.

There are no people on the face of the earth so adept at transforming a dream into reality as Americans. But they try their best to transform the dream into an ideal of their own. No people anywhere are so capable of absorbing a dream so thoroughly that it becomes a part of them, and they champion it, devote an amazing energy to it and transform it and, if you are not very careful, they destroy it. One of the reasons for this tendency toward the destruction of another's dream is the American's need to be loved, to be admired, to be approved, regardless of by whom, or in what circumstances. Approval, to a European, is a thing apart from everything else; to an American it is his whole reason for existence. Approval means *success*, and success is all to him.

Whether you as a European approve of me or not, of what I do or how I do it, is quite irrelevant to my attitude toward you. I can accept your disapproval and yet still like you as a person, and try to understand you. This, to an American, it seems, is so much gobbledygook.

I spent hours and hours trying to demonstrate that I approved of people as well as the ideas they were promulgating. It was like comforting souls who had been lost for weeks in a wilderness.

Yet no one else, no other people anywhere, could have made the effort that was made to ready *Outward Leg* for her voyage. No other people could have been so open, so original, or so generous. Nowhere else could heaven and earth have been shifted so rapidly, so enthusiastically, as they were shifted by all the Americans who helped *Outward Leg*. Once they got an idea firmly in their heads of how something should be found, or done, there was no stopping them. It would be found—it would be done.

In America, success is all. There is no middle way; the word *moderation* is anathema. To an American it stinks of failure. To be moderately successful is to fail. Failure, to them, is the most deadly sin of all. To an American, everything is possible, all is boundless, and not to have reached all that is possible, not to know all that is boundless, including love and respect, is anathema. They cannot conceive that the possible, the boundless, are only reachable and knowable by a very few elect of the earth. To them this is utter heresy—and yet, after being pressed hard, some of them will admit that there just might be a dash of truth in it.

To Americans—they are *all* middle class—reality is always *material* reality, something to grab hold of, hard, resistant, unformed, awkward, impenetrable and unpleasant—very much like the continent they have almost tamed, in its original state. The only mind that an American respects at all is very similar. It is the mind that reproduces the same sensations as this idea of reality. He has a tremendous guilt complex about the rape, as he sees it, of his country by his forebears, and is forever trying to transform himself, in his imagination, into a Red man, painted in a forest hunting deer, or riding the plains chasing buffalo. Few Americans are content merely to *be*.

A European can become accustomed to living happily in America and yet remain European, and so, in the possible future, he will find little difficulty in existing quite contentedly on a strange planet. He will become, say, a Euro-Martian. But an American in the same situation will first construct a Coca-Cola plant, build a fence, and remain American. He will worship all Martians between the ages of twelve and twenty, and despise all over the age of forty. Those he cannot convert into salesmen he will send off to the next planet as a sort of Peace Corps.

But, bless them—they performed miracles.

I, too, performed a miracle. In that boiler room of mind-twisting effort that was Star-base, I managed to keep the dream of Operation Star to its original simplicity and purity, to show that where there's life, there's hope. . . .

Yesterday I returned to the beach at the far end of Bahía Concha. It was windy and deserted, except for a patrol of the antinarcotics police, about fifteen strong, under the command of a lieutenant. All the privates were very young; I think none was over twenty. Cotes says this must be so, as the terrain they cover, over the mountains of the Sierra Nevada de Santa Marta, is very difficult to traverse. They must be as agile as goats. They were dressed in olive-drab outfits, with a sort of tropical Australian bush hat. The youngsters carried rifles, one to each two men, and the officer, a man of no more than twenty-four, wore a revolver. They were quite friendly to me, as it seems that one of the privates had been swimming in Santa Marta bay the other week, and I had allowed him to rest on our stern for a few minutes before he swam back to the beach. There Wally had talked to him, and now he even remembered the name in Spanish of one of my books. It is a good thing to be known by these people, and even better that they know the boat— that we have become part of the furniture here. They are notorious for nervous trigger fingers at night, and will attack anything that moves or that is strange. As Cotes paddled me back to Conchita I saw that the police scouts were strung all along the shoreline. I doubt if anything was happening, and to me it looked only like a demonstration of force.

A police private told me that his pay is $130 a month, out of which he pays $30 for his food, and $10 for the upkeep of his outfit and arms. The rest, $3 a day, is all his to send home or to spend as he pleases. He doesn't know it, but actually at the moment he is better off than I am. . . .

I located on the radio a station that broadcasts classical music for most of the day. On the portable I can listen to Beethoven, Chopin, Liszt, along with the eternal background surge of the surf on the shore, and the sough of the breeze in the trees. Sound and visionwise I am now one of the fortunates of the earth. All that concerns me is that Don Jesús return from the States with some money from my agent for me to continue the voyage of *Outward Leg,* and that people take note of what I write of the reasons for the ill repute—well deserved—of this coast, and its murderous name.

The far eastern corner of Bahía Concha would make an ideal site for a small-craft haven. It is well protected from all winds except westerly, which is so rare as to be discountable, and there is good holding ground. The beach is backed by flat sandy terrain, to which a road leads from Santa Marta. The bay is surrounded by hills about five hundred feet high. The beach is fine and sandy, with plenty of shady spots provided by cypress and palm trees. The main problems are: banditry, piracy, guerrilla warfare, a shortage of fresh water—and the use of the place at present by drug smugglers who, I am told, pay off the police to avoid being caught. There are about a hundred acres of flatland backing the beach, which would make a fine site for a properly designed and built marine facility with amenities for visiting craft. The view to the west, overlooking the island of Agaja, is superb—at dusk it is the stuff of fables.

The patenting process for the cool-tubes was started while I was still in San Diego. I sent what is grandly known as a Disclosure Document to the Patent Office in Washington, which, while it does not secure the patent, at least gives a historical record of the disclosure of the idea, and is acceptable as evidence in a court of law, should litigation come about. Later my agent engaged a lawyer to search the records and found, to his amazement and to my unsurprised satisfaction, that nothing like the cool-tubes has ever been patented in the whole five-thousand-year history of boat design and construction. I am sharing some of the proceeds of the invention, if there ever are any, with Leo Surtees, for his help in applying the idea to *Outward Leg*. I hope I make a fortune out of it but much more important to me is to have the credit for the idea— and that multihulls of the future should be safer than those of the past. I want to be remembered as the man who first realized that trimarans, should *sail through their own ballast*. God provided the ocean (among other reasons) so that trimarans would have a positive downward thrust imparted to the lower edge of the keel whenever it might be needed.

When the cool-tubes were in place, it was too early to divulge any information about them to those not already in the know. The carpenters thought they were some kind of afterburner—the tubes had a *Star Wars* look about them—while the Mexican painters thought they were hidey-holes for smuggling contraband—naturally!

The materials used for the cool-tubes were wonderfully simple: two six-inch PVC pipes, some copper sheeting to line them with, a couple of lengths of copper tube to line the water entry and exit holes, and round, rubber-ringed stopper hatches at the after end. The whole device was molded to the existing keel with fiberglass and resin until it was as strong as the keel itself, then flared into a fish, or torpedolike, configuration. There it sits, out of sight most of the time, but not out of mind. The total cost was about $120 plus labor.

The original mast was forty-six feet tall. I asked that the new mast be forty-two feet. This was to bring the mast in line with the hull length and to reduce the hobby-horsing motion to which trimarans are prone when beating in a seaway. Events proved that I was right.

It is a matter of personal inclination, but I prefer in a long-distance voyager, which will be encountering all kinds of weather conditions, to have a lower, longer mainsail. To make up for the reduction in height

I had the boom lengthened by two feet. This means that now when the main is reefed, it has more power than it would have had with the high-aspect rig, and it shoves where it should shove, down low, and the shorter mast means less useless and dangerous top-hamper aloft in a bad blow.

I made the mistake of not insisting on the removal of the large deck lights on the main deck. I was asking for so much more to be changed that I decided to give way on that score because of silly considerations of appearance. I was wrong. We have had nothing but continual leaks in those lights whenever it rained or whenever we beat to windward in anything of a sea. We are still looking for a solution to this problem. Big windows and small craft do not go together. After a few hours' beating the crew cannot sleep in their berths—they're wet through. But I've no doubt that we shall find the answer to this aggravating problem— one of the few problems in an otherwise almost perfect design.

Another minor fault was the lack of limber holes in the main hull frames. With the deck light leaking and seawater finding its way in, as it always will, no matter how fast a boat is closed up, this was a nuisance, because it meant swabbing out each section of the hull one at a time, first removing all the gear stowed in it. This is a very awkward task at sea, beating to windward, and especially for me, on one leg. This problem we are resolving by drilling limber holes for the water to drain into the galley bilge, whence it can be pumped out by the existing bilge pump.

8

Ready . . .

Hey, don't you see the black cloud rising?
Way, haul away—we'll haul away Joe!

Don't you see the black cloud rising?
Way, haul away, we'll haul away Joe!

Now when I was a little boy, and so my mother told me,
That if I didn't kiss the girls my lips would all grow mouldy,

I sailed the seas for many years not knowing what I was missing,
Then I set my sails afore the gales and started in a-kissing.

I find myself a Yankee girl and sure she wasn't civil,
I stuck a plaster on her ass and sent her to the devil,

Sheepskin, pitch and beeswax, they make a bully plaster,
The more she tried to get it off it only stuck the faster.

I courted then a Frenchie girl, she took things free and easy,
Then I found an English girl and sure she is a daisy.

So listen while I sing to you about my darling Nancy,
She's copper-bottomed, clipper bowed, she's just my style and fancy.

You may talk about your Yankee girls and round-the-corner Sallies,
But they wouldn't make the grade, my boys, with the girls from
     down our alley.

Oh, once I was in Ireland a digging turf and taties,
But now I'm in a limejuice ship a-hauling on the braces.

> "Haul Away Joe," tack and sheet shanty, mid-nineteenth century

The best moment in the day for a leg amputee, at least for me, is when I first wake up in the morning, or on board for my watch, whenever that may be. It is the only time when my leg is not in some kind of pain or discomfort—which goes to show, I believe, that pain and discomfort must be in the mind, all other things being equal. It is the only time when I am conscious of being relaxed.

The worst moment is right afterward, when I shift myself to stand, or to don my heavy false leg. Then the full import of my physical state comes right home to me, and I know that I have another day of hard struggle ahead. Struggle and effort. Effort in everything: to sit, to stand, to walk, to go to the toilet, to clamber up or down ladders or stairs, or in and out of dinghys, to *keep going.* I am told that a leg amputee of my age expends 130 percent more energy in mere ordinary movement than my ablebodied counterpart. I can well believe that.

After the first few minutes lying in a nirvana of painlessness, I look over for my leg and think to myself unless I am very careful, "Oh, God, another day with that thing!" But I drive the thought away from me, and think of the things to be done, and wonder what other, previously unnoticed wonders I shall discover before it is time to sleep, exhausted, again. Good music definitely helps. What also helps is to wake up surrounded by the tools and gear of my trade. I think it would be far harder for me to get started on my daily tasks if I had to commute to my work. My advice to other people who are, or who may become, handicapped is to find something you can do at home; and if you cannot, then shift yourself to where your work is. Surround yourself with it, soak yourself in it, and do it better than you ever did. More important though—live for others, just as much as for yourself. If you do that, their strength becomes, in some mysterious way, yours. There is always *somebody,* somewhere, who needs *you.* Never, for one minute, ever lose sight of that. If they are not with you, not near you now—*go and find them,* even if it means voyaging thousands of miles to do it.

In San Diego, the media turned up in full force, as usual after the hard work and struggle of preparation was over. As usual, they hinted and hoped that "events" be made to occur, and as usual did not realize that what was occurring *was* the event. As usual, they tried to make me say what I did not want to say, and do what I would never do. As usual, they tried to make a legend to their liking. I call it the "Popeye syndrome," this molding, this distortion, of the vision, the "image," of a responsible human being, fully aware of the terrible responsibility of bearing the dreams and the hopes of others upon his shoulders, into a foolish caricature of himself and all he stands for.

What with the doctors' lawyers hounding me, the American tax people aiming missiles at me, various credit-card companies insisting I had not paid what I had paid, and the magazines and TV people doing their best to drive me up the wall, and a complete lack of income prospects for some months, I decided to hare out from California as soon as Christ would let me. When in danger or in doubt hoist the sail and fuck off out. . . .

But I must not complain. Several organizations provided me with much-appreciated gear for the boat. Their names appear at the end of this book. What they provided were mere drops in an ocean of necessities but they were precious drops indeed.

It might be thought that I should consider myself very fortunate indeed to have had an almost complete vessel provided for my purpose (Operation Star) at such favorable rates. And so I was, but at the same time I was engaged in an activity toward which certain commitments had been made and which were now withdrawn. I had removed myself from the possibility, for example, of playwrighting a Broadway show, a monologue from *Ice,* which might well have given me a reasonable income for years to come. I had removed myself from the possibility, at least for the time being, of any European consortium providing me with a complete, ready-for-sea vessel and funds for the voyage. I had put everything I had into the venture, and mortgaged my future for three years. And I would do the same again—*I would have given my other leg* to get *Outward Leg* away on her voyage. I almost did.

I probably could have found another vessel in shorter time than that offered by the Europeans, but I had fallen in love with *Outward Leg.* I had, too, set out to make trimarans safer and—at no small risk—to prove that they can be safer. I was convinced, and still am, that apart from all the other aspects, this voyage will also prove that trimaran long-distance cruising is a viable prospect for the average couple with a family to sail many different areas of the ocean, and to do so safely. That alone makes all the extra worry and struggle that was thrust upon me worthwhile.

Leo Surtees was a wanderer for much of his young life. He found work in Canada for a while, where he became entranced with multihulls and their problems. He made a voyage from Vancouver, I think, to San Diego, and observed much and learned much about the movement of multihulls on the face of the waters in bad weather. He learned his lessons well and truly, and the sum of them stuck in his head. But he did not learn them in the company of a "traditional" sailor. That was a pity in some ways. Leo is an artist as well as a scientist. A rare combination indeed. Some of the ideas and innovations he designed into the Osprey class, of which *Outward Leg* is the prototype, are revolutionary and add much to the groundwork already laid in oceangoing multihull sailing craft by Arthur Piver, Walter Greene, Dick Newick, Eric Le Rouge and many others. One of Leo's brilliant innovations was, I think, the first ballasted keel to be built into a trimaran; he was already partly on the way to the cool-tubes development perhaps, when the flash of enlightenment struck me off the Californian Channel Islands.

Leo's ballasted keel, of fiberglass filled with concrete, provided the *Osprey* with 500 foot-pounds of downward thrust, in case the vessel reached the capsizing moment of angle. That might have been enough for general cruising purposes offshore, but I do not think it would have been sufficient for the huge Atlantic growlers, or the heavy gray seas of the Southern Ocean. For a forty-foot boat, 2,000–3,000 pounds of downward thrust, available at the instant of need, is much more like it.

Just as important as the trend toward available ballast, in Leo's philosophy, was his inclusion in the Osprey class of the very first built-in self-righting system for a trimaran. The method was not new, it had been tried out previously in Germany, but what was new was the provision of a seawater flooding and transfer system integral in the boat.

The self-righting system, if it should ever be needed, works by flooding the forward sections of the amas, so that the boat's forward part sinks, tilting her to a vertical position with her stern above water level. In this attitude she is kept until the seas calm down, or until the time to self-right is propitious. Thus the boat herself, bows down, serves as a life raft for her occupants.

At the right time the poles that form the A-frame, and which are normally stowed under the wing decks, are erected, and from them a 500-pound rubber water bag is suspended. This starts the self-righting moment when the bag is full. The weight of the water in the bag gives about 10 percent of the self-righting moment. All the rest is provided by the transfer of water within the boat by means of a 30-gallon-per-minute hand pump, permanently stowed under the berth in the after cabin.

Outward Leg is of foam sandwich construction, but if she were of say, aluminum or fiberglass, she would not, in fact, need the water bag to self-right. Nevertheless, I think foam sandwich is best, because it is buoyant in salt water. The boat simply cannot sink, even when fully swamped, even with a ton and a half of supplies and fresh water on board. Capsized, *Outward Leg* would become a life raft. A very expensive one, to be sure, but a good sturdy one, and if she stays afloat—which she will—then she can probably be self-righted.

The advantages of a center cockpit are obvious. The sails can mostly be handled from the wheel position. Running, there is a much more secure feeling in a center cockpit. There is always a high—and often dry, at least when running—view of everything all around the boat from the conning position. But another advantage to a center cockpit is that if she did capsize—an unlikely event, with her cool-tubes fitted—but if she did, then the center cockpit would dampen the heavy surge of water inside the main hull in rough weather.

An escape hatch is provided in the wing deck of the after cabin, in case of capsize, so that we can leave or enter the capsized boat. Even with the boat upside down the escape hatch is above water level, and always accessible. Normally, though, the escape hatch, opened up when the boat is alongside or at anchor, makes a wonderful ventilation hatch or fish observatory and a very convenient head for the skipper, at least in remote havens.

Leo made *Outward Leg* of Airex foam glass, with plywood crossarms, bulkheads and decks. This gives a tremendously strong yet simple construction with minimum maintenance necessary. Foam sandwich for the hulls means that we have a material that is 100 percent nonrotting, is fast to build, can take very heavy impacts, is not liable to condensation inside the boat, absorbs sound better than plywood, makes the hull self-supporting (*Outward Leg* has only six frames in the hull and four each in the amas), and will just about last forever.

She has two main cabins—one aft and one forward—and a roomy engine room in which I can stand and walk through. There is plenty of storage room—enough for a good four months' supply of food and fresh water for three people.

The rig that I asked for *Outward Leg* was similar to the cutter rig Leo originally provided, with the exceptions that I cut down the height of the mast by four feet, doubled up on all stays, and provided a clubfooted staysail and twin roller-reefing jibs for when running.

For cruising the best rig is cutter. It is simple to handle, especially with a clubfooted staysail and from a center cockpit, and it avoids that bane of self-steering wind-vane gears—a mizzen. With the staysail roller furling it also means that even if I had no hand with me I could sail the boat, using only the main and the staysail. I would not be able to sail fast with that rig, but it would get me there. Losing your crew should always be a consideration to bear in mind when you rig a long-distance voyaging vessel.

Because of *Outward Leg*'s wide beam she has no need of spreaders. The shrouds are brought straight down to the sides of the amas. This saves a certain amount of windage aloft in heavy winds. It also avoids the risk of damage to the rig caused by the collapse of a spreader.

On the rig that Leo and I designed, the running poles are fitted to swivels on deck, already six feet away from the base of the mast. With fourteen-foot-long poles, this gives me a full-width reach, from pole end to pole end, of forty feet. That's a very nice spread of sail when we are running downwind, wing on wing, with the two rolling headsails. One of the running poles can also be fitted to a track on the mast itself, to act as a derrick for lifting heavy gear on and off the boat, if I might be shorthanded.

I avoid a roller-furling mainboom. There is too much risk of a seize-up. Slab reefing is much simpler, and makes a tidier reef.

Both the backstays are also employed as aerials. One for the short-wave receiver, and one for a VHF radio, if we ever have one. Heavy-duty insulators are built into the backstay rig.

The sails provided were: mainsail, staysail, twin roller-furling jibs, yankee jib, spitfire jib, storm jib, genniker in light dacron.

The engine was a brand new Yanmar 24-horsepower diesel, with a sail drive. This means that there is no propeller shaft or gland aft. The propeller is almost directly below the gearbox, right abaft the keel, where it does the most good, especially in heavy head seas, and stays out the way of trailing warps and dropped sheets. Three electric batteries provide us with about 120 amp/hours of electricity. This is used mainly for cabin lights, the Weatherfax and the satellite-navigation set, also for the tape player, which is switched on for an hour or two a day at sea.

Leo put in an incredible amount of effort during the outfitting of *Outward Leg,* and worked all the hours that God sent him. The pressure on him and his family must have been intense, but we managed to work together, through thick and thin, for three months without severe conflict. Our aim was the same: to get the boat to sea as soon as could be, in as seaworthy condition as possible. I enticed him to even more effort, holding out the prospect of possible competition with other multihull sailors even then out on the ocean. This appealed to his youth and his Australian soul. But in reality it was only a sprat I was setting out to catch a mackerel. I was already thinking of much bigger fish to fry than the mere setting up of records, or the attainment of more and more speed under sail. I was thinking about the need for a psychological change in the reasons for voyaging.

There must be more to it than the mere setting out to sail from A to B via C. There must be exploration, not only of new areas of the ocean, but also of new parts of yourself.

If it is, then, to be an exploration, how can we know what it is to be until it is well under way? How can we even start to guess?

I told a reporter that we were bound for Pitcairn Island. So I was— to the Pitcairn Island of myself, with the wide ocean of the world, and all its joys and miseries, about me, and still another five hundred miles of the Equatorial Current and the reinforced trade winds to beat against, directly to windward, to reach Curaçao.

9

. . . Go!

Shanghaied in 'Frisco, we fetched up in Bombay,
They set us afloat in an old Leith boat,
That steered like a bale of hay.
Then away Susannah, my fair maid,
Oh! you New York Girls, can't you dance the polka?

We painted in the tropics,
While the pitch boiled up on deck,
We've saved our hides, little else besides,
From a freezing North Sea wreck.

We drank our rum in Portland,
We've thrashed through the Bering Strait,
And we've toed the mark on a Yankee bark,
With a hard case Down-east mate.

We know the quays of Glasgow,
And the boom of the lone Azores,
We've had our grub from a salt-horse tub,
Condemned by the Navy stores.

We know the track to Auckland,
And the lights of Kinsale Head,
And we've crept close-hauled while the leadsman called,
The depth of the Channel bed.

We know the streets of Santos,
The river at Saigon,
We've had our glass with a Chinese lass,
In Ship Street in Hong Kong.

'Tis goodbye Sal and Lucy,
'Tis time we were afloat,
With a straw-stuffed bed and an aching head,
A knife and an oilskin coat.

And when the purple disappears,
And only the blue is seen,
That'll take our bones to Davy Jones,
And our souls to Fiddler's Green.

"Away Susannah!" Capstan shanty, late nineteenth
century

This morning in Conchita it is raining—a slight drizzle driven in on the
wings of the trade. At this time of year, February, rain is rare indeed in
these parts. The rainy season is supposed to be from May until October.
Strong winds of forty knots and more yesterday blew in great rolling
fields and mountains of clouds, and all the night it blew and blew, and
the rain swished down on *Outward Leg*'s decks. There our rain-catch-
ment area, installed with insistence in San Diego, receives it, funnels
it down below, and into plastic jerricans. With luck, we shall refill the
boat's fresh water today—here, twenty miles from the nearest land supply.

Everyone involved in the outfitting of *Outward Leg* was, I think,
surprised—and no doubt relieved—at my not fitting big water tanks. Instead we carry eighty-five gallons in five- and three-gallon plastic containers. This means that there are no great weights sitting where they
cannot be shifted about. It means much greater flexibility, and it saves
a ton or so of water, all of a piece, sloshing about in a seaway. It also
saves the labor and expense of plumbing. And it imparts a psychological obstacle to using fresh water without good cause at sea; having to
lug a jerrican a few feet is vastly different from merely turning on a tap.
Right now we still have water we shipped in San Diego in October, and
only once have we taken a few gallons on board from ashore. All the
rest has been rainwater. In countries where the freshwater supply can
be considered always as suspect, that is important; it saves a lot of stomach troubles.

One of the great advantages of trimarans is also a disadvantage. The
big deck to catch rainwater, with lots of room to walk about on and to
stow gear on in harbor, also catches bird shit. But that's hardly a problem here as there are very few seabirds. With all the fish dynamited out
of the local waters, how could there be?

Here in Conchita, Wally and Ivan have been steadily working on
the boat—mainly painting areas left unpainted in the rush to make our
departure from San Diego. The after cabin is now pristine, bright and
airy. The galley bulkheads are dark navy blue, the same color as our
crockery. But besides tarting up the guts of the boat, we have also over-

hauled the self-righting gear, the winches and the self-steering gear. Now we are going to remove the big deck windows and replace them with wood and fiberglass. It is the only way we can stop the continual leaks when we are beating to windward.

For a small craft at anchor, I have the ideal crew. Ivan is very good with a paintbrush, clean and precise. Wally is handy with any tools. They are neither much good at cooking, they will never qualify for a Cordon Bleu certificate, but they will eat anything and without complaint. Neither of them smoke, which leaves the field clear for me. It is my only luxury apart from classical music. Give me a packet of cigarettes and Ludwig van Beethoven, and any kind of wind, and I am content. If tobacco was good enough for Sir Walter Raleigh, it's good enough for me. At any rate, it wasn't tobacco that killed him. I've been at it since the age of six, and I hope to be still smoking when they lay me out. Booze and tobacco were denied by Heinrich Himmler to recruits to the Nazi S.S. That alone is enough to highly recommend the consumption of both in quantity to anyone.

Another member of the crew of *Outward Leg* joined her only a day or so before we sailed. This was Ms. Brimstone, our cat. At the time she was very small and very black, and was rescued from an animal shelter. Now she is quite large, surely very desirable to male cats, and seems to think herself the owner and captain. She has recently taken to ignoring me and ordering Wally about. She is waiting for Ivan to learn more English before she starts on him, too. She likes Conchita—there is an almost continual supply of succulent fresh fish scraps on offer every day, and twenty feet of surf between her and the scruffy shore dogs, upon which she gazes scornfully as they bark their heads off at her for the first few minutes of her appearance on the deck, which is her stage. As the dogs yap neurotically, she purrs and grins to herself, as if she were bathing in applause. But once the boat is alongside, as she was on Colón, Ms. Brimstone loses all her élan and mostly hides down below in the daytime.

I hope one day to introduce her to a black male cat, whom we shall name Treacle. Ms. Brimstone seems to know this, and primps herself even more than usual every time we head into a haven.

Is it only four months and four thousand miles since we departed from San Diego?

On October 17 the well-wishers were out in force. Some of them set to helping us with the final necessary things like splicing the eyes into the ends of the two 150-foot-long drag warps, which we stowed in the after wing-deck holds. One of them gave us a dinghy racing knot meter—a sort of plastic pipe with a disc in it, which indicated speed. Wise one, that. He knew how dependable electronic logs are. . . . Others, including Wally's dad, drilled and hammered and sawed away well into the evening before we sailed, and started again the next morning before the sun rose. All the while this went on, the media crawled everywhere with their notebooks and cameras, forever getting in the way and holding up whatever was going on. They can't be blamed for that, of course; reporters are under intense pressure; but what they can be blamed for is putting their own construction on the thing that *is*. The radar alarm system in *Outward Leg*—one of the most advanced methods of giving warning of other craft in the area, was ignored—they wanted pictures of my wooden leg, which ornaments the mast-step. Again the "Popeye syndrome." The simplicity of the rig—simple and easily handled—was entirely missed: They wanted stories of death and disaster.

The stresses and strains of a fast, thorough outfitting, almost a rebuild, like *Outward Leg*'s, and the work involved in making sure that every part, every piece of the puzzle, fitted together thoroughly and well, were almost enough to make me forget that the preparation of the skipper and the crew are as important as, if not more so than, getting the boat shipshape.

Regardless of all the modern equipment fitted, and of all the advanced techniques built into the boat, the fact remains that a good blue-water skipper is still duty bound to make sure he's able to think rationally, and be able to convert that thought into responsible and sensible action or orders, no matter what is happening, or how concerned or even frightened he may feel.

Here it pays to remember that there are three kinds of problems: Those that will solve themselves regardless of any action, those that will remain regardless of what is done, and those that demand immediate attention to solve them. To sort them out needs a cool head, and attention only to the present circumstances.

It sometimes seemed that the tendency in San Diego was to consider that because the tools for solving some of the problems of the voyage were on board, the problems were solved. That is not so. In the end it all comes down to the skill, abilities and characters of the skipper and crew. You can have the most expensively fitted-out vessel ever built, but if the skipper and crew are dummkopfs—given the average amount of luck, good and bad, on a voyage of any length—the endeavor will fail.

To put into sensible order the welter of books and publications, charts and navigational lists in a period of three weeks is alone almost enough to send any sane man screaming along the jetty. To have him arrange and consider his weather information sources—on hurricanes, typhoons, willy-willies, cyclones, anticyclones, his warm fronts, cold fronts, his pressure gradients, strengths and shifts of squalls, his wind systems, ocean currents, harmattans, sharmals, cordonazos, Tehuantepecers—and to have reporters knocking on his deck all the while, borders on the unfair, if anything was ever fair about setting out on a long-distance voyage in a blaze of publicity.

Then I had to consider the welfare of my crew, some privacy for them, their food, medical kit (it ended up as a box of Band-Aids and aspirins from a local supermarket), making sure they were unworried about finances for the next few months, money itself, and where and how to get some, and when and where and how to get it sent out to me wherever *Outward Leg* might be, and my own health—I finally had to examine myself as best I could; there was no money for a doctor, or a dentist. Then there was the question of visas—most countries demand them of visitors, and especially of American visitors; there had been no time to inquire about them. It would have to be a case of arrive first and then ask. There were special cruising permits to inquire about, for countries like Ecuador or Indonesia, New Zealand or South Africa. There was no time for it all; it would have to be done on voyage, as we made our way. There were other papers, too, which we would require to have on board: registration documents, clearance documents, crew list, proof of financial solvency, which some countries require. The last was easy; there was none.

All the material requirements of the boat were in place, all the machinery and fittings, the life rails and the life raft, the dodger and the dinghy, all the hundreds of different items that go into a modern ocean-going cruising craft. By some kind of superhuman effort Leo had installed the fuel tank almost at the last minute. A heaving-to parachute arrived on board only an hour before we sailed. The Aries self-steering vane gear was in place. We had an electric drill so that the work could go on even at sea. All sails had been tried and tested. I had managed to have enough money to buy, at the last minute, a spare alternator. A three-hundred-foot trailing warp was now stowed below the wing decks. All this seemed to be incidental to replying to questions from reporters.

Four other yachts, two multihulls and two monohulls—I liked that touch—escorted us from San Diego Police Dock out to the offing. Practically everyone who had been involved in the outfitting of *Outward Leg* was there. Leo Surtees threw on board at the last moment a packet of split pins for the lower shrouds. They had been missed in the rush. The H. & S. partners excitedly cheered us, along with a hundred other people. Gradually *Outward Leg* drew ahead of the other boats, even heavily loaded as she was. As H. & S.'s boat pulled away to return to port I sang out, "God bless America!"

"God save the Queen!" came their reply, loud and clear. Not bad for people so true-blue American.

A sleepy murmur of waters was pushed aside as *Outward Leg,* under a quartering breeze, headed out to sea. Wally stood on the after deck, staring after the diminishing shapes of the chase boats. I stood in the after companionway for an hour, facing aft and the warm breeze, and watched as the dark water drowned the blinking harbor lights, until California was gone as if it had been a dream.

Aloft, the wind sighed, increasing as dusk descended. The turnbuckles whistled a high note, the stanchions a low note, a block on the main boom creaked, and the ship hummed at first, then sang her way as she curtseyed to the sea gods—southwest. Wally turned, red-eyed with staring into the gloaming, "Well, I'd better get some grub up," was all he said.

"That'll be nice, mate." I slithered down the steep after ladder, turned on the red light over the navigation table, and decided that this was not a dream, after all—the Coronado Islands were right in the way of our track.

During that first night out from San Diego I discovered that in a trimaran on a broad reach—what with her forward speed and the seas sloshing up through the vents between the main hull and the weather ama, and sometimes the leeward ama, too—what seemed down below to be a raging gale was, in fact, a steady, good sailing breeze. At first it is a strange sensation below in a loaded multihull under sail. The movement in any kind of seaway is like that of a benevolent camel treading daintily through a crowd of drunken football fans. But the fact remains that, uncomfortable as the jerking motion is and noisy as it seems to be aloft, the motion is far and away much easier than a monohull's would be.

Wally had never sailed with a wind-vane steering gear in charge of the course. He was astonished at the accuracy and faithfulness of the

Aries gear as it followed every slight change in wind direction and held the boat on a course no more than five degrees either side of that I had set. He sat for long periods during the next leg simply staring at the course lines and the wheel cables, the wind vane as it shivered, rose and collapsed time after time, and at the auxiliary rudder as it steered the boat as if by magic and left us free to gaze at it in wonder.

It was the first time I had ever departed on a long voyage without first communing with the land, somewhere away from the sea. I would have liked to, but I was not allowed to. There were too many people at hand, too many questions to answer, too many loose ends to be tied up, and I was wary in case something might happen on board that I would not know about. So it was sea, sea, sea, right from the word go.

One criticism had it that we were too early—the hurricane season was not over, and there was a fifteen-hundred-mile slog through the hurricane belt. But it would never have been too early to leave the tense ambience of San Diego. Never too early for me.

I didn't sleep at all that first night at sea—I never do on the first night. I seem to want the boat to know that I love her, and will guard her; that as she is awake so am I, and that nothing she suffers is not suffered by me.

Next morning light showed a brilliant day, with the low sun already shooting through the moderate seas at six o'clock, and the boat, with all her working rig—roller headsail, staysail and main—plunging away. I prepared breakfast and got a dollop of seawater in my porridge for my pains. The feeling of relief at being away from all the hullabaloo of San Diego was so intense that we just let her ride southwest, but with not much real care as to her precise course. To be free, at last, of the trammels of the land is something I wish everyone could experience. Compared to this, taking off along a highway in a souped-up car must be like being trapped in an iron lung. The boat is sound and sturdy, we are healthy (making allowances) and all the wide waters of the world are before us—and we do not yet know whither we are bound; the utmost freedom. It is like drinking sparkling champagne after years and years of flat beer. . . .

I was very pleased and most grateful for the provision of a Weatherfax radio. For those who do not know it, this is a radio set that prints on board a series of weather maps, and in most parts of the world, it can be tuned to a station that will broadcast forecasts for your particular area. Ours was provided by the Tai-Ping Society. I had adjusted it in

San Diego, along with a thousand other things, and it was working well, tuned in on San Francisco.

On the morning after we left San Diego the Weatherfax gave warning of Hurricane Tico, then forming up in the Gulf of Tehuantepec, in the south of Mexico, and heading northwest—straight up the Mexican coast and directly toward where we would be when it reached our latitude. I decided two things: first to head into Ensenada, Mexico, and second, that if Erik the Red or Columbus had carried Weatherfaxes the chances are that they would never have sailed. There was no point in staying out and trying to outrun the hurricane—not in the area we were in; the Mexican hurricanes are very fickle in direction and move fast, and their winds would blow the hair off a horse. We headed into Ensenada, and by dusk were feeling our chartless way around the end of the outer seawall. Then we crept in among ghostly tuna boats and dropped the hook. The hurricane needed nothing we could give it.

Ensenada has two things going for it, and two things against it. It is a safe anchorage, with lots of room and a good holding ground—mud—and the authorities there leave you alone. This, in a Latin country, is the highest recommendation that any haven can have. Against Ensenada are its geographical location, just south of the United States border, which means that hordes of American tourists visit the place and fleecing the gringos is thus the local preoccupation; and its lack of a good place to land from dinghies. Getting ashore there brought to mind pictures of British tommies floundering through the Flanders mud of World War I. I could see no reason why anyone would ever wish to visit Ensenada unless it was to take shelter in a small craft, or because things are cheaper there than they might be elsewhere. Apart from a thin strip of girly joints down by the waterfront, it seems to be mainly industrial, and there is nothing worse than industrial slums in a tropical climate.

Wally was quite at home in Ensenada and ignored it, mainly. We did a lot of work in the two days we anchored there. For one thing we fitted a head pipe for me in one of the cockpit cubby holes. A length of PVC pipe just stuck down straight through the wing deck. Into it I can now empty my toilet bucket, without having to risk my life going out onto the amas. We fitted the bilge pump so it gushes straight into the pipe, and so keeps it clean. This is an ideal toilet—apart from the bilge pump, there are no moving parts, and gravity never fails.

We then put in the reefing points in the main—all three hands of them—and secured the Avon life raft and the bows and arrows—our only arms—properly in the after cabin

It had become obvious that for any long spells at sea our fuel capacity, forty-two gallons, would not be enough to support an hour's daily engine running for battery charging and also allow us to keep a supply in hand for getting through dead calms. We needed to double the fuel stock on board. Wally and I went by taxi all around the town, looking for plastic fuel containers. We visited every hardware store; we called at every garage. Finally we tracked down a very shabby-looking ancient jerrican in a scrapyard. The sly-eyed owner knew we needed what he had. The price was thirty dollars. I gave him a talk on good relations between Great Britain and Mexico, and how I'd always admired Pancho Villa, not to mention Emilio Zapata, and the price came down to twenty dollars.

We returned, cursing under our breaths, to the waterfront. The taxi driver charged us twenty dollars, even though he'd previously agreed to an hour and a half for ten. We lugged the five-gallon container on board, hauled the hook and sailed out of Ensenada. The following day we found that the five-gallon container was empty. Whatever the sly-eyed scrap man had used to plug a crack had dissolved. Thus our officially unrecorded visit to Ensenada. It was just as well we didn't enter properly. The ship's papers had been mislaid in the rush to get away from San Diego.

Out we sailed, in the dusk again, out, out, southwest, in a freshening breeze, the wind again a low hum in the rigging.

I had tried again and again to raise someone in San Diego on the ham radio. Once, for a very brief exchange, I had succeeded. But from Ensenada I could only reach someone in Illinois. It seems that radio conditions on the west coast of Mexico were, at least at the time we were there, not ideal. Just as well, I suppose. There's enough noise at sea in a trimaran as it is. Every other noise is drowned in the constant swishing of water around the amas and up through the vents between them and the main hull. There are no smooth waters at sea.

In the offing of Ensenada, about eight miles out, in the darkness, I noticed that the water was behaving in a strange manner, swirling about in little whirlpools, sizzling and bubbling, and popping up vertically. For a second or two my heart jumped; I thought we might have strayed among rocks or reef, but since the chart showed deep water it could only be tide rips. I made myself a cup of tea and settled down on the cockpit seat, to while away the first watch until midnight. I thought about how the tides are gradually changing over the centuries; they are not now as they once were—not as strong now. As with everything that is of the earth, the days of the tides are numbered. The very movement of the water over the beds of the ocean, over the shallow ledges of the continental shelves, and over the inland seas, carries within itself the force that is destroying the tides; tidal friction is gradually slowing down the rotation of the earth. Then I shook myself, and recited silently some verses by Edward Lear to cheer myself up. There was still enough tidal movement to last you and me out, after all.

The departure from Ensenada was, to me at least, the real start of our voyage. It was not made in pomp and noise, but in a holy silence, as all pilgrimages should start.

In Conchita the rain has frizzled away—we caught only a quart or two on board. We are in the tropics, I remind myself, and we can expect nothing to last for long, except the sunshine: not rain, nor effort, nor memory, nor sincerity, nor truthfulness, nor love. Those are the things of the colder countries. In the tropics you should never have great expectations; only be prepared for great disappointments, always, and that goes for the people as well as the weather.

Jones's Law on Sincerity: Generally, the sincerity of people, their sense of compassion for others, can be measured in direct proportion to the distance of their home from the Equator.

Tomorrow I am going, with Ivan, into Santa Marta to buy supplies of food and gear needed for work on board. It means a trip by dug out canoe of a mile to the beach, and then a journey along *el camino de los muertos* of about eight miles. We could sail the boat around to Santa Marta, of course, but the trouble of getting the three anchors broken out, and then resetting them when we return, makes it hardly worth the effort. The anchors have bitten deep, after four attempts to set them properly. In these heavy February winds, directly onshore, it is best to leave the anchors be.

10

Naked Under the Stars

In Mexico where the land lies low,
Hoo-raw, boys, hoo-raw!
Where there ain't no snow and the whale fishes blow,
Heave away for the plains of Mexico!

In Mexico so I've heard say,
There's many a charming señorita gay.

'Twas there I met a maiden fair,
Black as night was her raven hair,

But she left me there, an' I did go,
Far away from the plains of Mexico.

In Mexico I long to be,
With my tight-waisted gal upon my knee.

In Mexico where I belong,
Them gals all sing this rousing song,

Oh, Mexico, my Mexico,
Oh, Mexico, where the land lies low.

"The Plains of Mexico," capstan shanty, nineteenth
century

The task of living from day to day in remote places hardly makes it worthwhile, especially in rainless places where game or fish are scarce. It took all of eight hours yesterday to head into Santa Marta and obtain enough fresh food to last out the next few days. But it was fun to swing down from a dusty Land-Rover outside the post office and send Ivan and Cotes's son Juan Carlos to the market while I hobbled inside the *correo* to argue with the officials. There was no mail, of course, and they seemed to take great delight in telling me so. The postal clerk who issued stamps for the letters I was mailing noticed the Operation Star logo on the envelopes and asked me if any jobs were available at our *empresa*. I told him no, so he reweighed the letters and charged me double the postage. "Gringos out—unless you can employ me!"

Now that the holiday season is over there are more ice-lollipop and coffee vendors on the town beach than there are tourists. The town is much more dark-complexioned than it was in early January, but it is far more easygoing and good-natured.

El camino de los muertos is a rough track, about eight miles long, mostly overhung by delicate-looking trees. In the daytime it looks like a fairy glen, with sunshine dancing between the shadows, and it is almost impossible to conceive the dread that the locals feel about it. Halfway along the road is a grandiose gatehouse, which is the entrance to "Villa Concha" urbanization. By this is meant the five ruined villas on the beach. But ruined as the villas may or may not be, the gatehouse (of course) is in full splendor, complete with gatekeeper, fence and dogs, and splendid notices which display all the advantages of living in Villa Concha and ask people not to take food into the restaurant.

I was reminded of a slang word used in Spain to describe people who have great plans, which they fail, but only just, to complete—it is *curti*. The best definition I have heard—it is not an "official" word—is someone who buys a Mercedes Benz car and then cannot afford gas.

We collected fifty-two gallons of fresh water in Santa Marta; we were lucky, for water is rationed there. We also brought back about fifty pounds of food. By the time we got all that loaded into the dugout, besides Ivan, Cotes, Mario, Juan Carlos and me, the canoe, only nine feet long, was—well, wobbly. Only Cotes could paddle against the wind and keep the boat balanced, so it took a good two hours to slowly inch our way back to Conchita and peace. I wondered what would happen if the boat capsized. Would my leg weigh me down? Or would it act as a float? Or would the seawater inside the leg have neutral buoyancy? I must try to swim with the leg on before we leave Conchita. I may have to bore holes in the ankle to drain the water out when I take the leg onto the boat or onshore.

The ship's electronic log was worse than useless, as is everything that makes great stir and promise, and then fails. It starts off all right but after a while it gives up counting of its own accord. Even when switched to the "speed" mode, when it should show the boat's speed through the water, it stops indicating differences whenever it wants to. I came to the conclusion that it was part of a plot to confound ocean navigators.

The little dinghy log a kind soul gave us in San Diego worked a treat until some big fish got at it down near Panama. But for the whole way from California to the Gulf of Panama, this is what we used to indicate speed. It is beautifully simple, and measures speed up to twelve knots. For dead reckoning, even with Sat-nav on board, some form of speed log is a necessity. Sat-nav can only give a position according to its latest "satellite grab" and the dead-reckoning input put into it by the navigator. If you don't know your speed, or can only make a wild guess at it, the chances are that if there are a few hours to wait for a "grab," then the sat-nav can be miles out in its position. Without a speed log it is foolish to navigate close to the shore at night—or even in the day-time unless you pick off each landmark ashore one by one. The only thing to do is stand well offshore and stay there until you are off your destination. And keep well clear of all other hazards, like rocks and islands, reefs and sandbanks, too.

The wind-speed indicator, when the breeze was less than four knots, was also useless—the boat outran the wind in those times—so I tied a bit of wool on the lower shroud and reverted to good, simple telltales. You can soon gauge by the angle of the wool and by its fluttering, within a half-knot or so, the wind speed in light airs just as effectively as any electronic instrument, and in calms far better.

Really, apart from the sat-nav, the only electronic instrument that has served us well and truly is the depth-sounder. That is the only navigational dead-reckoning function that cannot be done better by old, simple means than by "modern" electronic methods. All the rest—speed indication, wind speed, wind direction, relative wind direction, satellite navigation—are merely lazy ways of doing some things that could be done just as easily, and far more dependably, by taking a bit of time and trouble, in the time-tested old-fashioned ways. I suppose the electronic salesmen find it fairly easy to sell gauges to people who are accustomed to haring along highways at sixty miles an hour and having a set of dials in front of them to give them an illusion of mastery and power. At sea in a small craft sailing below twenty knots, "power" is all pure illusion. The wind is its own speed and direction indicator.

All the way from Ensenada to Cabo San Lucas, on the southern tip of Baja California, we had northwest winds at about ten knots. Sometimes at night this would increase to fifteen knots, but this was rare. Much of the distance—four days and nights, four hundred and seventy-five miles—we had the twin roller-headsails hoisted, and they pulled the boat along almost too well; time and again she outran her own wind. Time and again her speed away from the wind deprived the Aries gear of enough wind to operate it properly. Then we merely rolled up the headsails a touch and slowed her down, or hand-steered. I am not a fast sailor except when it is very necessary. I would sooner slow the boat down any day, and take it easy, than wear out the crew hand-steering. It is better to get there at six knots, healthy and refreshed, than to make it at eight knots and hardly be able to crawl ashore at the destination.

The voyage from San Diego south was more in the nature of a trial than anything else. When we left San Diego we had only vague ideas of what the boat could do and what she couldn't. Sailingwise, we found her to be top-rate, but powerwise she had a flaw. The electricity drain on her batteries, from the electronic gear and from the ham radio, was too much for her fuel supply as it was then. For a sixty-day ocean passage, and making allowances for a six-hundred-mile push under power through doldrums (which every ocean-voyaging craft should allow for), her fuel capacity was short by about half.

When this became clearer, I decided to stay at sea long enough to prove it, and then make into a port and obtain more fuel, and the means for stowing it. We cannot expect a family to take off on a long passage without having sufficient fuel to maintain the battery power for the whole voyage. Here we come into the philosophical argument: that the biggest advantage of multihulls is their speed, and that fuel means weight— and so on. But the basis of my argument is that we cannot expect families to take to the oceans in multihulls and have to be *forced* to sail at maximum speed in order to ensure a sufficient supply of fuel and food for the whole passage and to ensure that the craft can pass through calm stretches safely. We must demonstrate that multihulls can be faster than monohulls yet just as safe and, if anything, more comfortable. If less fuel is carried, then any sensible skipper is going to carry more food, to avoid starving in calms. The people we want to see out in multihulls are family people—and a skipper must ensure that his family is, above all, *safe*. No skipper in his right mind is going to take off across an ocean with his family in a craft that *has* to be sailed at maximum speed. For more elderly sailors, it is doubtful if they could maintain maximum speed for any length of time anyway. I know that the vociferous minority of hell-bent multihullers is going to say "too bad," but the point is that if we are to prove and try the ocean-cruising boat of the next century, then we have to prove and try it for *everyone*. She has to be proved in the sailing grounds where everyone would sail, not just the hair-shirt minority, nor the glory seekers alone.

A hundred and fifty miles south of Cabo San Lucas the wind diminished, and we were lucky to get five knots. Up went the genniker, and that pushed us along very nicely, over the blue sparkling tropical sea, at a steady rate for three days and nights.

By this time Ms. Brimstone had decided to make friends with us, both Wally and me. She slept mostly in the daytime, but at dusk came alive and gamboled on deck until dark; then she crept onto our knees in the cockpit and gazed, slit-eyed, at the watching stars and the moving clouds.

Now, after a week at sea, the clouds, the sea, the face of the sky, the weather, all took on personality. I looked into the face of nature as the courtier looks into the face of the tyrant. I was becoming again a primitive who gives names and character to these mute forces. Sometimes I was curiously aware of the steady, subtle pressure of something that undermines our own character; something that favors the growth of primitive virtues that know only one duty—duty to ourselves. Then a maverick sea slopped up through the ama vent in the night and left a sloppy phosphorescence on the wing deck, and I jerked my head back into the cockpit.

Many and many a time, during that first long stretch at sea, well out in the offing—three hundred and more miles out—I found myself wondering what I was doing here, in these small confines (even the biggest sailboat is small at sea), crawling and scrambling about at tasks that anywhere else would be considered foolish and futile, but that out there took on the complexion of necessity. Many a time I asked myself what I was doing, jerking about in a tiny compartment far less comfortable than the meanest motel room; and less spacious, too. Many a time when I stumbled and fell painfully, I cursed myself for being such a fool as to return to sea crippled. But then my mind's eye saw again those youngsters in St. Vincent's Hospital; again I read the hundreds of letters that had told me that I could do it—if anyone could. Besides, I asked myself how could I work for them if I was hobbling around ashore somewhere—and the old, old question in my life—if I didn't do it, whom could I ask to do it for me?

I'd had a new leg made in San Diego. It was supposed to be the latest state-of-the-art thing. It had a knee that could be stiffened at the pull of a lever, and it had no foot, so that obstacles would not catch it and trip me. Instead it had a thick rubber padding in place of a foot. It also had a suction arrangement, so that cloth stump socks need not be worn with the leg. I wore it for two days, in intense agony, until it collapsed on me as I clumped down the after companionway and toppled me down into the cabin, straight onto the stump. I saw stars, then I invented a hundred new curse words, unstrapped the leg and threw it into the starboard after-cabin stowage. It is still there.

I donned my old street leg, "New York's finest," and I am still wearing it. It has never let me down.

I decided to make into Acapulco, to have the stump checked to see if there were any complications caused by the fall, and to solve the fuel problem. That meant another week at sea.

At this time, on the first two and a half thousand miles from San Diego, Wally and I had been keeping six-hour watches. With the Aries gear steering the boat for much of the time, that was no physical strain, but the watch for shipping meant that we must stay awake. One of the problems on that particular run, down the west coast of Mexico, is that it is a main shipping route from the Panama Canal to the U.S. west coast and to Asia. There is no getting away from the odd ship—and there is no trusting them, not even with a radar alarm on board. Most of them are on automatic pilot, and sometimes the men at the wheel seem to have about as much sea sense as Mickey Mouse, from what I have experienced. One ship, in 19° north, 106° west, came straight at us, even though our navigation lights were lit and the night was clear. She steamed right for us and only sheered off when I aimed the powerful searchlight beam straight at her bridge. She could not have been more than three hundred yards off when she changed course. By that time, our sails were backed in the freshening breeze, and the language from our cockpit would have turned the Pacific Ocean sky-blue pink.

Porpoises joined us on the tenth day out of San Diego, I could not help comparing their twinkling, leaping, slashing joy with the drilled contortions of the poor animals I had seen in Sea World in Florida the year before. That was enough reason, for me, to be back at sea. I went down below with light in my eyes—until I found that Ms. Brimstone had chewed away at one corner of my chart.

All this time Wally was almost not on board; when I was on watch he was sleeping, and the other way round. With the long six-hour watches I hardly saw him except for our social get-together at five in the afternoon. Then we shared a tot of Pusser's rum in fresh water, to liven up the sunset and the prepackaged food for dinner. At sea on a long voyage the ideal mate is one who is hardly ever noticed until something goes wrong, or until his company is welcomed. The same goes for a skipper, too.

On the first of November, in latitude 17° north, the wind finally expired. We had reached the doldrums, which at that time were slowly heading south, following the sun. We were almost fifteen hundred miles from San Diego, and had used the engine for a mere twenty-five hours. I started the thing, and we headed east, east, toward Acapulco. That took two days and nights, at five knots and with a sea as flat and unbecoming as an empty parking lot in Kansas. The doldrums are not encountered; they grip the boat and hold it, under a hot, steely sky. Bare metal becomes too hot to touch. When the boat is stopped the sails hang listlessly from the spars and halyards; the cockpit is like a furnace under the dodger-top. Our only amusement was to scan the face of the brazen heavens and whistle for a wind. At times the sky became overcast, a black thundercloud overspreading everything and then, without a moment's warning, down came the deluge! The cloud seemed to collapse, the rain fell in sheets, in torrents, with such intensity that it was impossible to see more than a few yards—sometimes impossible to see over the side of the amas—and the sea gave off a continual hissing roar under the violence of the downpour. Then, as suddenly as it began, the rain stopped, the clouds rolled away and the sun shone again with undiminished vehemence upon our drenched and steaming boat. Then we sweated away the rest of the day, until night fell upon us like a benison from the gods.

To see the lights of Acapulco rise from behind the seagirt hills, listening to Beethoven's "Eroica" symphony . . . ah, you may talk of fine foods and wines and the banks of Shalimar, but this was a real feast!

I had no chart of Acapulco, and no indication of the shape of things apart from a tiny flyspeck on my general chart of the Mexican coast. The town lights, millions of them, of all colors, are confusing to an eye looking for buoy flashes. I stopped the engine, handed the main, and lay to, awaiting come what might. This was in the shape of a small pleasure-fishing craft, which unwittingly led us in to the Mexican Naval Base, on the south side of Acapulco's vast and calm bay. There we dropped the hook, stripped off and, naked under the stars, washed off the yeast of two weeks at sea. I don't know whether bashing your head against a brick wall for the relief when it stops is worth it, but that evening it seemed so.

Now in Conchita Mario is drawing a cat, a dog, a house and a fish, and writing their names quite legibly alongside them. Wally and Ivan are working at replacing the large deck windows with plywood patches. They work fast, and will have it all completed by dusk.

I will wait for Don Jesús to arrive either today or tomorrow, with perhaps money and news from New York. Failing that, I will have to try to sell him our Avon life raft. That's not as irresponsible as it looks at first sight. A trimaran is its own life raft. It's comforting, perhaps, to have one stowed on board, but it's the first one I've ever sailed with; the cool-tubes work, and if the boat is flooded she will not sink, so why a life raft? It is more important for us to have food and stores in order to carry on with the voyage. I need one thousand dollars, to last over until more income is due. Then I need five hundred dollars a month to support a circumnavigation. That's the minimum nowadays, with three people to feed and the craft to maintain in a seaworthy state.

Today is the first day here at Conchita without heavy gusts blowing onshore and into the house. The flies are having a field day.

I cannot get out of my mind the reasons that I returned to sea. It was not only to set an example to others who have shared misfortune; it was also because the sea is a great consoler: She has been the consolation of man over the centuries, ever since the first log was paddled out. She is the companion and the receiver of men. She may beguile us, she may challenge us, she may destroy us, but she never refuses us. The sea has moods for men to fill the storehouses of their minds, perils for trials or even for an ending, and calms for the good emblems of death. There, on the sea, we are nearest to our own making, and in communion with that from which we came and to which we shall return. Out of salt water all things came and back to it we shall return. The sea is the matrix of our creation and we have the memory of her in our blood.

I returned to the sea despite myself—and because of myself.

11

Mexican Encounters

A is for the anchor, that lies on our bow,
B is for the bowsprit, and the jibs all lie low, oh,
C is for the capstan we all run around,
D is for the davits, to low'r the boats down, so!

Chorus:
Merrily, so merrily, so merrily sail we,
There's no mortal on earth like a sailor at sea,
Blow high or blow low! as the ship rolls along,
Give a sailor his grog and there's nothing goes wrong!

E is for the earring, when reefing we haul,
F is for the fo'c'sle where bullies do brawl,
Oh! G is for the galley where the saltjunk smells so strong,
H is for the halyard we hoist with a song.

I is for the eyebolt, bloody awful for the feet,
J is for the jibs, boys, stand by the lee sheet,
Oh! K is for the knightheads, where the shantyman stands.
L is for the leeside, hard found by new hands.

M is for the mainmast so sound and so strong,
N is for the compass needle, it never points wrong,
Oh! O is for the orlop, 'neath the 'tweendecks it lays,
P is for the Peter, flown on sailing days.

Q is for the quadrant, to the wheel it lies near,
R is for the rudder, it helps us to steer,
Oh! S is for the sheerpole, over which we must climb,
T is for the topmen, 'way aloft every time.

U is for Uniform, only worn aft,
V is for the vangs running from the main gaff,
Oh! W is for the water, we're on pint and pound,
X marks the spot where old Stormy was drowned.

Y is for the yardarm, needs a good sailorman,
Z is for Zoe and I'm her fancy man,
So this is the end of my jolly old song,
Heave away, bullies, oh, heave long and strong!

"The Bosun's Alphabet." This is a forebitter, that is, a
sailor's song not heard during heavy work. It was sung only
for pleasure. It was popular in the square-riggers during the
latter half of the nineteenth century and early this century.

Here at Conchita we had a blowout last night and supped on some of
the spoils from our trip to Santa Marta: a baked chicken, baked potatoes and rice, with a genuine and expensive Washington apple apiece.
Our usual diet is dried food from the boat—rice and dried potatoes—
and fish when Cotes's catch has been good. Our safeguard against scurvy
is Rose's lime juice or lemon concentrate. I made sure we had enough
in the boat, before we sailed from San Diego, to last for six months.
Every time I taste the lime juice it reminds me of my time in Royal
Navy destroyers, when the saying was that breakfast in rough weather
would be two draws of a cigarette and one reef in your belt; and I remember the time in the Indian Ocean, on a Dutch ketch, when our
water went bad, and all we had to drink for a week was pure, undiluted
lime juice straight out of the bottle. If you ever become sanguine about
your water supplies, try neat lime juice.

Our substitute for bread on this voyage, and ashore here at Conchita most of the time, is a kind of sea biscuit, but sweeter and softer
than the original version, which you could build houses with or patch
a holed deck. Our biscuit was issued by the United States government
for storage in case of nuclear attack, in 1962. It was packed in airtight
tin boxes, khaki-colored, and it has kept its original staleness through
the years. We have on board about a year's supply. I found them in a
surplus store in outer San Diego, and bought them at fifteen dollars for
the whole year. Cheap at half the price.

I am proud of our marmalade; it was made in Acapulco. We bought
a few pounds of oranges, saved the peel, and boiled it. Then we poured
off the water from the first boiling and added more water. The secret of
good marmalade is to change the water. Add plenty of sugar of course,
and stew the whole lot down until it looks like a gooey mess. Slap it
into jars, and make it airtight, and there is your marmalade, better than
anything that ever came out of a factory.

The main fish here is bonito, and a week ago we made a memorable meal from a fair-sized one. We cut the dark red meat into cubes, then soaked them in lime juice, salt water, and sliced onion for a few minutes until the meat was bleached white. Then we drained the fish, added a sauce of coconut milk and salt water—and there was a dish fit for kings. It was not at all fishy tasting; if anything it resembled fresh beef.

Wally's star dish is pancakes. He makes them from flour or oatmeal or anything else that can be mixed with water and flattened into a floppy paste, shoved into a frying pan, and tossed. The matter of flavor with our flapjacks is mostly a question of pot luck.

In Acapulco we woke to find *Outward Leg* surrounded by ships of the Mexican Navy. It seems to be, compared to the Royal Navy, a very casual service, to say the least. At first it was confusing trying to distinguish the ship's ensigns from the clothes hung out to dry. But the navy people were a friendly lot, and waved to us cheerfully from the liberty boats returning from shore. As we ate breakfast in the early morning sunshine, one quartermaster, aged about fifty and with a face like the Acapulco waterfront, hailed us and told us where the yacht club was, on the other side of the bay. *Outward Leg* hoisted her Royal Naval Sailing Association burgee and made for the club, where there are plenty of alongside berths, running water and electricity, and a Mexican dockhand for every foot-length of the boat. Fending off eager dockhands and would-be deck-hands is the most difficult task when going alongside.

After two weeks solid in the boat, I needed to exercise my leg. We took one of the twelve thousand taxis in Acapulco and we headed for the Socalo, the old town square, drank coffee in the Caballero Bar—a marvelous place for people-watching—and I stumped up and down under the shady trees for a couple of hours. Wally took off to see the cliff-diving elimination bouts for the forthcoming championship finals, which were to be held the next week. That, along with a couple of good, hefty, cheap meals ashore, was the sum total of our shoreside activities, and as soon as we had taken in diesel fuel we headed out again, cheered by friends on board the Dutch liner *Niew Amsterdam*, which also was paying a visit. I had found two fuel containers, each holding thirteen gallons. These we fitted inside the ama vents on each side of the main hull. Now we had a total capacity of sixty-four gallons—and that would be the minimum needed for an ocean crossing, with a reserve of half that amount for crossing doldrums. Events proved that I was right.

From Acapulco, all the three hundred miles to Salina Cruz, we had hardly a breath of wind. We motored the whole way and that took almost three days, until we were in one of the dreariest ports in the whole of Latin America, at least so far as I know.

There was more than one reason for heading to Salina Cruz: apart from its being at the head of the notorious Gulf of Tehuantepec, the birthplace of Pacific hurricanes, it is also the southernmost Pacific port in Mexico, and a place to obtain fuel. To the southeast of Salina Cruz lie Nicaragua, El Salvador, and Honduras. In the political climate of late 1983, any craft approaching the waters of those three countries would simply be asking for trouble. Because of the notoriously calm weather conditions off these coasts—up to five hundred miles out—enough fuel has to be carried to push past, and so make southing and the comparative safety of the shores of Costa Rica.

But more important to us, a northerly gale—often up to storm conditions—in the Gulf of Tehuantepec, would be ideal for testing the boat at running before the wind in short, sharp seas; and especially for trying out the effects of the cool-tubes in such weather.

The port of Salina Cruz must have been constructed by a landlubber lunatic. It is about the most unseaworthy haven in the whole of Mexico—and that's saying something. It is stuck at the end of a huge gulf, with the prevailing wind blowing hard onshore, right into the entrance most of the time, and when the wind shifts around to the north and flows at forty knots, it is almost impossible to leave the place because of the shallow, nasty seas that are set up. The port itself is only miles from the actual spawning ground of dozens of hurricanes annually. It was also the dirtiest port I have been in since Assab, in Ethiopia. The whole inner harbor, to which small craft must go, was covered in a foot or so of thick black oil.

Now life became complicated as only Latin American officialdom can complicate it. Because we had "entered" Mexico at Acapulco Yacht Club, and because there had been a fiesta on the day we left and therefore the entry had not been made by the club officials, and because we had no *zarpe* (permit to sail) from Acapulco, we must go through the whole painful, slow routine again. In Salina Cruz that meant spending two whole days taking taxis from the Port Office to the Port Captain's office, to the Immigration Office, to the Fuel Supply Office, to the Port Police Office . . . and as each office was a couple of miles from the other, taxis cost about one hundred dollars.

Anyone who has not experienced the frustration, the despair, the agony, of trying to make sense out of a Mad Hatter's Tea Party should try hobbling around the hot, dusty streets of Salina Cruz for a couple of days, from one obstacle-erecting, jumped-up clerk to the next. Each time we returned to the Port Captain's Office we found that portly gentleman asleep in his hammock slung between the trees in his garden, and had to wait until he awoke at three P.M. Then we were charged "overtime" fees.

The town of Salina Cruz itself has nothing to recommend it except for the central market, which is a prime example of how not to build a public place in a hot climate. The building is open above so the breeze, along with all the dust for miles around, is swept in and covers everything with a fine patina of Mexican soil. Then, in between dust storms, rain pours in through the roof and soaks everything. The restaurants of the town are all object lessons in what to avoid when seeking a meal ashore. The people are unfriendly to the point of surliness, very different from Acapulco.

Salina Cruz has two saving graces, though: the friendliness of the fishermen in the port—you have to watch out or the boat will be full of them in five seconds flat, and their friendliness is the type that takes off with souvenirs—and the police guard imposed on the boat from the moment she enters until the moment she leaves. The guards are all teenagers armed with machine pistols, who take their job very seriously. I chatted with one of them, and kept a record of the conversation.

"Where are you from?" I asked him.

"Tehuantepec." He grabbed another of my cigarettes.

"What do you do there?"

"Nothing."

"What does your family do?"

"Nothing."

"Is your mother there?" (You can always break ice in Latin America talking about mothers.)

"Yes."

"What does she do?"

"Nothing."

"What does your father do?"

"Well—there's Mother . . ."

Finally, after three days of trying to purchase fuel in the port, Wally went off in a taxi and bought thirty gallons from a roadside gas station outside the town, which is what we should have done in the first place, had we known it.

As soon as the fuel was on board we took off. There was a hard northerly blowing at up to forty knots at the time, but anything was better—nothing could be worse—than staying in Salina Cruz.

As soon as *Outward Leg* made a hundred yards out into the offing we reefed down the main. The wind was then blowing at thirty-five knots, and the seas were so steep and sharp and close to each other that at times a merchant ship, steaming to her anchor only a quarter of a mile away, was hidden by the waves; I mean completely hidden, right to the trucks of her masts. It was like being enclosed by moving walls, shifting violently up and down and ahead. Once we were a mile from the harbor entrance, there was no possibility of turning back. Neither was there any chance of turning beam on to those seas; they were so close together that the boat would have endured insufferable strains. They were no more than twenty feet apart and fifteen feet high, and the boat's beam is twenty-six feet.

It was four in the afternoon when we departed from Salina Cruz, and we ran directly before the gale, due south, for thirty-six hours. We could not chance using the Aries self-steering for the first sixty miles or so until we got out into deeper water and the seas lengthened to about thirty feet apart, so it was hand-steering all night—a wearisome grind in that hard, heavy movement. We were under reefed main- and stay-sail the whole time, and the boat's speed was eight knots on average, but shooting up to ten and even twelve at times. In the dusk it was sad to see land birds, driven out to sea, fighting to stay above the waves and reach our decks, but almost always going down and once down never coming up again.

Outward Leg was very steady in these conditions; she jerked and shook as sea after sea assaulted her stern, but she did not wallow, nor did she broach, although a few times the threat was suddenly upon us; but a fast, deep heave on the wheel and her deep rudder soon held her back on course before that wind, now howling at fifty knots on and off. By the following morning, even with the wind at forty knots and a really wicked sea, all foam and anger, we could lock in the Aries gear. It steered her perfectly well, with a veering of only ten degrees or so either side of due south, and we crashed and bashed our way out into the deep reaches of the ocean. That night I balanced myself in the after cabin, half sitting on the table—try it some day on one leg—in the jerking, dark cabin, trying to raise California on the ham radio, cursing the drain on the batteries, and listening carefully for the Greenwich time-signal pips, and all the while up and down, and jerk, jerk, jerk.

Several times during the night, the following seas caught up with the boat and threatened to roll right over her decks from aft, but each time she lifted and surfed at terrific speed on the sea, and outran it, but the rudder held its grip always, and we never once lost steerage way, although in this trial it was a constant concern, in case the loss should bring about a broach; but *Outward Leg* held true.

The twenty-four-hour run, from four P.M. to four P.M., was one hundred and seventy-three miles.

On the second day of the Tehuantepec storm, I somehow scrambled and crawled out on to the starboard ama to observe carefully, and very wetly, the action of the cool-tubes on the bottom of the keel. The movement of the boat was a violent rocking motion up bow, down stern, up stern, down bow, and so on. Never once, in the three hours I was out clinging to lower shrouds, staring at the hull, did the keel show out of the water. Never once did more than half the rudder expose itself. Running before the storm, the cockpit was as dry as in harbor, except for flying spindrift now and again. With the galley hatch boards in place, this was no problem.

On the evening of the second day out of Salina Cruz, we were accompanied for a time by a whale—I think it was a sperm whale—and this was an additional concern, for at times he was so close that we could hear the creaking of his flipper bones. But he left us before the sun sank leaving the sky looking like a bucket of blood. We came to the conclusion that there is far better company at sea than a sixty-foot-long animal shifting its hundred and fifty tons of bulk only yards away from us in a heavy seaway.

That night the wind expired and left us floundering around in a sulky sea, thanking the heavens that we were not in a monohull. It was bad enough in *Outward Leg,* but in a monohull the mast would have been waving about like a metronome. We hauled everything in taut, and turned in to catch up with sleep lost the previous night, and with the radar alarm switched on, slept the sleep of the just.

From then on, for eight days, it was flat calm, heavy rain squalls with winds for brief periods sometimes reaching forty knots in ten seconds, and hot sunshine, all the way to Puntarenas, in Costa Rica. The squalls seemed to come out of nowhere, especially at night, and by the time we reached Punta we were experts at reefing down in no time at all. Sometimes we crept forward on a slight breeze at two knots, then a few minutes later, reefed right down, we would be surfing at ten knots while I explained to Wally how it is that we should always make for the lee side of a squall that is passing ahead, and never for the weather side.

In the calm spells, shuddering on under power, we fitted a small emergency tiller to the rudder post, and to it we hooked up the Tiller-master electric steering unit. This proved a blessing in the hundreds of miles of motoring ahead of us, much of the way to Panama. It freed us, even with no wind, from the tyranny of the tiller, from long, hot day-time hours at the wheel.

I had an attack of toothache for most of this period. I had two bro-ken stumps in my gums, and I had neither the time nor the money in San Diego to get them fixed. To get Operation Star under way was much more important to me, and I had plenty of painkiller tablets, but it made eating very painful at times, and often I had to abandon meals half eaten. I should have gone to a dentist in San Diego, but buying a life raft and getting the life rails fitted was much more vital. I planned to see a dentist in the West Indies or New York before we took off on the transatlantic voyage, though. When the toothache attacked, it somehow relieved the phantom pains in my leg. In that way there is an advantage to toothache, for it was far less bothersome than the leg pain. If it had been ordinary toothache, I could have cured it by taking the teeth out myself, or with Wally's help, but there was nothing I could do about stumps but suffer and be patient. There's nothing like tooth-ache, though, for destroying romantic thought.

Heat below in the cabin—especially the after cabin, which was not insulated because we lacked funds and time in San Diego—was another problem. It meant that at sea, with the temperature below rising to over a hundred degrees in the afternoons, I could not stay in the cabin with-out running a fan, and that was an extra drain on the batteries. It also meant that I could not write down below for more than a few minutes at a stretch at most times and places in the tropics. The color of the deck above was part of the cause, and this would have to be changed as soon as I could afford some paint. Nothing is more miserable than trying to work in a hot boat. Give me the Arctic any day. At least you can always make yourself warmer by wrapping up in a blanket, but from heat there is no relief, except when going to windward—but that's a tale for later.

By the time we sighted Cabo Blanco, on the coast of Costa Rica, after a voyage of eleven hundred miles from Salina Cruz, we had been jerked, soaked, and boiled alternately for twelve days; I was ready, just about, for a cold beer, and some walking exercise.

Presumably, the name Costa Rica—Rich Coast—was given by the Spaniards to the Caribbean shore of that country, but it would even more have suited the Pacific shore. It is a rich-looking coast indeed, with enough rainfall (and more) to make the land green and inviting.

We felt our way into the Gulf of Nicoya in heavy rainstorms, and saw nothing of the coast until we were a scant two miles from the port of Puntarenas. Then, suddenly and brilliantly, the sun exposed himself and shone hard, as hard and as hot as he could, until the day we left.

By now I had made up my mind as to our route for this circumnavigation. I like to feel the wind. Running before it, the wind in *Outward Leg* can hardly be felt. I would go to windward, right around the world. Chile was out—it was too late to reach the southern end much before the middle of February, loaded as we were. The crossing of the Pacific from east to west was attractive; but the challenge of heading through the Caribbean against the Equatorial Current for a thousand miles, and across the Atlantic and the Mediterranean from west to east, seemed much more so. Besides, there were some things that I had promised myself I would do if I ever got the chance—and to revisit Colombia was one of them. Another was to follow the tracks of the treasure fleets of Spain, from the New World to the Old. But first, there was Costa Rica.

12

The Rich Coast

Oh the times are hard and the wages low,
Leave her, Johnny, leave her!
But now once more ashore we'll go,
And it's time for us to leave her!
For the voyage is done and the winds don't blow,
And it's time for us to leave her!

Oh, I thought I heard the Old Man say,
Tomorrow you will get your pay,

We'd be better off in a nice clean jail,
With all nights in and plenty of ale.

She's poverty stricken and parish-rigged,
The bloomin' crew is fever strick.

The mate was a bucko and the Old Man a Turk,
The bosun was a bugger with the middle name of Work.

The Old Man swears and the mate swears too,
The crew all swear and so would you.

The ship won't steer, nor stay, nor wear,
And so us shellbacks learned to swear.

We was made to pump all night and day,
And we, half-dead, had bugger-all to say.

We'll leave her tight and we'll leave her trim,
We'll heave the hungry bastard in.

The sails are furled and our work is done,
And now ashore we'll have some fun.

Leave her, Johnny, leave her like a man,
Leave her Johnny, leave her while you can.

"Leave Her, Johnny," a pumping shanty, mid-nineteenth century

Money is generally a problem for remote-cruising people. Even if they have sufficient funds back home to finance the voyage well, there are generally some difficulties in getting the money transferred. The best way, I suppose, is to carry a letter of credit, if you have credit; but even then it often involves long waits while the local bank checks your credit with the bank at home. Another method of having money to hand when needed is to carry traveler's checks, but they expire after six months and have to be renewed, and that's not easy if you are at sea at the time. Probably the best way to deal with the problem is to have an American Express account so that with your card you can head for the local office, wherever you may be, and draw money on a personal check from your own bank at home. But even this has its difficulties. The American Express office closest to you might be hundreds of miles from the coast.

Carrying large amounts of cash is risky. If the boat is broken into, then you may lose the whole amount. One great asset is to have someone at home you can trust to send money out to you by the fastest means possible, in case of a sudden emergency.

It is foolish dreaming to think that you can sail off into the blue with no money in a boat. All kinds of expenses crop up, like harbor dues and immigration entry deposits, or emergency repairs and replacements of essential bits of equipment. Nowadays the minimum amount needed in hand is $500—and even that is cutting it fine.

Two hundred dollars is the amount that I am down to now, in Colombia, in mid-February. I have sent for money to my agent. Don Jesús is to try to bring it back from New York with him. It will be about $600. That will be my cruising money for the next two months, until we are at the eastern end of the Caribbean and ready to turn off the wind and head for Puerto Rico, the Virgins, and New York, where we shall stock up for the Atlantic crossing, to commence at the end of June.

That is the strategy—simple and straightforward. The tactics are a very different kettle of fish. These involve beating to windward four hundred miles for Venezuela as soon as practicable; the Venezuelan bolivar has just been devalued again, and the rate of exchange against the dollar is very favorable to us. By moving along to Venezuela we can probably double the value of every dollar on board and hold out there until mid-April, when I may have some income due from royalties. This will pay for the transatlantic supplies.

When long-distance voyaging, a skipper must think ahead and foresee problems before they arise—especially when he has a hungry crew to feed. The amount of food *Outward Leg* carries is sufficient, now, to provide staples for the next six weeks, and with the fish we might catch, we can probably last out for two months. But supplements to diet—fresh vegetables and fruit—have to be allowed for, too. Generally, every trip ashore or into town involves the spending of some money, and it is idle to imagine that cruising can be done at no expense; even the boat's stores have to be replaced at some time.

In the past I have cruised with no money at all, and little prospect of earning any for months, but that was when I voyaged alone—indeed that was generally *why* I was alone. That way there is far less concern than when other people are involved. Alone, you can regulate your diet and skimp as much as you like, but with other people this is more difficult, especially with young men who are expending much energy and need to replace it. How I regret, now, spending my money on the life raft and the radar alarm! That two thousand dollars would see us well over the next four months or so—all the way to Europe.

The big problem with poverty is that it means we must devote so much energy to mere survival, to the detriment of any advance in techniques or creativity. That is poverty's real crime: It kills progress. Costa Ricans call themselves *Ticos* for short. Women are *Ticas*. Puntarenas means "Sandy Point"—and it is just that. The town has been built on a long spit of sand, and nowhere is it wider than four city blocks, with a length of about two miles. Being ashore there is like being in a big ship. You can see clear across town along any street, from river to sea. During the week the place is a sleepy tropical port, dozing in the sun, but at weekends it is jammed with holiday makers from the highlands of Costa Rica: city folk from San José and planters from the mountains. Then the place is pulsing with music and laughter, and the waterfront *malecón*, on the Gulf side of town, is crowded with merrymakers and lovers strolling arm in arm.

The anchorage for yachts is on the river side of the town. The best anchorage was the one we went to; off the Club Acuático, which charges a mere one dollar per day for the use of a dinghy dock and showers, and there is a small bar and restaurant, and a night guard to watch the anchored craft.

The port authorities dealt with formalities with a refreshing efficiency—except for the Customs. All five officials piled on board and
after drinking a half-bottle of whiskey—all I had—they demanded
"presents." I offered them my spare leg, which offer they declined and,
office hours being almost over, sulkily retired ashore. That was the only
unpleasant episode in Puntarenas. For the rest, I went ashore daily and
exercised my leg in the heat of the afternoon, and Wally and I ate curried shrimp with beer on the *malecón*.

On the third day in Costa Rica I did one of the things I have wanted
to do for years—I went inland, up through the mountains, to San José,
the capital, to visit the opera house and see the city, which is one of
the few genuine Spanish cities remaining in Latin America. The two-
hour bus ride was well worth the two-dollar fare, if only to get away for
a few hours from the sultry heat of Puntarenas. In San José it rained,
and as it is not easy for me to walk in rain along not-too-well-paved
streets, I stayed mainly in the foyer of the San José hotel and watched
the gringos spend their money. The opera house was only across the
square, so I chose a propitious moment between showers and limped
over to look it over. The beauty of this building, the faith of the men
who built and decorated it, the delicacy of the ornamentation alone made
the sail to Costa Rica worthwhile.

On the way back to Puntarenas in the bus I was accosted by a
Frenchman and his wife, thirtyish, both wearing spectacles and back-
packs and speaking at first bad English, then terrible Spanish. I pretended to be Bulgarian, and so avoided having to converse with them.
It's bad enough having to encounter the French in anchorages, without
having them drain you dry in buses. The last I saw of those two they
were disappearing along a palm-tree-lined esplanade in the company of
a disreputable-looking hotel pimp. In the bus, Wally was in close conversation with a young *Tica* and so escaped the French couple's attention.

There were several other yachts in Puntarenas, mostly American,
and one Canadian sloop, which had secured a charter service for the
Costa Rican government, taking scientists back and forth to and from
Cocos Island, a Costa Rican possession three hundred miles offshore. It
does little else in Cocos, I was told, but rain, and there is little else to
do but hunt wild pig, or converse very basically with the three Costa
Rican policemen who guard the place and who, when drunk, are liable
to fire their rifles indiscriminately at anything that moves.

There was also an American-built sloop in Puntarenas, under the
Swiss flag, whose owner was trying to sell the boat to two deserters from
the Spanish army. Along with the two Spaniards was a young man, Ivan,

who seemed at first meeting to be a little out of his depth among these rather exotic characters. He was polite, attentive, and helpful.

On my last day in Puntarenas, crossing a street on my way back from the harbor-master's office (which is situated, of course, on the other side of the town from the anchorage), I stumbled over a rough patch. Ivan ran up, grabbed my arm, and helped me across the street. Now I usually resent being helped as though I were dependent, but his gesture impressed me so much that I decided there and then that Ivan González would be the third member of Outward Leg's crew. It only remained to suborn him away from his friends and from his brother's chicken farm at Puerto Jiménez, farther down the coast, near Golfito.

But apart from his manners, and his slight sailing experience, there were other reasons why I picked Ivan for my second deckhand. Wally is very averse to any domestic chores, cooking and such. Ivan would take over these jobs. Also, his Castilian Spanish can be understood anywhere that the Spanish language is spoken, and more important, in some areas where the local Spanish is impossible for a gringo to understand at all unless he has lived there for years, Ivan would be able to understand; he would be my ears in Panama and Colombia—especially Colombia. Events to date have proved that I was right to bring Ivan along. I learn many things that otherwise would be completely missed. But first Ivan had to sail with his countrymen to Golfito, to try out the Swiss sloop that was for sale. We would see him in Golfito, and we left it at that.

I picked up diesel oil and fresh food in Puntarenas and headed out into the Gulf of Nicoya.

The gulf is deep—about thirty miles or so—and littered with black-beached islands (this is volcanic land) lush with tropical vegetation, the haunt of howler monkeys and parakeets. All these islands and islets can be visited safely, I was told, with the exception of the largest, San Lucas. That is a prison island, and yachts approaching too closely have been shot at in the past. San Lucas is the island closest to Puntarenas, so there is no mistaking it.

The Gulf of Nicoya would make an ideal sail-charter area. At the moment it is almost completely undeveloped in any way. The waters of the gulf are protected, there are good anchorages every few miles, and for the most part the locals are friendly. The main problem is lack of wind for most of the year, so a good engine is needed. The scenery around the gulf is striking, with mountain ranges to the north and east, the hills of Cabo Blanco to the west, and the wide open waters of the Pacific Ocean to the south. Navigation markers and lights are non-existent, and it is very easy to imagine yourself as one of the first conquistadors to arrive on this coast five hundred years ago. Fishing is fair, I was told. There are a few places where waterfalls pour straight into the sea, and so there is no problem of a freshwater supply.

We went to anchor at Isla Jesusita where there is a small hotel, government owned but run by an American yachtsman who was "taking a break" en route from the West Indies to the West Coast. His tales of violence and his continual talk of "blowing their heads off" were so depressing that I sailed the next day. His fourteen-year-old nubile, well-developed, blond daughter was running around all day in a skimpy bikini, sending the local lads wild with lust—they do not understand a female prancing around practically naked unless it is a direct invitation to dally. Already one of the local youngsters had tried during the night to clamber on board the hotel manager's yacht, where the daughter slept alone. The whole scene was so stupid, unseeing, and sordid that I could not witness any more, but took off. She wasn't doing wrong, neither were the lads, but Dad was.

That night we anchored off Caño Island, where the holding ground is just about as bad as anywhere. After dragging several times, Wally dived down and wrapped the anchor cable around a convenient rock, which held us in the incessant swell. There is little of interest on the island except for its pristine natural condition and two waterfalls down to the beach, from which good, clean fresh water pours, fed by the heavy rain showers. When you've seen one rainbelt jungle-covered island, you've seen them all. But the views of the mainland are remarkable for their splendor, in between the thrashing falls of rain. I stayed below most of the time at anchor off Caño, and read The Diaries of Evelyn Waugh. There are times when you can have quite enough of staring at wet trees and waterfalls, and it is good to imagine being in the bar of a London club, or in a good restaurant in Soho. Fish and rice, sun and rain are all very well, but there are, after all, other things in life.

Very few navigation lights work in Costa Rica. The main one, Cabo Blanco, had not operated for twenty years, I was told. Off any Latin American coast, don't expect any help from shoreside navigational aids. Look and listen for them, but don't expect them to work. The only one I saw working in Costa Rica was off the jetty on the seaside of Puntarenas, and that was a mile out of its position on the chart. It's little things like that that make visits to "quaint" countries all the more interesting and intriguing, I feel. Plot all your courses off Costa Rica so that you leave in light, unless there is a clear offing, and arrive before dusk; or if you cannot arrive in daylight, then stand off well clear, all night, and wait until dawn. After all, that's one of the things God made boats for—to wait in.

Some of the names of headlands on the Costa Rican coast tell their own tale: Salsipuede (Leave if you can) and Matapalo (Mast-killer)— but our main hazard in the calm season was not wind but rain. It bucketed, it poured, it *Niagara'd* down, time after time after time, and there are few things as miserable as being in a boat under power in pouring tropical rain, unless it's being under sail in fog. In cold climates you can hate the rain, or even be afraid of it. In the tropics the water is somehow sticky and it gets everywhere; the only thing to do is detest it and the clamminess that it brings about belowdecks because the hatches have to be kept shut.

Off Cabo Matapalo, about midnight, I noticed, as Wally took over the wheel, that although there was no moon, the water gradually changed from the India-ink color of deep water to a pale whitish color. It was as if there were moonlight over a shoal all around us, below. It was as if we were hovering over a white sandy bottom. The line of the horizon, to the west, disappeared in a pale reflected light. I switched on the depth meter. There was no bottom at twenty fathoms. I took a bearing on the cape, which I could see clearly reflected in the pale light from the sea. We were over a depth of six hundred fathoms, for certain. I hobbled and scrambled over to the port ama and dropped the sounding lead, in case the depth meter was defective. It left no phosphorescent trail of sparks; yet it was clearly visible, suspended, in the water, right down to the weight on the end of the line. As I stood there, holding on to the guardrail to keep my balance, a school of porpoises rushed across the bow, and the reflected light from the sea showed their blowholes as clearly as if they had been in broad daylight. The decks and the guardrails, the spars and the sails, all stood out distinctly, and I could see Wally's face as clearly as if under an electric light. It was lighter than a full-moon night, yet there was no moon and few stars showed between the passing clouds. The light came not from above but from the water. Shadows were inverted, which is why I had stared so hard at Wally's face; it was being lit from down below, up through the gap between the ama and the main hull, and the shadows of the netting webs crisscrossed his features. Weird is the word for it.

It was raining hard when we sailed—or motored—into the Golfo Dulce, and it did not ease up until we were narrowly missed by a large fishing boat only yards from the entrance to the narrow strait that leads into the beautiful, and hazardous, port of Golfito. Ivan was to join us there.

Among the letters that have reached Conchita today is one to tell me that yet another baby has been named after me. I am very proud of these occasions, and my pride never palls, even though I know that Tristan D'Lugosz, who was born on December 1 last year, and who lives in another world called Golden, Colorado, is the twenty-fifth baby to be named after me—that I know of—in the past four years. God bless him and keep him safe, I pray, in my little windswept cell here among the cliffs of northern Colombia; God bless him and keep madmen from running his world, so that he may enjoy it as much as, if not more than, I have done.

Also there were letters from Larry and Lyn Pardy, who have recently launched their new boat *Taleisin*, and from Bernard Moitessier, who is in Honolulu on board his new boat *Tamata*, and from a hostel for handicapped youngsters in Montpellier, in France, wishing me well. This last cheers me greatly. It means that my efforts are becoming known among the people who mean the most in my endeavors. It means that the rays of the star of hope are reaching them. When I read their letter I felt the extra strength of their knowing enter me. It was better than a double brandy. I replied, begging them to start their own Operation Star, to conceive it, plan it, *do* it. Self-help is the only way. Justice is not merely received, it is earned.

There are other letters too: one from a mad ship's captain, who curses me for pointing out that both Joshua Slocum and Howard Blackburn were Canadian born. For this he accuses me of being anti-American and a drunken liar to boot. The rest I will reply to in my time this week. You should not write letters merely in reply to a letter; a letter should be a surprise as much to the writer as to the receiver. I mean letters to friends of course, not business letters. You should never know when you should write to a friend until the moment comes; and then the urge should be irresistible. The only good thing about not being able to be with friends is that you can write to them. It should always be a pleasure, never a duty. Never tell your friends what they already know—but always write of something that is new to them. Never write a letter if you feel bored, just for something to do; there is nothing worse than a boring letter. Never be afraid to write about yourself and your own feelings in your letters to friends; after all, it is like a visit from you when your letter arrives, and *you* are what your friends want to know about. If you cannot overcome modesty, don't write letters—if you do, it will be a contradiction in terms. A sailor can write a letter at sea just as well as he can in harbor, weather allowing. Write letters when you feel like it. Never forget that it takes two to make a good letter—or any kind of letter—the writer and the reader.

Here endeth the first-ever mention, I believe, on the subject of letters in the whole literature of small-craft voyaging. It is one very important matter that all the other writing voyagers have missed. I include it with no apology.

13

A Nest of Thieves

Tommy's gone, what shall I do?
Away, you Hilo!
Oh, Tommy's gone, and I'll go too.
Tom's gone to Hilo!

Tommy's gone to Hill town,
Where all the girls they do come down.

Tommy's gone to Liverpool,
To Liverpool, that packet school.

Yankee shellbacks you'll see there,
With red-topped boots and short cut hair.

Tommy's gone to Cally-o,
He won't come back from there I know.

Tommy's gone to Pernambuck,
He's gone to get a real good fuck.

Now hoist her up and show her clew,
Oh, we're the bastards to kick her through.

One more pull, lads, then belay,
Oh! One more pull and then belay!

"Tom's Gone to Hilo." Tops'l halyard
shanty, mid-nineteenth century. Cally-o
was Callao, in Peru. Pernambuck was Per-
nambuco, in Brazil. Hilo was a port on the
coast of Chile, now defunct. A packet was
a sailing ship that made a regular voyage—
usually to and from New York or Boston
and Liverpool.

At night here in Conchita I listen to the radio receiver, which I brought ashore from the boat. Mainly I tune in to the BBC in London, or to the Voice of America, for the news, and to radio Moscow now and again for the other side's point of view. This week Moscow is celebrating the anniversary of the first-ever airplane flight across the North Pole from the USSR to the USA in the thirties. The flyers, with Chicagov in charge, were certainly brave men. I also get radio Havana and hear, fascinated, the extraordinary voice of Fidel Castro haranguing his crowds. He is probably the greatest demagogue since Adolf Hitler. Everything he says is absolutely convincing, until he's finished, and I consider the price evidently paid in Cuba for social security of the most basic kinds.

Another thing I hear this week is that the United Nations is having a conference—in Switzerland of all places—on the growing menace of sea piracy. In three days, all that has come out at the conference is that piracy exists, according to the U.N., mainly in the South China Sea, the Gulf of Thailand, and the Straits of Malacca. Brief mention was also made, in the BBC broadcast, of Colombia, too. The U.N. has been told that piracy is directed against merchant ships awaiting berths in major ports and steaming slowly around in the offing. The pirates, it is said, hover offshore in mostly inflatable craft, motor up under the sterns of the ships, sling grappling hooks on board, attack the vessel silently, hold the crews at knife- or gunpoint, kill anyone who resists, and rifle the cabins and the ship's safe. Then they take off just as fast as they arrived. Mention was also made of the pirates in the Gulf of Thailand who attack the so-called boat people, raping and killing. The U.N., as usual, can think of nothing more to do about this matter than form yet another committee to study "means of increasing security" in offshore areas of the sea outside major ports. What that means, so far as I can see, is that nothing will be done about piracy at sea for another ten years or so, if ever. The BBC told the account of one British skipper who made a kind of mortar out of a steel pipe and led a high-pressure air hose to it, to lob half-full beer bottles at the pirates as they approached his vessel. The Oxford accents of the announcers made it all sound like "jolly good fun, chaps." There was no conveyance of the fact that these sea pirates are murderous scoundrels who should be either shot on sight or hanged in public after trial. There was no mention, either, of attacks on yachts.

At the same time, yesterday, President Reagan, addressing a meeting to celebrate his birthday and to open his campaign for reelection, states that "now American citizens can no longer be attacked or held hostage with impunity." Well, perhaps we shall see the worth of that claim. *Outward Leg* is American registered, and Wally is an American citizen. What will happen if we are attacked? Will the British and U.S. navies steam into Colombian waters to demonstrate our governments' displeasure? Will reparations be demanded? Or, as has happened so often in the past, will the matter be known only to our relatives and to other yachtsmen? Are yachtsmen supposed to feel guilt because they are not engaged in commercial activity? Is that why we are so silent about lack of government protection? But what would happen if a planeload of tourists landing in Colombia were attacked, raped, beaten up, shot at, and killed?

The governments might take the example of the "Q" ships of the first and second world wars, sailing ships armed with hidden guns that were only revealed, to their surprise and consternation, to attacking U-boats. A trimaran would make a splendid platform for a couple of heavy machine guns and a mortar or two. We might even consider adding spreaders to the mast so that the bastards not killed could be promptly hanged. If the governments won't do this, perhaps some Texan oil magnate might care to fit out a Texas Navy to deal with the pirate problem in the Caribbean? He can have my services any day.

Golfito, the southernmost port in Costa Rica, on the Pacific side, is rainy, hot, humid, dreary, dirty, and a nest of boat thieves. As a haven for small craft, it could be crossed off any discerning yachtsman's chart without being missed. The town itself has only one saving grace, and that is the view out over the bay, which is surrounded by forest-covered mountains and is very beautiful. There is much more evident poverty in Golfito than in Puntarenas, and in Latin America that means much more "Marxist" influence. I put the word in quotes because from what I could hear and see, I very much doubt if most of the "left-wingers" I met in Costa Rica have ever read anything at all by Marx, or have any idea of what he was propounding. It seems to me that in Latin America, the term *Marxist* really means someone who is inciting race warfare. Rob the gringos, kill the whites, share out the loot. That's not going to be a very popular view, but it seems to me to be the truth.

To a certain degree I can empathize with the revolutionaries' aims. Most of the gringos I encountered in Golfito could talk only of how much they were going to make out of Costa Rica. They are mostly Americans, and collect together in exclusive little cliques under the rain-noisy roof of a small hotel that proclaims itself a "Yacht Club," and there the coffee tastes like Amazon River water. It all made me think of "limbo."

I'd fallen on board and shaken up my stump, so I could not walk very far on our arrival in Golfito. Wally bravely tackled the task of entering the boat at the Aduana—the Customs Office. You have to enter at each port in Costa Rica separately. Don't expect to get away with anything as easy or convenient as a national sailing carnet, as in advanced countries—not in Latin America. Bureaucracy there, as in most of the Third World, does not exist to help but to hinder, and in Latin America it has official carte blanche to hinder to its shriveled heart's content. Wally arrived at the immigration at 3.30 P.M. The immigration officer asked him for ten dollars for "overtime." He claimed that the office was "closed." Wally didn't have ten dollars on him; he told the immigration officer he would return next day. In the morning, back Wally went, all the three miles to the immigration office. We were leaving soon after, so he got our passports stamped and wished the immigration officer "goodbye."

That worthy didn't even look up from his desk. "*Vete*" was all he said. "Go away, *gringo.*"

He was angry because he hadn't squeezed ten dollars from us. That is the kind of thing that puts a black gloom on cruising in Latin America, and in many other Third World areas, too. When Wally told me, I found myself wishing there would be a revolution in Costa Rica and that I could take part—that immigration officer would be the first bugger I'd stick up against the wall.

But the beauty of the bay itself makes a visit to Golfito worthwhile. It reminded me of some of the fjords of Norway, and at night with a rising moon and Beethoven sounding off down below, the vista is dreamy. We didn't let the view keep our eyes from the deck and the dinghy, though. I was told that the thieves hide in the trees above the bay and watch yachts through binoculars. As soon as the crew go ashore the thieves make their preparations to strip the boat—and I mean strip. Ropes, sails, booms, winches—the works. The only place a dinghy may be left fairly safely is on the steps of the small hotel–yacht club, but even then you must sit where you can keep your eye on it.

My main impression of Golfito was hours and hours of thick rain downpour, and a sad view of the tin roofs of the town houses rusting above peeling paint and the stinking mud of the outgoing tide. The citizens have none of the jollity or merriment of the people of the Puntarenas. As soon as you walk down the one long street of the straggling town, you are aware of stares of hostility or sly glances reckoning up your worth—in dollars, of course. The reason is obvious as soon as you reach the end of the street: There is a United Fruit Company jetty, alongside which the banana boats berth. The whole town has lived for decades on what the men could sweat out of the UFC and what the women could squeeze out of the merchant seamen from the ships. The people of Golfito are about the most uncivil I have ever come across anywhere in Latin America. They make New Yorkers look like long-lost relatives when it comes to making you feel welcome. Along with Salina Cruz it gets my accolade of the second worst haven in all the Americas. The place hums with hate and envy and avariciousness. This is amazing, because anywhere else in Costa Rica I found the *Ticos* and *Ticas* to be friendly, charming, and helpful. Being in Golfito is like being in some kind of tropical penal colony as a visiting guard. I thoroughly unrecommend it to anyone.

But nature always holds its balance, and around Golfito it does so by bestowing on the place a breathless natural beauty in between rain storms—and Captain Tom.

It took me a day to find Captain Tom's place, which is at Playa Cacao, just inside the entrance to the bay of Golfito, on the northern side. There is a sandy beach backed by palm trees, and among them a small settlement, the leading light of which is Tom Claremont. He is another amputee, having lost a leg at the battle of Iwo Jima, when he was a young U.S. marine in World War II. He, too, didn't let a small thing like the loss of a leg stop him; he bought an ex–U.S. Navy sub-chaser (they were cheap in those days) and sailed her down to Costa Rica, where, he says, he "engaged in a bit of trade here and there" until the engine gave up the ghost in 1954. Captain Tom beached his boat at Playa Cacao, and has been there ever since. He lugged a lot of the fittings onto the beach and built his abode around them there among the palms, married twice, and is now surrounded by his offspring and the mementos of the subchaser. A big man, he uses crutches now to get around on; he finds it easier than his false leg, which he hasn't worn since the subchaser went aground.

Captain Tom is slowly converting an old harbor launch into a small hotel—the Shipwreck Hotel. He has grounded the old boat on the beach and is building onto it sleeping accommodation for six people. I can think of nowhere better for anyone to go for a quiet, interesting vacation "away from it all"—as long as they keep out of Golfito town; if they don't, they may as well vacation on the Lower East Side of Manhattan. All the yachtsmen who visit Golfito call on Captain Tom. He is renowned and remembered all over the world. His visitors' book, which he has kept for thirty years, is crammed with names of sailing boats and sailors from every corner of every ocean. His "jungleburgers" are delicious and his beer is very cold. His "house" reminded me of Dicken's description of the Old Curiosity Shop. It is jam-packed with all sorts of relics and ornaments, mostly nautical. Tom Claremont is a mine of information about the coast of Pacific Central America, and he told us about many vessels that had passed through Golfito in the previous thirty years.

Ivan Gonzáles joined us in Golfito, on a day's notice. He took off from Golfito for Puerto Jiménez, across Golfo Dulce, and collected his gear from his brother's ranch. He was back on board the following day. Puerto Jiménez is the gold-mining capital of Costa Rica. From Ivan's accounts it is a very rough place, full of drunks, whores, and bandits, and life is held at a very low premium indeed. Everyone else I spoke to about the place warned me not to go there. If I'd had more time, I would have called there just to check it out, but the Caribbean and Colombia were calling; the heavy wind season was due to start in December, and it was now almost the end of November. I wanted to be clear of Panama and the high cost of staying there before hard, reinforced trade winds made passage east a hard, hard beat.

On the way from Golfito to Balboa, Panama, is the island of Coiba. We steered well clear of it—it's a Panamanian prison colony, and yachts that approach too close may be shot at.

The first thing that was pleasantly obvious on the night passage south from Golfito was that Panamanian navigation lights work. It is always more cheerful to be passing a point or a cape in a rainstorm at night if you can see flashes of the light in between downpours. Your cigarette may be wet, and your tea may be watered down in seconds, and your trousers soaking and cold, but at least you can see where the main hazards are. As we wore Punta Burica, on the Panamian frontier, I said a couple of prayers for the soul of the unknown ancient Egyptian who built the first lighthouse.

In between rain squalls the night was shining bright, with a million lights gleaming from the sky and even more millions flashing in the wake astern. Squall clouds, black and menacing, marched down on us from the northern horizon like a disorganized army fleeing an enemy, and the larger masses of them had tentacles that groped toward the sea below at one time, and ranged from little cones to full-fledged vortices that drew up the sea to the breast of the cloud and roared out their challenge in the otherwise silent night. Ever the homeless clouds passed over us on their way to the vast reaches of the Pacific, and ever, as they passed over us, we buttoned up the dodger sides and cursed the rain.

The wind rose in the morning and we scooted along under running rig all day, bound for the Secas (Dry) Islands, there to anchor and clean the bottom of the boat, which was growing green moustaches all along the waterline. Wally woke me at six as usual, and I made tea, then went out to the cockpit. Clouds were beginning to form over the Secas on the southern horizon—this is a birthplace of clouds—and I sat and watched the birth of fair-weather cumulus.

A light haze lifted from between the islands, and a mist that had been hanging over one of the bigger islands drifted toward it. An unseen dip in the big island discharged, like a cannon, a small puff of smoke. The islands were beginning to warm, and soon every hillside, every cave, every fold was firing white shells into the air. The cloud above the islands thickened and darkened faster than anyone accustomed to temperate climes would ever believe. The wind blew the cloud sideways, and as it rose it toppled into the shape of an old man's head. In half an hour it was full grown, and it drifted out to sea to join the other morning clouds on their way to the Tuamotus.

I don't know why the Secas Islands are so called. They were anything but dry when we were there. My guess is that the Spaniards in the old days named them to discourage pirates and privateers from hiding among them. There are waterfalls, fed by the frequent rain showers, on every one of the bigger islands, which are all rocky except for a few sandy beaches here and there, and probably teeming with lobsters and fish. We stayed at anchor only long enough to clean the bottom, so we didn't get the chance to find the lobsters or the fish and made do, instead, with bananas from our already rotting supply. That's the problem with buying a whole stalk of the things—actually ours were a gift from Ivan's brother—they all go bad at once, and the only remedy is for everyone on board to set to and eat them. We held a banana-eating contest, which Wally won hands down—twenty-five in fifteen minutes.

We anchored in the lee of the middle Secas Island, off a sandy beach with a waterfall tumbling down the cliff behind it. The jungle growth of the island was so thick that it was impenetrable beyond a few feet. Even though we were well tucked in behind the southern side of the island, and surrounded completely by other islands, rocks and islets, the ocean swell still reached us. If we had been in a monohull, the berth would have been uncomfortable. As it was we stayed the night and rested levely under the stars in between rain showers.

The sail from the Secas to Taboga Island, off Balboa, was a fair one with a stern wind and sea that pushed us at a good rate past the notorious Cabo Mala and so to an unnamed islet off Punta Purio, a heaven of wildlife: thousands of birds of a hundred kinds and fish galore—but a hell of an anchorage, with a fast-sweeping tidal current and soft sandy bottom. Here we grounded, but softly, during the night for a few minutes, and as soon as we floated again, took off for Taboga Island in the Gulf of Panama. It was a rainy but fast sail, and that evening we dropped the hook only yards from the Taboga town jetty. There we stayed level in the swell, while all around us other ocean yachts, all monohulls, rolled out their guts so much that, watching their masts describe wild arcs continually, I wondered how I'd ever be able to put up with that on one leg.

The Sailing Directions state that the passage we made from the ocean southwest of Cabo Mala to Taboga is usually fraught with calms or strong head winds. They recommend that you avoid Cabo Mala by a good distance—even up to thirty miles—and then head across the bight of the Gulf of Panama as far as the offing of the Perlas Islands, so as to pick up the straggly remnants of the northeast trades that have managed to struggle over the high mountains of Darien, and so make a broad reach to Taboga. But we found a westerly off Cabo Mala that pushed us close past that notorious headland like an express train and then hefted us on a broad reach in almost flat water all the way to Taboga, in brilliant sunshine interspersed with heavy rain showers; we exulted or swore alternately all the livelong day in the Gulf of Panama but we did arrive with all our freshwater jugs full. That's the way to arrive: not bedraggled and weary, nor with relief, but with nothing less in the boat than when she started and with some of the food and fuel that was on board when she left her last port.

We were quietly content. We had made a passage of very close to four thousand miles from San Diego, most of it well out from the coast; we had bypassed a politically hazardous area off Central America; we had set our aims, were targeted and right on course; and the boat was in good order, all her gear in first-class shape.

By the time I reached Taboga I had convinced myself that we were right to let others chase ephemeral "records." I knew that I had some useful contributions to make to sail cruising: for one, to find out the truth about the Colombian coast; and for another, to prove the design of *Outward Leg* by beating her against the reinforced trades of the Caribbean for over a thousand miles, right along the northern coast of South America—one of the most difficult sail passages in the world. If she could do that, we knew she could do practically anything. In the words of Sherlock Holmes: "The game was afoot."

Arriving at Taboga was a special occasion for me. I was now at a place I had called at in *Sea Dart*, on that voyage described in my book *The Incredible Voyage.* As dusk fell I searched the distance to see through the binoculars the bay where I had leaned *Sea Dart* against an old jetty to clean her bottom. The old jetty was still there—still black and rusting in the fading sunlight. I felt very fond of the place; it was eleven years since we had been there, *Sea Dart* and I, yet I had a strange feeling of belonging—or as if the jetty belonged to *Sea Dart.*

The wakes of passing ships on their way into and out of the Panama Canal rocked and rolled the monohulls all night, but we in *Outward Leg* slept like logs on flat beds, level and unmoving.

For days after we arrived here in Conchita, the sound of the waves breaking on the pebbly beach to one side of our little baylet was very disturbing to me. I never did like the sound, having spent hours and hours and hours listening in dread for it during foggy nights and days from Sptizbergen to Magellan Strait.

I am beginning to be accustomed to it now, and this concerns me a mite, in case I should lose that sixth sense—it's not quite *hearing*—about being too close to shore. I keep remembering the times in fog when, for no obvious reason, I've sheered off a course and later, sure enough, when the fog has lifted I've seen that I'd been heading for disaster, had I not changed the tack. There's nothing in the world better for sharpening the senses—all of them—than a couple of days stuck in the middle of the English Channel, or Long Island Sound, in a thick pea-souper fog. It would liven up a corpse.

14

Old Haunts

There's a saucy wild packet, a packet of fame,
She belongs to New York, and the *Dreadnaught*'s her name;
She's bound to the westward where the wide waters flow,
Bound away to the westward in the *Dreadnaught* we'll go!

The time of her sailing is now drawing nigh,
Farewell, pretty maids, we must bid you goodbye;
Farewell to old England and all we hold dear,
Bound away to the westward in the *Dreadnaught* we'll steer.

And now we are hauling out of Waterloo dock,
The boys and the girls on the pier they do flock;
They'll give us three cheers while their tears they do flow,
Saying "God bless the *Dreadnaught* where'er she may go!"

Now the *Dreadnaught*'s a-sailing the Atlantic so wide,
Where the high rolling seas roll along her black side;
With her sails tautly set for the Red Cross to show,
She's a saucy flash packet—O Lord let her go!

Now the *Dreadnaught*'s arrived in New York once more,
So we'll go ashore, shipmates, to the land we adore;
With wives and with sweethearts so merry we'll be,
And drink to the *Dreadnaught* where'er she may be.

Now my story is ended and my tale it is told,
Forgive me, old shipmates, if you think that I'm bold;
For this song was composed while the watch was below,
Bound away to the westward in the *Dreadnaught* we'll go!

"The Dreadnaught," a forebitter (nonworking song), mid-
nineteenth century

We guard the boat day and night here at Conchita. There is not one moment of the twenty-four hours when either Wally, Ivan, Cotes, or I am not watching her. Every craft that enters the bay is scrutinized and, if Cotes cannot identify it, watched carefully. If the craft comes any-where near *Outward Leg*, the bows and arrows—they are not a boy's playthings; they can put a shaft right through a man at fifty yards—are placed ready: one in the cockpit on board, one at the barred window of the small room ashore I use as a study. Thus the boat is covered from two directions, day and night. During the night hours, Cotes maintains watch from the beach, only twenty feet from *Outward Leg*, until mid-night; then the crew take over. Both Wally and Ivan sleep with long knives in their belts, and with the ship's flare gun to hand and Molotov cocktails primed and ready, together with a powerful electric headlamp.

The Aries vane gear, in its folded-up position, looks from a distance very much like some kind of armament poking out from the stern—that, too, may be a discouragement to intruders. In the port and star-board wing-deck lockers, Molotov cocktails, four of them, are prepared ready to repel night boarders. These are mineral-water bottles (Coke or Pepsi bottles will not do; they are too tough and do not break easily) half full of gasoline, with a rag pendant thrust into the neck. If an at-tack takes place, the rag will be shoved down into the bottle (it absorbs the gasoline very quickly), the cork will be rammed in atop the rag, lit, and the bottle, with the flaming rag atop, will be heaved at the attack-er's boat. That is the plan.

Daily, we have "repel boarders" practice on board, and onshore Wally and Ivan shoot arrows at targets every afternoon—if possible while lo-cals are nearby. A deterrent must be known to exist, and to work.

I often wish here that we had a good guard dog on board, but the local hounds are so dejected and beaten-looking that I doubt if any of them would serve any purpose except to eat and make a noise. The best kinds of dog would have been an English bulldog or a Doberman, ex-cept that the latter is so big and eats so much. The bulldog is ugly, and slobbers a lot, but God help anyone it gets its teeth into.

Today we are going to repaint the deck of my after cabin, this time light gray, the same color as the ship's side, in an attempt to make the deck—and therefore the cabin—cooler. Until now, in bright, relentless tropical sunshine, the deck has been too hot for bare feet, and the tem-perature below shoots up to over a hundred in midmorning, making it almost impossible to work below. This was in a way my fault, as I asked for turquoise decks; it's the most antiglare color of all. But then I was allowing for being in the far south for a few months. Now that the plan of the voyage has been changed, so can the color of the afterdeck.

* * *

At first sight, from a distance, Balboa, at the Pacific end of the Panama Canal, was much the same as it had been on my previous visits, but on closer approach it was obvious that some deterioration had set in. The mooring buoys at the Balboa Yacht Club were more rusty than they used to be; the foreshore was covered with a thick patina of oil fuel, black and sinister; the fueling dock, where the club ferry lands (you are now allowed to use your own dinghy) was much scruffier and littered with garbage; and the attendants even surlier than they were—which is saying something.

In the old days, before the Panamanians took over the administration of the yacht club, local non–club members were allowed to use the long pier to fish, and it was always a pleasure to greet them and be greeted, to gossip about how much bigger fish used to be and how much better the catch was. But now the pier was deserted. Locals are no longer allowed on now that it is a point of entry into the Republic of Panama, and so the old fisherman must traipse miles to find a place to cast their rods, while the kids probably don't know that the pier was once open to everyone. Officialdom has taken over. Long live freedom! *Viva la independencia!*

I had encountered enough of official obstructionism on the way down the Pacific coast. I had met a young American in Costa Rica who is operating Panama Canal Yacht Services, from Balboa. He is a canal pilot, and thus well connected. His charges are moderate, and he helps in everything from the merry-go-round of filling in forms and getting them stamped to obtaining propane gas and groceries, along with anything else that the boat might need. From past experience I knew what hassles there can be when taking a vessel through Panama—it was always a long, long, sweaty traipse from one nest of bureaucracy to the others, *ad infinitum*. I paid my money—about eighty dollars to PCYS for arranging everything—and saved myself at least a thousand dollars, I estimate, on the cost of medical treatment for ulcers later in the year.

The only people I had to deal with in the fantasy world of papers and stamps were the immigration officer in his little spy post at the end of the pier in Balboa and the yacht-club clerks. On the immigration form, in reply to the question "Purpose of visit" I wrote, "To pass yacht *Outward Leg* through the Panama Canal." This was not allowed. The little man told me to write down "Tourism." So I did. I was now officially a tourist, and felt much better for it as you may imagine. I hobbled back along the pier to the boat and changed into shorts. I might as well look the tourist.

At the office I found that the charge for the mooring was high; in fact, for swinging around in an oily goo to a rusty buoy only yards from the busiest shipping lane in the world, subject to the violent wash of thirty or forty ships a day, it was very high: twelve dollars a day. Not only was it very high, it was extortionate. It was extortionate because there is nowhere else that anyone can moor a yacht without having to land the dinghy miles from the yacht-club pier—and you must land at the yacht club to pass through the immigration office. It's a Catch 22 situation. Traditionally, there has always been a free anchorage on the north side of the canal channel, on the far side from the yacht-club pier. But the yacht-club ferry does not serve this anchorage, and the yacht-club officials are trying to shut down the free anchorage so that visiting vessels will be forced to use the yacht-club moorings—and pay outrageous fees for doing so. The nearest free anchorage will then be Taboga Island, twelve miles away. But that's another Catch 22—because the Canal Authority admeasurers, who reckon up the dimensions of the boat and thus the charge for transiting the canal, will not do it in Taboga. Your boat has to go to Balboa—and that means you have to pay the extortionate charges for the yacht-club moorings. I protested at this, of course, to the chief clerk in the office. He shook his head and murmured, "Well, that's the way it is, take it or leave it. '

"Then I will plead *force majeure,*" said I.

"What's that?" asked the clerk, puzzled.

"Forced by act of God," I explained. "By traditional laws of the sea, if you are forced into a haven by circumstances beyond your control, the port authorities must allow you to shelter without payment until the circumstances allow you to leave in safety. . . ."

"It's not an act of God," replied the clerk. "It's the yacht-club rules."

"But God put the American continent here, didn't He? Isn't that an act of God?"

The clerk, very dark complexioned, grinned hugely. I thought his face was going to crack wide open. He stared down at my walking stick and my leg showing raw and mechanistic below my shorts. Then he leaned over and whispered, "How long did you say your boat was? Twenty-six feet?"

"No—that's the beam."

"She's a trimaran, eh?"

"Yes."

"I never know, with those things, which is the length and which is the beam." He shook his head conspiratorially. "I'll tell you what, it looks like we mistook the beam for the length and vice versa. I'll put you down for nine dollars a day. How's that?"

My faith in humanity restored a mite, I then went to my next job: to telephone my agent in New York and let him know where we were. I found the yacht-club visitors' telephone in the entrance passage to the toilets behind the bar, a dusty, dirty place with an inch of water on the floor. I waited there for an hour, hanging on to an overhead iron pipe, rusty and leaking, while my call went through. Afterward I returned to the office to protest at the siting of the telephone and was referred to the Commodore, who was sitting at a table on the bar veranda.

The Commodore was pleasant enough, but his reply, in fair English, was that "after all, you are now in the land of *mañana*." He was a portly gentleman, and courteous along with his sarcasm.

"But, señor," I replied, "if you expect sailors, after slogging all the way to Panama from God only knows where, to pay such high rates for the privilege of staying here on their way to and from the canal, surely the visitors' telephone can be put in a better place?"

"We don't ask them to use the telephone," he replied. "And they can use the office phone, anyway."

"But the office closes for lunch and at five o'clock, and at weekends."

"Then it's too bad. There are telephones outside the club—" and with that the Commodore rose and walked away.

Now you may think that it was pretentious of me to complain about a little matter of standing in—I won't say it was urine—water in a dark toilet passage for an hour; you may even think that I am going soft in my old age, perhaps demanding more comfort than is my due, and you may be right. But when things are obviously not right—wherever people are being overcharged and underserved, wherever sloth or downright discourtesy is offered—it is up to each and every one of us to protest. If I make attempts to treat my visitors on board with a modicum of courtesy and civility and care for their comfort, surely I may be allowed to expect the same from others—and especially when I am paying for it? Standards are the responsibility not only of those providing them but of those receiving them, too.

It is wrong for cruising yachtspeople outside their own country to feel that they are wherever they are on sufferance. It is wrong for them, as I have observed so often, to cringe before bullying or incivility, or to make excuses for their presence in another land than their own. It is even wrong, to a certain extent, for them to feel that it is a privilege to be in someone else's country. So long as they conform with the laws of that country it is their *right* to be there. By tradition and usage immemorial it is their *right*. In many, many cases that I know of, it is the privilege, the precious privilege, of the country being visited to have some of the people I know even deign to drop their hook on their miserable, stinking, mosquito-infested, corruption-ridden coasts. Now, I've said what needs to be said on that matter, and so far as I know never has been, so I'll leave it at that and to hell with the pompous arrogant farts who run more than a few of the world's havens.

The admeasurer who came onboard *Outward Leg* was, like all the canal officials left over from the previous administration, civil, friendly and efficient, but he had a bad sniffling cold. He laid his tapes and sniffled all over the wide decks, and talked about Lake Tahoe and canoeing on the Canadian rivers. I gave him the last of my Pusser's rum to help his cold, and sympathized with him on his exile, which cheered him.

The next day I hoisted my spare leg up the forestay and we took off for the Panama Canal entrance at Pedro Domínguez lock. We had on board two extra line handlers and two pilots—one an apprentice who, under the supervision of the older one, took us through with no problems at all. There's always a big song and dance about the canal passage—and rightly so—but really it's very easy and simple. You have a long line at each corner of the boat. These are tied to long light lines, which are thrown to the boat when she reaches her position inside the lock, and then the line walkers on the dock fix the lines to the bollards so that they hold the boat in place. Then, when the boat moves out of one lock, the line handlers walk along to the next lock with the lines, and let them go when the job's done and the boat is at the new level.

The canal is not as well kept as it used to be. The grass on the grounds around it is not as kempt, and the paintwork on some of the buildings is peeling here and there, but the efficiency and wonder of the enterprise is still there. It was, to me, a bit like meeting an old shipmate who had always been smart and well groomed, but who now has a day's growth on his chin and trousers a bit frayed, and is keeping company that you feel just *might* be better.

Outward Leg entered the first lock at nine o'clock in the morning and emerged from the last lock, on the Caribbean (everyone else calls it the Atlantic) side at four in the afternoon. I pushed the boat hard through the lakes, under power and later sail, and at times reached over ten knots with a fair northerly breeze. Some of the houses on the islands of the lakes, which used to be weekend and holiday retreats for the canal officials, now look abandoned and neglected. I'm not thinking that it was right there should have been such privileges, but surely the houses could be put to some good purpose, like turning them into sailing schools for the youngsters from the cities of Panama?

On the way through the canal we passed eight yachts heading the other way. Two were American, one British, and five were French. You can always tell a French boat long before you sight her ensign; there are always people moving frenziedly around her deck and there are always *too many* of them. That's apart from the noise they make.

All the yachts saluted *Outward Leg,* and the British even waved, which clearly showed to me that they must have been undergoing a tremendously emotional experience, passing from one ocean to another. Either that or they were running out of tea and were trying to attract our attention. I see no other excuse for making confusing hand signals.

I remembered, each step of the way through the canal, the last time I had passed through, with little *Sea Dart;* she came to my mind so often, as we passed through locks and lakes. Half the time I was back with her, imagining how she would feel if she saw me now, in this new, strange-looking vessel. I tried to imagine how she looked now, and hoped that the Wooden Boat Society had at last succeeded in rescuing her from her obscurity.

As we passed through the canal I imagined how it must look to my young crew—all fresh and new. When the last lock gate opened they had before them the waters of the Caribbean, the Atlantic—a whole new world before their eyes. I quietly rolled up the Pacific Ocean charts and stowed them safely away. We would not need them for quite a while.

Last night in Conchita I drew little mute Mario a picture of a stickman holding up a fat fish. Behind him I drew the sun, with a grin on its face, rising from the horizon. Then, with much pantomime, Wally and I greeted each other, and gave Mario to understand that this all meant "Good morning!"—*Buenos días!* He knows that when a fish is caught by Cotes it's a good day, a good morning. But when I turned in I was doubtful whether he had trapped in his mind the sense of what we were trying to teach him. . . .

Imagine my delight when Mario turned up only minutes ago, holding a tattered piece of paper in his hand, which he gave me; I looked up from my typewriter, and saw that he had written in very shaky letters, but still legibly enough. *"Buenos días."*

I am elated. We have taught Mario to make a greeting. Wally was so pleased that he grabbed Mario and ran him down to the water's edge, as if to throw him in, and Mario laughed, because he knows he belongs to humanity, and is not imprisoned in himself any longer.

My critics will probably flay me for mixing the present with the past—for mentioning little Mario's triumph along with telling about our passage through the Panama Canal, but I want you to know that there are passages to make every day, for everyone, and that the star that guided me to Balboa is the same one that we are trying to show to Mario. And as you visit Conchita, and we gaze across the blue bay to the mountains beyond, and wonder who that is walking along the beach in the distance, and listen to the *carpinteros* nagging each other in the gnarled trees, I want you to know about the little current of pure excitement that runs through the house, along the whitewashed stone corridors, and makes the spider webs shiver. I want you to know that the star of hope shines here, just as it can everywhere else. Sometimes the light needs a bit of help to get through the dark clouds around us—and that's up to you.

To hell with the critics, anyway. There's them that can, them that can't and them that criticizes. I don't give a fiddler's toot whether I can or can't, as long as Mario can wish me *Buenos días!*

15

Old Friends

To Panama we are bound away, *oh roll!*
To Panama we are bound away, *oh roll!*
We're bound away from Liverpool Bay,
Oh, them *putas* from Colón will grab all our pay,
Oh, roll, rock your bars!
Heave her high, oh roll!

Old Pedro the crimp, boys, we know him of old,
Old Pedro the crimp, boys, we know him of old,
He's priming his *vino* and doping his beer,
To Valparaiso we'll ship, boys, if we don't steer clear,

Them *putas* of Colón, they're hard to beat,
Them *putas* of Colón, they're hard to beat,
They'll greet us and love us and treat us to wine,
But them bastards is robbing us most of the time.

"Colón shanty." Pumping shanty, early twentieth century. It derives from the "Saltpeter shanty" of the mid-nineteenth century. *Crimp* was the term for a re-cruiter of seamen for sailing ships. *Puta* means whore in Spanish. The term *rock and roll* is not modern—it was used in dozens of sea shanties from the early nineteenth century onward. It meant to put great ef-fort into a hauling or pumping job.

Yesterday afternoon a Colombian navy gunboat steamed into Bahía Concha and anchored at the eastern end of the bay, by the ruined mole. She was not very large, about the size of an inshore minesweeper. A short while after she anchored, one of her tenders—an inflatable din-ghy—motored over to Conchita and hailed *Outward Leg.* Wally greeted them; there were three men on board the tender, all in their twenties and all dressed only in bathing trunks. One of them, thin and younger than the rest but obviously in charge, asked rather brusquely to go aboard to inspect the vessel. Wally, carrying out my instructions, refused; he told him to come ashore and see me first. He also showed the officer the note Don Jesús has written for us, which states that we are his guests at Conchita. The officer's demeanor changed immediately, says Wally.

When the officer arrived ashore at the house, he was most civil, and courteously asked if he and his men could go aboard to inspect the boat. I said, "Certainly," and in passing asked him what they were looking for.

"Contraband, señor."

"You mean drugs?" I suggested.

"Sí—or arms," he replied. He was no more than twenty-two, slender, well spoken, and I guessed he was well educated.

"But surely, any vessel," I said, "which was smuggling drugs or arms would not wait around on the coast of Colombia for a month in full view of all the authorities? Surely they would come in at night, load up or unload, and get out again by morning, wouldn't they?"

The officer was nonplussed for a moment, then his face brightened. "Ah, but you see, señor, we have never seen a boat like yours, with three hulls, and we are wondering what she is like; how she is built—and we thought we'd come over and see."

"Well, certainly, señor. I'll come over with you with great pleasure."

The three officers—for that is what they were, the captain, the executive officer and the engineer—went through the motions of inspecting the boat for contraband, but it was a halfhearted effort. They were more interested in the construction of *Outward Leg*, and her self-righting capabilities, her rig and her engine installation. While the captain and the engineer poked around with Wally down below, the executive officer told me that the last non-Colombian yacht they had been on board was four years before. She had been French, and they had stopped her outside of Cartagena—and found a kilo of heroin on board. They had arrested the Frenchman and his crew of two sailors from Guadeloupe, and they had been deservedly sent to prison, and the vessel was sold.

"But what about all the tales I have heard about the mistreatment of visiting yachts by Colombian authorities?" I asked him. "Tales about being boarded by gun-toting sailors, and the boat ransacked, and women being insulted and terrified?"

The young man was surprised at this. He spoke quickly with the captain, and a short discussion ensued. They talked far too fast for me to understand them distinctly, but afterward the captain said, "The only people who come here in yachts and have any reason to be afraid of the Colombian navy are those who are either carrying drugs on board for their own use, or who are coming here to pick up drugs."

The engineer added, "Or who might come here with arms on board for which they have no permission."

"What about attacks on boats by local craft?" I tackled them. "What about piracy?"

The captain answered, "Most of those attacks take place between groups of people involved in the drugs or the arms contraband. There is no honor among the *mafiosos*, despite what people say. They are always at each other's throats. There have been some armed attacks on foreign yachts, but that has mainly died down now. We patrol the coast all the time. Up to now we have had six vessels to do the job—four out on patrol, one refitting, and one standing by for emergency calls, in Cartagena. That has not really been enough, but now we have three new coastal vessels, bigger than ours, built in Germany and fast. We commissioned them only last month. Now we hope to be able to cover the waters of Colombia much better. Tell your people that if their boats are clean—if they are not carrying drugs or arms—there is no reason why they cannot enter our waters in reasonable confidence."

With that, we shook hands all round and the officers left *Outward Leg*, and we, her crew, returned to our tasks—but we still kept an eye on her.

At the Panama Canal Yacht Club in Cristóbal, the attitude to visiting craft was the direct opposite of the money gouging at Balboa. The officers at Cristóbal are themselves sailing people and most have made longish passages; therefore, they understand and appreciate the difficulties and needs of ocean sailors. Even before Commodore Grey sought me out to welcome me, the dockmaster had allotted *Outward Leg* a berth that took into consideration my handicap and where it was easy for me to clamber on board and ashore. The inch of oil atop the waters around the club, and all along the shores and pilings, was not the fault of the yacht club—there had been an oil spill from a broken valve on the ship-oiling dock right opposite the club only three days before our arrival. Hands were busy cleaning it all up.

Much of the club membership is made up of canal employees and ex-employees, mostly Americans, but with a few European steamship-line officials of various nationalities, too. There are Panamanians as well.

They keenly appreciate the great variety of interesting characters who arrive at their club in yachts from all over the world, north, east and west. They know, as we do, that no other activity known to man has such a great assortment of human nature as does ocean sailing. They know, as we do, that there are very few places where so many interesting people congregate, at one time or other, as the bar of their club. In Cristóbal Yacht Club, unlike in Balboa, the ocean sailors sense that they are welcome, and so they frequent the bar and the restaurant and they spend their money—if they have any—there. As opposed to Balboa's, the office staff at the Panama Canal Yacht Club is helpful, understanding and friendly. There is no servility about them, and sailors wouldn't want it; but they do understand our peculiar problems—mail, money transfers, engine and deck spares, charts—all the myriad necessities a sailor needs to pass from ocean to ocean, and the staff helps as well as it possibly can. Any yacht that must delay in Panama should do so at Cristóbal, and not at Balboa. Pass through Balboa as fast as you can, whichever way you are going, east or west, is my sincere advice.

The Cristóbal club members, most of them, seem to appreciate that there is an innocence, a perennial optimism, that ocean sailors have, which is contagious; a visit to the bar seems to be, for them, a remedy for all the pain of exile—and there is no pain of exile worse than an American one. They pile in, every evening, to hear the sailors exercising their second profession—rhetoric. They seem to know that while the ocean sailors can listen sympathetically to their problems of work, and living in exile—for some a lifelong exile—the sailors can also distract them from morbid thoughts with their talk of Gibraltar and Sydney and Antigua and Borneo. For them an hour or two in their bar must be like a world tour. They seem to know that the sailors do not sail in vain; that the sailors, too, are exiles naturalized with the universe, the companions of the stars, sailing the blue ocean as the stars sail their azure sky. They seem to know that when they shake the hand of an ocean sailor, hardened hand and broken nails, they never shook truer hands. They seem to know, as the sailors chat over their draft beer, that they are hearing the patter of hailstones on icebergs, and not the dull thump of career men, plodding their way from the cradle to the grave. With us, they seem to sniff the sea breeze and feel the slash of the spray. Working with ships and seamen for a lifetime, how could it be otherwise? How often must the canal pilots, treading the bridge deck of a tanker, dream of all the small ships and their constellation of voyages? They know, as do we, that we are but orphans of the immensity of the sea, and that with them we find, if only for a few days, a home ashore at last. They know that our ways are not the ways of landsmen, nor perhaps are our morals, nor our creeds in the main, and yet they know too that we are no better nor worse than our counterparts ashore. They know that our values change at sea, and so they do not ask us about the dangers and hazards, for they know we will answer with a joke; and for that they respect us. We in our turn respect them, for we know that their exile daily conquers a continent. They also know, it seems to me, that no fool, no dilettante, can arrive in Panama with a full-blown ocean-sailing vessel, pass through their canal and leave on the far side. Nothing is said about that, mind, but they know. They know that by the time we arrive there we have already paid high dues, and there is no need to gouge us further, but to charge us, and let us pay, fairly.

Among the visiting yatties there was the mixture that will usually be found in any of the great crossroads of the sailing world. There was the English couple, in their sixties, who had not changed one bit since they last sailed with me in the Mediterranean twenty years before. Cockneys to the core, he disguised an expert knowledge of all things maritime under a veneer of London cheeriness; she was the East End housewife who would always make a nice " 'ot dinner for 'er 'ubby (an' a nice 'ot cuppa tea)" in the middle of a raging gale, down in the galley of their ketch. They told me the tale of their visit to New York harbor, after they had crossed the Atlantic from England. They had sailed over to anchor off Liberty Island, to pay homage to the Statue, but the U.S. Coast Guard had warned them off, telling them that it was "federal territory" . . . "an' there we was, in the land of the blummin' free and the 'ome of the blinkin' brave, an' we wasn't allowed to anchor off their blessed Statue of Liberty—cor blimey!"

Then there was the young Englishman, with his charming little Chinese lady cook, who had converted a ship's lifeboat in Borneo and, with no previous experience, done an excellent job. He had intended to sail east from Borneo to the South Pacific islands; but when he tried the boat out under sail he found she wouldn't go to windward. So he sailed west, on his way around the world, across the Indonesian archipelago, the Indian Ocean, around the Cape of Good Hope, across the South Atlantic and the Caribbean, and now was about to cross the wide Pacific Ocean in his thirty-foot lifeboat, to reach the islands of his dreams. John was big and blond and a natural wanderer, and I nicknamed him "Lord Jim," but that was wrong. The Jim in Conrad's tale was practically incoherent—John was anything but that. I set him to work writing about his voyage, which was his main ambition. He hadn't been able to spark himself off; he needed a shove, and I did my best to provide it. I only hope it was enough.

John was what the average American may think of as a typical Englishman. Handsome, debonair and well spoken with a Home Counties accent full of "Eh what, chaps?" and "I say, well done, chaps!" Yet he was as tough as nails, and my crew were fascinated. They had never before encountered John's kind of Britisher.

John's charming Chinese companion was a miracle of efficiency. She could make a tasty meal out of almost nothing in ten minutes flat and John was always clean and tidy. I have never seen an ocean yachtsman from a small craft with such clean clothes as John's. She looked after him like a sailor's dream, and they obviously thought the world of each other. But unlike most lovers when they are together, they didn't let their interest in each other intrude on their interest in other people. It was always a pleasure to be in their company. I made up my mind on the spot to head for Borneo when I'm too old to fend for myself, and find a little Chinese companion. I've known for a long time that Chinese people are ideal shipmates. They know how to withdraw into themselves, and they have a wonderful sense of humor. They also have the sailor's prime necessity, patience. I once sailed with a Chinese deckhand, years ago. His name was Au Shu Ying, and he was a model of diligence.

Another remarkable crew was that of an American thirty-six-foot sloop being delivered from the Caribbean coast of Mexico to Acapulco, on the Pacific side. They were all French, and I doubt if a sailboat ever had a more motley crew. The skipper was about thirty, and of clean-cut appearance. His main complaint, he told me, was seasickness; it attacked him, he said, incessantly. I told him he had two choices: sail in multihulls, or swallow raw bacon fat on the end of a length of hairy string so he could regurgitate it easily. His wife was wild looking, with dyed white hair and a sharp sparrow face. She always dressed like something out of a surrealist stage show. She was also the most uncouth person I have yet met on the whole of this voyage so far. I went to speak to her husband about a technical matter in the club bar. She told me curtly to clear off—she was talking privately. I told her that France *deserves* her.

Two other members of the French crew were clean-cut, too; the first deckhand and the cook, who said he had worked as a chef in the best restaurants in Paris (even though he was only nineteen). The third crewman, whose main job seemed to be to decorate the deck, was a young Breton, who carried a volume of Baudelaire wherever he went, and whose hair was dyed blond over the back part of his head, and who wore a bikinilike contrivance during the day, and who at first sought out my company to go into dreary diatribes about philosophy. I told him that the only French philosopher whom I respected at all—indeed the only Frenchman, apart from Bernard Moitessier and Eric Le-Rouge—was Voltaire, and the reason I respected him was because he had the good sense to leave France as soon as he could and go to live in Switzerland. That got rid of the male bikini.

Another remarkable encounter at Cristóbal Yacht Club happened one morning, very rainy and very early. Hearing a commotion outside the boat, on the far side of our jetty, I roused myself and gazed out of the after companionway hatch. There were six men standing on the jetty, all staring down at something in the water. One of them turned around, shaking his head as if in disbelief. Intrigued, I hopped onto the jetty and looked down at the object of their gaze. She was tiny—only nine feet long, and the cabin roof took up most of the hull. Her hatch was open to the rain, and inside was a mess of dirty clothing and sodden paper—charts and such. No one was in the boat, and the name on her side was *Wind's Will.* I asked one of the younger men to climb down and shut her hatch. It would have been awkward for me on one leg. This, after much heaving and puffing, he managed to do. Then I returned on board *Outward Leg.*

A few minutes later the owner of *Wind's Will* showed up and introduced himself. We had heard of each other, but this was the first time we had met. He was a big man, and I wondered how he managed to fit himself into such a tiny boat.

"Bill Dunlop, Tristan," he said, and thrust forth a huge mitt for me to shake. His eyes were baby-blue Irish, the spirit of innocence.

"How was the trip, Bill?" I knew he'd already crossed the Atlantic in *Wind's Will,* but I had not heard of his latest voyage.

"OK, but the police gave me a hard time in Jamaica, and I had a bit of gear stolen."

I felt a quiet anger, a sudden gush of hatred for any bastard who could rob such a craft and such a man. Is there no limit? I thought to myself.

"How's the boat sail, Bill?"

"Oh, OK, and if it blows too much I just hand the sails and let her drift with the weather."

"Need anything?" I asked him.

"Charts of the Galápagos, if you have any," he replied.

I dug out my set of Galápagos charts and passed them to Bill. Then we sat and yarned over breakfast for an hour. He was talkative, as people are who have been alone for days, and I sat and listened patiently. Finally I asked him, "Why do you do it, Bill?"

"The money," he said, and winked one of his baby-blue eyes. We both grinned at that.

Then I gave Bill Dunlop a lecture on the need to exercise his warwound-scarred leg (from Vietnam) whenever he could get ashore, and gave him some Sloane's liniment, which might ease his pains after several days in his cramped cabin on his way around the world.

There are a lot of folk who say that Bill Dunlop is foolish, even suicidal, to make such voyages in such a small craft as *Wind's Will* and there are others who want legislation to prevent such endeavors. I think that the most dangerous people on earth are those who try to protect people from themselves, as they put it. I think that as long as someone does not expect outside help to come to his assistance if an emergency crops up, and as long as he or she is not harming anyone else, or society in general, he or she should be allowed to do anything they damn well want to. It is impossible for one person, alone in the ocean in a tiny boat, to harm anyone else. To say that he is a hazard to the navigation of other vessels must surely be a joke. I say that the human race badly needs examples of ingenuity and courage; they need to know that the days of individual effort and achievement are not over.

Astronauts can fly in space and the matter is trumpeted all over earth. But people know in their hearts that the astronauts are not really free— that they are tied to and controlled by hundreds of other people here on earth. But once Bill Dunlop is alone at sea in his tiny vessel, he is one of the truly free human beings of this age. He is beyond the control of authority—and authoritarians hate the thought of that. People like Bill Dunlop resist, more than any other people in the world, the approach of the bureaucrat's idea of an ideal world, with everyone prevented from being himself, truly himself, and Big Brother watching benignly over all.

God bless you, Bill, and send *Wind's Will* safely home again to Maine!

16

The Springboard

Come all you fair ones, come all my fond ones,
Come and listen to me;
Could you fancy a bonny sailor lad,
That's just come home from sea?
Could you fancy a bonny sailor lad,
That's just come home from sea?

No indeed I'll wed no sailor, for they smell too much of tar.
You are ragged, you are sassy, get you gone, you Jackie Tar,
You are ragged, you are sassy, get you gone, you Jackie Tar!

From "The Saucy Sailor Boy," eighteenth-century pump
shanty

Wally and I went into Santa Marta yesterday to get our visas for our
stay in Colombia extended, to collect mail and buy fresh food. After
checking the three anchors, we left Ivan on board to guard the boat,
along with Carlos on the shore. Cotes and little Mario accompanied us
to the beach in the big dugout canoe. It is a heavy boat, and impossible
to paddle against the heavy gusts that swoop around the southern headland, loaded as it was with three men, a boy and our gear, including
ten water containers. There is no fresh water here; we must collect it
from the town, seven miles away, every drop.

Wally and Cotes paddled like mad in between the gusts, while I hung
on to the dugout gunwales forward, surrounded by jerricans and boxes,
and our icebox. Without our dinghy (more about that later) we revert
to the same mode of transport the Indians have used here for centuries.
In my mind's eye, as the dugout moved slowly around the headland, I
imagined what we must look like: some kind of Victorian botanical ex-
pedition.

Beyond the south headland there is another baylet, bigger than ours at Conchita, and on the rising land among the bone-dry trees and cacti, some of which rise thirty feet straight up from the rocks, are two fishing camps used by local men. One of them has a rude hut, outside which someone is always on watch, but the other is only a bare piece of ground, with tree branches erected into a net-drying frame. Above the headland is a windblown tree, and atop that sits a frame lookout, where the fishermen keep watch for bonito and pompano entering their baylet. Perched up there, they look like sentinels or medicine men waiting for the sun to set. It is all weird-looking, dramatic, and very quiet.

Waiting on the beach was an ancient Land-Rover, and the driver, a large, dark, fat man, insisted on raising his usual fee for the trip, ten dollars to fifteen dollars. This is because he visited Cotes the day before at Conchita, and saw our boat. That makes us, in his mind, "rich gringos." There was no talking him out of it, and no alternative. In this windy season I don't want to disturb the anchors until I have finished the tasks in hand, which will take about another week. Otherwise I would have turned back to Conchita and taken *Outward Leg* around to Santa Marta. These days fifteen dollars is a lot of money.

At the end of *el camino de los muertos* we regained "civilization" by passing through the collection of half-built shacks, then past whole districts of newly built small houses crawling with small kids. On the road there was a man with a donkey pulling a small cart, selling kerosene, and he was surrounded by housewives bearing bottles and cans. This shows that the electricity supply evidently has not caught up with the building rate.

But despite the delay in the arrival of electricity, many of the shacks had on display in the living room, right in front of the main door, that status symbol of the Third World—a refrigerator, shining and polished. These, I discovered, are smuggled in from Venezuela, part of the cargo of a ship that "accidentally" went aground in the Gulf of Maracaibo. The delay in the supply of electricity is caused by the upcoming general elections. Candidates already in office buy the votes of the poor by promising to get the electric supply connected up as soon as they are voted back into office, so I was told.

In the outer barrios, pigs and chickens roam the streets at will. On one corner stood an iced-drink-vendor's cart. Water dripped down from the ice block and was licked off a wheel by a huge black sow. Around the syrup taps, swarms of wasps buzzed busily, and as we waited for a light to change (it didn't, and our driver eventually shot over the crossing, missing a bus by a hairbreadth), the drink vendor with one lazy hand casually brushed a great ball of wasps off a tap.

On practically every street corner in the barrios youths stood idly and complimented or catcalled at passing young, and some not so young, females. From the corner bars, salsas and corimbas blared so loud that they merged with the music from the bar on the next corner, a city block away. Every gang of men at work usually had one man doing something and the rest standing around, resting. It seems that the only time the locals move at a rate faster than a tortoise is when they are playing soccer or dancing. Then they spring to life. Otherwise they move like exhausted, undernourished shadows.

On the way into Santa Marta we passed several truckloads of soldiers, all very young, all gazing around with seemingly unseeing eyes, all dressed in drab brown uniforms that usually had nothing to do with the shape of the wearer, and all toting rifles. Their officers looked well fed, were well dressed, and toted pistols.

The buses, like most local buses in Latin America, are all gaily painted—garish might be more the word—and they have names like "Let me love her," and "Here comes one who loves you," and "Dance with me." They are always crowded, and there is no order when people mount or leave. It's all push, push and the devil take the hindmost. But somehow everyone gets aboard.

Farther on, we passed schools, through the open windows of which we could see children busy at their work. They were all in uniform. Hundreds of people were walking in the same direction as we were, headed toward the town from the direction of the barrios. No doubt this is good for their health, but it also indicates the poverty here, because the bus fares are only about fifteen cents to and from anywhere in and around the city. The temperature in the sun, by ten in the forenoon, must have been at least ninety. At an estimate, at least three out of ten people walking were carrying something—a box or a tray or a bundle of things to sell in the town; a good half of them were women, and the other half small children. The rest of the pedestrians were mainly men, mostly dressed in clean shirts, trousers and highly polished shoes, and carrying some form of case for papers.

We stopped briefly at the Casa de Cambios opposite the Port Office, and I was greeted by name by no fewer than three pistol-toting policemen. They were all friendly, and asked after the boat and Ivan, and this gave me a craven feeling of some kind of security. Wally they knew, too, because he is now a legend in Santa Marta where he is known either as *El Palito* or *El Escalador* ("The Mast-Man" or "The Climber").

The fat Land-Rover driver, despite my twenty-minute lecture to him on the correct performance of his duties, refused to carry us to the post office. His excuse was that he "had no pass" to drive in the town center, and I told him I thought he was lying. But he persisted, and dropped us off at my favorite rendezvous in Santa Marta, El Molino restaurant. It is only a hole in a wall, dirty, with a pet turkey, old and dog-bitten, which pecks and shits among the customers at the outside tables under the trees, but there is a fine view across the beach, the harbor, the bay and right out to the ocean seas in the distance, white topped and wild. Also, El Molino is very convenient for short hobbles to everywhere in Santa Marta that matters to me.

Another great asset that Cristóbal has, and a very unusual one in the yachtsman's world, is a civil, polite, human immigration officer. I do not know his name, but he is a small dark man of about fifty who operates from a tiny office on the foreshore by the yacht club. He treats everyone alike, with a warmth and courtesy so genuine that it is almost incredible. When our boat cleared for sea he even took the trouble to come down to the jetty and wish us fair winds and a good voyage. That I write this is a sad commentary on the attitude of most of the other government officials who preside over the ins and outs of most Third World major yachting centers—and minor ones, too. This Panamanian government official left a deep impression on me, and I'm sure on everyone else who passes through. When will governments realize that yatties *talk*? For everyone who is treated badly, subjected to long, unnecessary waits in hot anterooms, or lectured on correct behavior by some tin-pot, jumped-up bureaucrat who is usually not even fit to sell lottery tickets—hundreds of other people, all over the world, will sooner or later know about it. How many governments of tourism-minded islands in the Caribbean, for example, know the untold damage that is done by the scurvy treatment of cruising people on arrival, some of whom have made tremendous efforts to reach their shores?

In Cristóbal I met several people, like ghosts from the past, who had at one time or other sailed with me. Among these were a Dutch couple, now sailing their ketch, which they had built in Portugal, to Indonesia. They were anchored at the little-known Yate Club Carib, on the other side of the peninsula where the city of Colón sits, alternately soaked and fried in the heavy downpours and glaring sun. I decided, to break the monotony while we waited for mail (that never arrived), to join them for a couple of days. The Yate Club Carib is a mainly Panamanian organization. It has a small anchorage, with fair holding in not-too-deep mud, but there is a reef right in the middle of the roadstead, marked by a buoy. It is open to the north wind, and therefore cooler than the berth in Cristóbal. The Carib club has large buildings, a good bar, friendly but not pushy members, and a welcoming staff. Its rates are reasonable for an alongside berth at the short jetty, but its toilets are untenable. It holds social functions often, and it is a fine place to observe the customs and listen to the music of Panamanians enjoying themselves. It is situated in the "best" part of Colón, and there is a pretty, breezy seafront promenade close by, where I hobbled daily under the rain-soaked, wind-bent palms. It is guarded at every corner by machine-pistol-armed policemen, most of whom look hardly old enough to have left school. Nevertheless, we were warned not to wander about outside the club grounds after dark, for fear of robbers and murderers.

At the Yate Club Carib we were boarded, late at night, by four men dressed in civilian clothes. One of them produced a badge, and this showed that they were *aduaneros*, customs officials. They searched the boat thoroughly, in every crevice. They told me that drug smugglers used the Carib anchorage. I said that the smugglers must be pretty stupid to come to a place where there was usually no other yacht. If I were smuggling I would go into the Cristóbal Yacht Club, where I would not be so prominent. But by this time the boss Customs man had spied a couple of my books, and so a literary discussion ensued that ended only at about three A.M. I could see, from this episode, how problems could arise, how a dangerous incident might occur. To be woken at midnight by four men in civilian clothes creeping around the deck, each with a pistol in his belt—I told them that I thought it was asking for trouble. But they said that they had to maintain the element of surprise. I said they would get a surprise, all right, if some paranoic North American, with a Fort Knox arsenal down below, was visiting the Yate Club Carib. The boss man said that he would think about that, and try to figure out a way to encounter yachts without frightening the living daylights out of the crew, and we parted on the best of terms.

The anchorage at the Yate Club Carib has one advantage that the Cristóbal berths do not; it is clean. There we cleaned off the muck left on the ship's side and on the mooring lines by the oil spill, so that the boat would look well for Christmas, then we returned to Cristóbal, to what we thought of as a sort of umbilical cord: the letterless mailbox at the yacht-club office.

One of the deepest wrenches cruising people feel after they set off on a long voyage is the difficulty of receiving mail. This is especially so if there was no clear plan of the voyage upon setting out. Then it is very much a matter of playing it by ear and trying to get word to the folks back home of where you will be at some particular time. Lord only knows how many letters arrive for people after they have departed for their next port of call. You can always leave behind instructions for the mail to be forwarded, but whether this will be done or not is in the hands of the gods—and especially in the Third World. There were letters in the Cristóbal mailbox—which yatties sort out for themselves—that had been originally posted in Europe, the USA and Australia as far back as 1980!

In Colón, as the rain pounded on deck, I inspected my tattered charts of the South American coasts in the Caribbean. The charts are tattered because they have been traded for charts of the Pacific, and some of them have probably crossed the Caribbean half a dozen times. One of the greatest rises in the costs of voyaging in the past few years has been the increase in the cost of navigation charts. When I first went small-boat voyaging, in 1952, the average British Admiralty chart cost five shillings—that was then equivalent to about one dollar and twenty cents. Now the average cost is about eighteen dollars. This means that the cost of a full set of proper charts for the area he is going to sail is beyond the means of the average yattie. This leads to the exchange of a set of charts for an area already sailed for that of another someone else has passed through. After charts have changed hands a few times, they are probably out-of-date, and newly found hazards or wrecks and other obstructions are not shown.

Another way of avoiding the cost of new charts is to copy old ones, and although this is illegal, the practice is growing. Some of these illegal chart copiers even advertise in the yachting press in the United States. Both these ways of getting charts are risky. The old charts may be out-of-date; the copied charts may be so badly printed that much of the vital data is unreadable. If this goes on, lives are going to be lost, vessels are going to be put at risk and founder.

This situation is caused by the usual bureaucratic attitude to yachting: "If you own a yacht you must be rich, and therefore you are fair game." It is exactly the same attitude as that of an ignorant fisherman-peasant-turned-pirate on the coast of Colombia or in the Malacca Strait. To my mind there is little to choose between attacking a cruising craft physically with guns and hoisting the price of life-preserving navigation charts to unaffordable prices.

Most of the charts printed today are based on the heroic labors of men long dead. It's hardly costing these governments one penny to include all that data from the nineteenth and most of the twentieth centuries on their products. They make additions, much of it inaccurate so far as I can see, which have been gathered through cloud by satellite, and then they have the gall to pile on costs, all on to the seafarer. They subsidize their airlines hand over fist, and yet lose sight of the fact that most of the world's cargoes are shifted by seamen—and then these "advanced countries" wonder why their merchant fleets are diminishing in size at such a rate as to disappear within the next two decades.

In the USA alone there are something close to *eighteen million* privately registered small craft. I have no idea how many are registered in the European community, but it must be close to that. That's a lot of political clout. It's up to all yachtsmen, everywhere, to protest to their representatives in the halls of power about this ever-increasing cost of safety at sea in the shape of nautical charts, and other official publications such as lights lists and tide tables; and to point out that any regulatory activity that leads to the creation of criminality where none existed before must be bad. There is no excuse for making a situation whereby people are forced to voyage without sufficient charts.

My general chart of the Caribbean Sea is ripped, torn and tattered beyond belief. In parts it has most intriguing stains and patches of dried liquids such as coffee, tea and lubricating oil. Whenever I fall to studying it, I find myself wondering what the weather was like, what the boat was and where she was bound when that particular coffee stain discolored the south coast of Haiti, or that blob of oil spilled over Grenada.

There in Colón I studied the coast of Colombia. I had to work out the best place to approach her shores with the best chance of safe arrival in some port or other.

Turbo, in the Gulf of Darien, was discounted from my calculations. It is known to be a hotbed of small-craft piracy; a murderous hellhole at the deep end of a hazardous gulf. Isla Fuerte, which I knew from *Sea Dart's* voyage was a good anchorage, was also out; it is remote from any port, and I could not go close to the Colombian shores without first officially entering. The San Bernardo Islands, while there was a police post there, might be dicey; it was reputed to be a major haunt of *marijuanistas* who run the drug out to larger ships waiting offshore. Cartagena was out; although it has a well-guarded yacht basin at the Club de Pescas, the port sites at the far end of a long, intricate landlocked bay, with many holes from which attackers might sally. Barranquilla was out;

it had the worst name of all the Colombian ports for violence; it was reputed to be the home of the drug mafia.

The one place that met my criteria was Santa Marta. It is in the lee of the hard eastern winds, it is out of the three-knot westerly-going current, it has an open approach from the sea so the risk of surprise is lessened, and I remembered the approaches and the harbor well.

In Colón, as the yacht club celebrated Christmas, we on board *Outward Leg* made preparations for sailing to one of the most notoriously risky coasts on earth, by all accounts—Colombia.

The crew and I held our first archery practice on the foreshore at Cristóbal, and I bought six Pepsi-Colas in the bar. No doubt when the yatties and canal staff at the bar saw that, they thought that I was turning teetotal in my old age. I did not think it right to inform them that the bottles were for making Molotov cocktails.

The toilet seat in the visiting-yacht lavatory at Cristóbal was cracked. I presented Commodore Greg with a new one, which I'd bought in San Diego with the idea of having a fancy head on board. We couldn't find the space to fit it, and it's always better, I think, to give *useful* gifts, anyway.

The Ley supermarket in Santa Marta is almost next door to the main post office. The selection of supplies is not bad at all. It is nowhere up to North American standards, of course; the fresh vegetables and fruit are somewhat flyblown and the frozen chickens are thin and tiny, but the people are friendly. Everything on biggish order—and ours must be that for I am feeding three men for two weeks—was checked out twice; but this, I think, was mainly because the young lady at the check-out was so fascinated by Wally's fair hair, blue eyes and merry demeanor.

While Wally packed the stuff in boxes, I read the first letter I have received in Colombia, after being in this country for a month. It is from a British editor of a yachting magazine. The first words are, "Colombia, for God's sake!" and it ends up with the line "Don't get yourself shot, blasted or raped"—and I knew I had come to the right place. I knew that the job I am doing is worthwhile. I realized that if I can turn rumor into facts, then all the problems and troubles that we have overcome to get here, and to stay here, are worthwhile.

At the Immigration Office Señor Mario Torres, the officer in charge, was courteous, civil and helpful, as always. Here again, thank God, is another government official who does not use his post as an excuse to be bad-mannered or bullying, as so many elsewhere do. It is always a pleasure to visit him. I talked again with him about the possibilities of opening up Santa Marta to visiting yachts; the protection they will need, and the facilities that ought to be afforded them, in return for the extra income that they will bring to the town. Again he heard me carefully, and again he promised to bring my points up before the next meeting of the City Fathers . . . and again he accompanied me to the main door and bade me a gracious good-day.

When we returned from Concha beach to Conchita in our dugout, well loaded down with food, water and diesel fuel, so that it had only three inches of freeboard above the waves, the two lookouts at the fishing camp were still at their post, high up the wind-leaned tree, almost naked the pair of them, staring into the sunset, like a scene from a million years ago.

Wally and I were away from *Outward Leg* and Conchita for nine hours; it seemed, in our concern for the rising wind and the risk of piracy in our absence, like nine years. Next time we leave Conchita it will be in *Outward Leg*. When we reached the boat we found Ivan in the cockpit, with bow and arrows, flare gun and Molotov cocktails ready. To him our absence must have seemed like nine centuries.

To tease Ivan, I told him that the young waitress at El Molino, with whom he flirted last week, has now fallen for Wally.

"In Colombia," he retorted, "with a dozen women for every man, that's not going to worry me too much!"

So much for Spanish jealousy.

17

The Spanish Main

Did you know old Ruben Ranzo?
Good-bye, farewell, good-bye, farewell!
The one who fishes for bonito?
Hoorah, oh Mexico!

He has three daughters, they're all the same,
He has three daughters, all on the game.

One in Liverpool, one in New York,
The third lives in Colom-bye-oh!

From "Goodbye, Farewell." This was originally a French shanty. It is the only one I
know of that mentions Colombia.

At breakfast in Conchita this morning—we eat on the house patio while
the boat's galley is being painted—we were roused suddenly by a loud
explosion from the direction of *Outward Leg*. We all three hopped swiftly
from our plates of black pudding and fried egg, and jumped to stare over
the patio wall. A hundred yards astern of the boat, a canoe with four
men in it was drifting, while directly under the stern a big patch of discolored water on the surface of the sea told the tale: They were dynamiting fish. In the water, by the dugout, a masked diver was holding
on to its gunwhale. Almost immediately, as if from nowhere, a flock of
pelicans zoomed in over the dugout and circled, slowly, searching the
surface of the water for dead or stunned fish. These were the first pelicans we have seen here. Their leaders were overhead before the echoes
of the explosion had finished reverberating from the hills across the bay.
Minutes later the pelicans were joined by another kind of bird, black-
and-white, with a wingspan about three feet across. These were less
graceful in their flight than the pelicans—what bird is not?—and

swooped, climbed and plunged above and into the discolored patch of sea.

Soon the men had gathered a score or so of fish. They paddled over to our beach to fling a couple of cadavers to Cotes—I suppose they consider it his bay—and then made their way around the point and out of sight.

Wally swam over to dive around *Outward Leg* to check that there had been no damage to her underwater parts from the shock of the explosion. All was well. The pelicans sat patiently on the sea surface, riding the swells over the shallowing bay, for hours afterward, waiting for the bloated stomachs of the dead fish to lift them to the surface. They did not sit together in a flock, but singly in a circle surrounding the place where the dynamite had been set off. Hour in, hour out, they waited, like mothers outside a school, until at last the sea gave up the last of the fish; then they took off, all together again in a graceful squadron, out to seaward. The black-and-white divers stayed around for hardly more than the time the men in the canoe were gathering fish, but the pelicans knew that the sea takes its time to surrender dead things. They had seen all this before, many times, obviously.

As for the dynamiting, we can complain, I suppose, about the waste, and the destruction of yet another part of nature's network, but we can hardly hold opinions on the morals of the fishermen. Hunger knows no conscience. When your annual income might be two hundred dollars if you have a good year, food is food, from wherever it comes. When your family's bellies are empty today it's futile to think about tomorrow or next year or ten years hence. My guess is that within a short time, maybe two years, fish will be a thing of the past on the inshore coast of Colombia. Fish may be slower than pelicans at learning but they will learn, eventually, to avoid this coast. Then it will be as starkly beautiful—and as lifeless—as the Dead Sea.

The Caribbean coast of Panama, east of Colón, has always fascinated me, even from a distance, even when I am poring over an atlas half a world away from it. For sixty miles or so it is replete with historical interest from the days when it was known as the Spanish Main, and there are old Spanish forts and pirate havens every few miles along the shore, and the wind and the sea beat up incessantly against wild rocks and golden sandy beaches, all to a backdrop of waving palms and blue, misty mountains, gloomy, mysterious and haunting.

Farther east along this coast, beyond Punta San Blas, is the Archipiélago de las Mulatas, a chain of islands and islets, hundreds of them, lying offshore along the coast as it trends southeast, for ninety miles. This is the home of the San Blas Indians who live more or less as they have done for centuries, hunting and gathering, fishing and supporting themselves in practically every manner, independent for the most part of the siren call of "modern technology." Toward the eastern end of the island chain lies one of the least known areas of the Americas, although it is nowadays, more and more, the subject of exploratory probes, and the mountains inland are being slowly but surely, yard by yard, penetrated by the Pan-American Highway.

I was anxious to find somewhere to hole up for the worst of the heavy wind season, January and February, and to do this in Colombia. In late December the winds were already rising and blowing hard from the northeast and setting up a strong-running westerly-going current in the southern Caribbean. I decided to make for Punta Manzanillo, and then head east across the Golfo de Urabá, which bites deeply between Panama and Colombia. Easting was the thing. Grab everything *east*.

Christmas, and celebrating it among other exiles, had left us downcast and ready for sea. None of us on board *Outward Leg* wanted to spend New Year in Colón; no mail was arriving, there seemed to be no interest in our progress or welfare from the people who had seen us off at San Diego and who had promised to keep in touch, there was no money forthcoming from my interests ashore, the mobiles operation, which was supposed to support the voyage in its first few months and which was supposedly being handled by someone, seemed to have been forgotten. It was obvious that if Operation Star—the voyage of *Outward Leg*—was to be kept going, I would, somehow, with God's help, have to do it myself. Joe Gribbins of *Nautical Quarterly* magazine had sent me five hundred dollars in payment for some work I had done for him. With this in hand, I set off from Cristóbal, to tackle all the vicissitudes, hazards and dangers of a winter passage east along the pirate-ridden Caribbean shores of Colombia, and all the expenses of keeping an oceangoing vessel in good, seaworthy trim, at the same time feeding two hungry young men and keeping up their spirits until I could find a place where I might work undisturbed to try to earn some money for the next stage of the voyage. No wonder my leg had a resurgence of phantom pains on the night before we departed from Cristóbal. No wonder I spent hours in silent agony, unable to sit, stand or lie down for more than a few minutes at a stretch. As I clamped my remaining teeth in the after cabin I figured that I had to last out until I could somehow earn income to replace the money I had had to lay out in San Diego to complete the outfitting of *Outward Leg* as a proper, safe, oceangoing vessel. Knights of old used to spend a vigil before they set off on quests or pilgrimages, praying in a chapel. I spent my vigil fighting off my need for a pain-killing tablet, in case it should interfere with my navigational judgment after we slipped the berth in the small hours of the morning and wended our way through the still busy, vast harbor of Colón, and so out into the offing.

Then, after we had made the offing, past the blinking harbor entrance beacons, the wind rose and the sea with it, directly on the nose, and slapped me for being such a fool as to believe in anything engendered by, for and with publicity. All the hype—all the oaths and promises ever made—mean sweet bugger all to the wind and the sea. They say only "Be true to yourself," and that's all that really matters. That is the sea's grace, and that night she blessed *Outward Leg* and we three *caballeros* thrice over. She pounded us and flayed us, and the wind lacerated out of us any remaining romantic notions we might have had about landlubbers and their promises. Then the dawn came from below the heaving, wind-whipped sea, blood red, and comforted us coldly with the knowledge that out here we had been restored to our own resources, our own devices, and that we had not to depend on anyone else, anywhere. This is the only freedom of spirit that is truly real—because it is earned. On land there is no such thing as "justice"—as men know it at sea—because there justice is handed down by other men as a sop to preserve their own situation. The sea doesn't care if you win or lose, and that is the only real justice; if you ask for it you get it—and we had asked for it all right, and we got it.

Portobelo is only about twenty miles or so northeast in a straight line from Colón, but tacking this increased it to about thirty, and it took us from dawn to dusk to bash and crash our way there. The wind was about thirty knots, straight out of the northeast, and sometimes the gusts reached forty knots. The seas, on the continental shelf, were about eighteen feet high on average and spuming wickedly. We found that the boat, with her cruising load on board of necessity, was wet. We found some protection from the whipping spray, and the seas rolling right over the bow, behind the dodger, which we could ill afford but I had insisted on having fitted, but it was obvious that the hundreds of miles to windward across the Caribbean Sea were going to be wet indeed and, for me, hot too. The door to the after cabin would have to be shut the whole time we were headed into the wind and sea in any kind of seaway—otherwise my cabin, and everything in it, would be soaking wet. On this hop, until we found a place where we would have the time and the material to cure these problems, we would just have to pound away and suffer.

Breakfast is always cheering, and after that breakfast we set to, pretending we were out for a day-sail (which is the best way to cure first-day-out blues) and let her bash for Portobelo. Apart from its being a good anchorage, I wanted to see what Ivan's reaction to the well-preserved Spanish fortifications would be; Portobelo is a place of historical legend and courageous endeavor in Spanish history.

In the forenoon, as the ship heaved and pounded with each big sea, I ruminated that after all she was alive again after three weeks sleeping in the dead waters of the Panama Canal. She rubbed her cheeks fondly then against the high swells and pounded less, or so it seemed to me, and I reflected that it was good to smell the open sea again and feel the boat respond to every welcome of the foam-flecked blue.

In the afternoon it rained and rained and rained. At times the rain was so thick and heavy, and slashed so hard in the wind, that it was impossible for long stretches of time to see the plunging bow from the rearing center cockpit, a distance of about fourteen feet. It was like hurling around in a gray-painted iron box. But in between the heavy showers, the view of misty mountains, blue and gray, rearing up into the rain-laden clouds, was dramatic and magnificent. The mountains of Panama are on the receiving end of all the trade-wind weather, blown all the way across the Atlantic Ocean, all the way from Africa. Here the weather is killed. On the other side of Panama, on the Pacific side, it is reborn, to hurl its way anew across that mighty ocean on its way around the world.

This was the first time we had sailed *Outward Leg* loaded for any distance directly to windward—close hauled. She went like a witch, at times making eight knots and more even through that steep-piled sea. She was wet, but she was so because she was *fast*. The seas that came on board over the bow and rolled right up over into the cockpit were rare, perhaps only three the whole way from Colón to Portobelo, but you only need one to soak everything in the cockpit and if the hatchway to the after cabin is open, there, too.

My main concern on this leg was my dead reckoning. The speed log was hopeless. It switched itself off, as if maliciously, at odd times, as it had done the whole voyage so far. I'd had no money to get it seen to in Panama. On the open ocean and with fair visibility, this is not too

serious, but in coastal waters you must keep careful track of your courses
and boards, of course, to avoid hazards and to arrive safely at your destination. In rainy conditions, if the sat-nav packs up, there is no chance
of a sextant sight for longitude, and without some method of knowing
your speed, how can you tell where you are? Or even when you think
you might be? If I'd had sufficient money in Panama I would have bought
a taffrail log, a mechanical log, but I couldn't, so I was back to gauging
the speed of the boat by staring for a few seconds at the water rushing
under the gap between the ama and the main hull. Also I took regular
bearings on landmarks ashore that I could identify from the chart.

In between rainstorms I sighted a ketch on the horizon, driving to
the west astern of us. I tried to imagine what she could be, and from
whence she had hailed, and the excitement of those on board as they
reached nearer and nearer to Panama and a new ocean beyond. Then
she was gone into a low bank of thick rain, and I saw no more of her.

The northern point of the mile-wide fjordlike bay that is Portobelo
harbor is still called by the name bestowed on it by British privateers
centuries ago: Iron Castle Point. On both sides of the fjord there are
extensive ruins of old Spanish forts, and at the end of the bay, too.
They were constructed to defend the warehouses of Portobelo, where
the gold and silver looted from a whole continent was piled, and also
to cover the loading of the galleons with treasures before their long and
hazardous voyages back to Spain to refill the coffers of the king. Now
the fortresses are empty husks, with fallen cannon lying everywhere, but
the grass is kept mowed. Ivan and I wandered around the ruins, trying
to imagine what it must have been like to have been a Spanish soldier
stationed there so long ago. As in most of the ancient castles back home
in Wales, the doorways and rooms of the ruins are very small by modern standards, and I realized again how much bigger modern people are
compared to their predecessors of five hundred years ago. We must be
at least a foot taller on average.

"That's not really a good thing," I told Ivan. "We really ought to
be growing smaller, for everybody's sake."

"?" When Ivan looks puzzled his face screws up as if he had swallowed a frog.

"Well, then we wouldn't need so much food, and there'd be more
to go round; and not only food, but other materials, too. Just imagine,
if everyone was only three feet high the resources of the earth would be
double what they are now!"

Ivan escaped this thought by climbing a nearby hill to inspect an old Spanish lookout tower. He's not very tall himself, yet he has twice the energy of many a young man much taller. In general, I have found over the years that shorter people make better sailors. They certainly seem to have more stamina than tall people, but there are exceptions, of course, among both short and tall.

The anchorage at Portobelo is right in front of the old fort on the southern side of the fjord. The bottom is hard sand and good. In the small cabin right by the fortress gate lives a man who will guard dinghies, and if he is not there his wife or one of his numerous offspring will perform this necessary task with diligence for a dollar.

The town itself is about a quarter of a mile or so from the anchorage. I found that it had hardly changed since I was there in *Sea Dart* eleven years before. There were a few more bicycles, a few more garish buses and cars which use the now-paved road to Colón, much more racket from transistor radios blaring everywhere, and a few television aerials atop the tin roofs of the cottages. Otherwise everything was about the same. There was the same poor selection of victuals in the tiny shops, the same watery coffee in the roadside stands, the same sleepy town square, the same few worshipers of the black Christ in the old Spanish church, and the same gently courteous people and curious laughing children everywhere. I still say that the people of Portobelo are the happiest and friendliest-to-strangers anywhere north of Brazil. It is a pleasure still to be among them, and for this alone Portobelo is well worth a visit.

One of the little tin houses had a notice posted over the doorway, in Spanish of course: "The black Christ does not like burglars."

The next day was New Year's Eve. We weighed at dawn and, in the lazier wind of the morning, made our way along the beautiful coast, threading our way through the stark Duarte Cays so as to stay out of the heavy seas as much as we could, to Isla Grande. This was to be our departure point for Santa Marta, three hundred miles as the crow flies, almost directly to windward. I decided that New Year's Day might be propitious for the start of our new venture, and so we stayed in Isla Grande only one night.

Isla Grande is a pretty place, straight out of a travel company's tropical vacation brochure, it seems. It lies about half a mile offshore, and the channel between it and the mainland is flat, blue and busy with small colorful ferry boats. There is a small jetty poking out from the village, right in front of the only store. The best anchorage is to the west of the jetty about fifty yards, between it and the reef, against which the heavy seas outside the strait break—alarmingly from a distance. The holding ground is hard sand and good in any wind.

The inhabitants are mainly descendants of black slaves from colonial days, and Jamaicans brought over for the digging of the Panama Canal at the end of the last century. This shows in the number of tiny chapels in the village. It seemed there was a chapel for every family. The people are very friendly and helpful to visitors, and they appreciate that the town survives almost wholly on what tourism is attracted there by the vacation village on the eastern end of the sandy beach.

At the anchorage a good fresh breeze blows in from the sea, and keeps the boat cool, but ashore it is hot and sultry. I could manage to hobble a few yards along the palm-tree-lined track behind the beach. Then I had to sit down, and found myself staring into the distance, at the misty bay five miles away where Francis Drake's bones lie "slung amid the round shot in Nombre Dios Bay." That was where the British and Dutch privateers used to lie in wait for the galleons of Spain to leave Portobelo, treasure laden, and from where they emerged from hiding, to track the big ships on their way north, like bloodhounds on the trail.

So ended the year 1983. The new year seemed full of promise—and hazard, at least the first part of it. But what is a life without risk, I thought, under the waving palms, and what else would I want to be doing?

Now Don Jesús has arrived at Conchita again. He has decided not to bring his boat Amorua here because it is "too dangerous." His boat was outfitted here—completely rebuilt—and afterward she was stripped of all her new gear by pirates, aided and abetted by the then watchman.

I owe it to Don Jesús to help him, as much as we in Outward Leg can, to resolve his leak problem. Then Amorua will have to wait until we can find a good, hardworking, honest sailor somewhere who will be willing to come to Santa Marta and help prepare Amorua for sea and sail her around the world. We both know, Don Jesús and I, that there are a host of young men who might jump at the opportunity to live here on board a boat in the tropics without expense, but we also know that whoever does come must be prepared for long hours of hard work and be capable of solving all the worrisome problems of outfitting a vessel in an as yet undeveloped country, along with people who are relatively inexperienced and unaware of the demands of the sea.

I have told Wally and Ivan to prepare the boat for sailing on Thursday morning. We shall leave Conchita and head for Tacanga, where we shall be much closer to Santa Marta, yet not under the vulture eye of the Port Captain, and from where we can try to solve the problem of the leak in *Amorua*'s keel.

We shall also, I hope, be safer from the possibility of pirate attack for the first time in a month.

18

Out in the Blue

The brave west wind it filled our mainsail,
And bore us outward bound,
Outward bound across the ocean,
Outward bound, alive oh!
Sheet her home, the big main tops'l,
Sheet her home, boys, good and true,
For we're bound for Mother Carey's,
She feeds her chicks out in the blue!

From "Mother Carey's." Capstan shanty,
late nineteenth century. Mother Carey's
chickens are a species of ocean birds.

Don Jesús stayed for the afternoon yesterday. He showed me pictures of
how his craft *Amorua* was completely rebuilt here at Conchita. He had
first to build a concrete slip seventy feet long and ten feet wide, to support the heavy boat on the foreshore. Then he built two towers of steel
piping, each ninety feet high, so that he could remove her mast vertically and replace it when the refurbishing was done. The whole job took
four years; and all the while the refitting crew had to be supplied with
fresh water and victuals.

We also talked about the reasons that yachtsmen do not come to
Colombia anymore. Don Jesús claims that the worst of the drug-related
violence is now under control, more or less, but there are still areas
where it would be very dangerous to go, and of these the Gulf of Urabá,
close to the Panama frontier, and the Guajira Peninsula, next to the
Venezuelan frontier—about one hundred and fifty miles east of Santa
Marta—are the worst. On Guajira, which is about a hundred miles across
each way, there are an estimated seven hundred private landing strips,
where the drug smugglers' planes land. The peninsula is inhabited by
Guajira Indians and *mestizos*, who are practically without law and who

live by violence, pure and simple. Blood feuds among them are common, and murder is as common and as unimportant there as the common cold. People are shot for the slightest insult. Strangers are murdered for a mere jug of water.

An estimated two hundred drug-smuggling planes, Don Jesús tells me, have crashed in Guajira in the past ten years. The Indians dig a ditch alongside the wreck, pile the machine in along with the dead pilot, cover it up and go on their way.

Three years ago Don Jesús saw a plane pass over Conchita and drop a parachutist with suitcases on the beach—probably loaded with dollars. He was picked up by a jeep and speeded away into the hills along *el camino de los muertos.* Until a couple of years ago, when the antidrug patrols were beefed up, Don Jesús used to watch the drug-smuggling craft leave Bahía Concha practically every night, on their way out to sea to pass the marijuana on to bigger ships for onward consignment to the USA. Now, he says, those days are over; the trade has shifted to Guajira.

For the past three decades a civil war has been fought in the interior of Colombia, amid the mountains. At this moment there are an estimated ten thousand guerrillas fighting the army. Until recently this has been a problem separate from drugs exportation. But now that the government efforts to tighten up against the coastal drug traffic is slowly taking effect, the mafia is in contact with the guerrillas: supplying them with arms and other needs in return for cargoes of pot and cocaine. Thus the trade is moving inland.

Only the other day an American DC-10 plane crashed in the mountains of the Sierra Santa Marta, loaded with rifles and submachine guns. Now the bastards who have been busy distorting the minds of kids in the States and Canada are supplying the means of death for South American kids, too. The guerrillas still play their game, pretending to be the forces of social enlightenment, while all the time they are dealing with the ultracapitalist drug mafia of the United States and the Bahamas. These bandits, under the leadership of middle-class street-corner boys stomp through the jungles and mountains of Colombia murdering and terrorizing the country folk, seeking nothing but pure power in the easiest way they can get it. And they do it with American arms, supplied by Americans, in return for drugs to stupefy the minds of American youngsters.

But for sailors the move of the drug trade away from the coast is a good thing. The strengthening of the coastal watch may mean that by 1985 the area around Santa Marta may be reasonably safe to visit. That is, if the coast guard is not corrupted again. There will still be local thievery, of course, but that can be expected now anywhere. It means that a good watch must be kept on the vessel at all times. It means that new alarm systems will have to be developed, and new ways of discouraging unwanted visitors thought out and put into practice. It means, too, that the Colombian authorities will have to take much greater interest in the welfare of visiting craft, and afford them every protection possible.

We agreed that the average landsman might wonder why the Colombian authorities should concern themselves over the welfare of a few yachtsmen on their coast—and then we agreed that if the figures were shown to them they would be interested all right. If twenty yachts a month visited Santa Marta, and each had on board four people, and each person spent as much money here as we have in a month—and we have been by no means profligate—it would mean a monthly income for the town of Santa Marta of *ten thousand dollars*. In a place where the average monthly income is thirty dollars, that is not to be scoffed at. It would be clean money, too, and the decent, progressive Colombians here know that. Already Don Jesús has been talking to the Chamber of Commerce in Santa Marta, telling them what I have been saying about this potential, telling them that Santa Marta could become a yachting center on the Colombian coast; and already they are forming plans for a proper marina, well constructed, with decent facilities and guarded, to be built at Rodadero. I am not sure that this is the right place to build it, and for that reason I want to visit Tacanga, where there is better protection from the hard winter winds.

When Don Jesús and his party left Conchita I felt much better about my stay in Colombia. I came here to test the truth of rumors, to find out the truth about piracy hereabouts.

Back on the coast of Panama, as soon as the sun was high enough to show up the reef on the eastern side of Isla Grande strait, we hauled up the hook and shoved off. It was New Year's Day. Inside the strait the waters were placid—a playground for toy boats—but outside we could plainly see the undulating faces of the heavy seas as they piled themselves against the continent. And so through the narrow passage between the reef and the cliff, into the morning, the wind still with indignation at our temerity, the seas piling against us, and *Outward Leg* trooping, trying hard, pounding, pounding, working her way into the distance of the day and bright sunlight in the offing of Panama.

Then, for six days and seven hundred and eighty miles, it was drive, drive, watch after watch, down yankee, up spitfire, two reefs in the main, shake out the reefs; up main, down spitfire, up yankee, watch, in, watch out, day and night, night and day, drive, drive—here's a crack boat with a crack crew, her outrigger keels sparkling sheets of rainbow colors, the seas crashing up against her three bows, sending showers of spray right over her time after time, hour after hour, day after day, drive, drive, *oh Lord let her go!* There's one thing about bashing to windward—you never forget, for one minute, that you are at sea in a sailing boat. There is none of the lethargy, the temptation to boredom at times, that you might encounter going downwind after a few days at sea. There is none of the feeling, in the mornings especially, at dawn, of "Oh, well, another day . . ." Now in the mornings, at dawn or at any other time, you awake for your watch and it's "My Christ! Another watch?"

This was my first beat to windward for any real distance in a multihull vessel. The one big advantage, apart from the much greater speed as compared to the monohull of the same length going to windward, is the lack of any heel more than about five degrees—except, of course when *Outward Leg* slides down a big sea. Then the heel can increase to anything up to twenty degrees. I cuddled the thought of the cool-tubes down below, locking the boat to gravity. The closest description of the movement of *Outward Leg* when she is hurrying—there's no other word for it—to windward, is as I imagine it would be if I were sitting atop the roof of an express train hurtling through a rainstorm. She has a swayback motion, a quick waddle. Think of a hula-hula girl's movements when she shakes her hips, and that's about how it feels to move at eight or nine knots, forty-eight degrees off the wind, in *Outward Leg*. Then imagine the hula-hula girl doing that on a platform that is rising and falling steadily anything up to twenty feet, up and down; then imagine doing that on one leg, and imagine the platform stopping dead every minute or so with a crash.

Soon we had left the coast of Panama to look after itself under the incessant rain, and I was plotting to be in the Gulf of Urabá at night, without lights, so that we would not be seen by any roving *bandido* foolish enough to be out in that weather, one who might be innocent enough of the ways of normal cruising yatties to imagine that there might be a yacht out in it, too. At noon I ditched the 1983 Almanac into a shivering rainbow as spray hurled over the port ama, and dug out the 1984 Almanac. So we celebrated the new year.

After noon, as usual in the trades, the wind roused itself to a really hard blow. The seas were a great confusion of blue, exploding, white-capped, wall on wall, as far as my salt-spray-blinded eyes could see, ranged against us. The sun lit the sweep of the sea right out to the horizon, and the wind, glowing under an immense light of turquoise, banged us on the nose time and again brutally, as if in payment for our audacity. *Outward Leg* bit back at the wind, gnashed her teeth at it, worried it, gnarled it, and spit it out, time after time, hour after hour. Here was *fight!*

Now *Outward Leg*'s mast bent under the pressure of the wind, a strong, steady pressure, increasing only when she slid down a sea, but mostly at forty-five knots on the wind-speed gauge. Her reefed mainsail, taut and strained, shoved her, pushed her, rammed her, from sea to sea, and every sea tossed her, then passed quickly under her keels, subdued and humbled by her power.

The following few hours soon showed up two minor weaknesses in *Outward Leg*'s fore hatch and two big windows in her main deck; they all leaked. There are always small discrepancies in the construction of any sailing vessel, which will not be found until she is really up against it and the chips are down. As she pounded the seas, and as sea after sea mounted her low bows and streamed, rolled, gushed, over her foredeck, so the joints in the hatch and the windows worked loose, as they always do, and soon stream after stream of water was pouring into the crew's cabin forward. From then on it was bail out every few hours or so, and Wally's berth became sodden and untenable, so that he was forced to sleep alternately in my berth when I was on watch or on the sole of the forward cabin. Ivan's berth, too, was soaked all the time, and he slept where he could find a dry spot—mostly on the sole of the engine-room passageway.

Bailing out was a matter of shifting all the gear stowed in the bilges and scooping the water out of each separate bay between the frames, a soppy, futile job, for no sooner was the hull bailed out than there was another half ton of water down below in the bilges again. I had asked for limber holes to be drilled in the frames in San Diego, so that any water in the boat would drain aft to the galley bilge from where it could be pumped out by a long hose from the engine-room bilge suction, but neither the holes nor the long suction hose were provided for one reason or another. Now we were paying the price of perforce missing these two necessary items in any craft. We all three took turns in hefting around food supplies and cans, from bay to bay in the bilge, to keep the water level within the boat down, so as not to weigh her down too much. With a weaker crew, on a lee shore, this could have been serious. The amount of water pouring on board by the third day of beating could have had her completely waterlogged in a few hours.

As it was, we could not heave to to bail her out. The current runs at three knots, westerly, and in the southwest Caribbean you simply do not give one yard to the wind or the sea when you are making a passage east. It's go, go, go, from dawn to dusk to dawn, all the way, until you fetch your destination.

I made up my mind to cure the problems at the first possible opportunity. The forward hatch was a simple matter of adding a gasket at the after edge of the hatch—it had been overlooked. The windows would have to be replaced by solid plywood, and glassed over.

Now, as she pounded along from sea to sea, the crew and I crawled out onto the lee ama, slowly hauling ourselves out to the upper shroud turnbuckles against heavy, rolling seas sweeping on board, and we clipped our lifelines to the cables and, soaked to the skin, laughing, we gloried in the sight of all three keels shooting from a sea, clear in the air, a foot of the main keel showing, all three keels rainbows! This was sailing, by God! She wasn't sailing—she was flying!

I turned aft, away from the clobbering seas, and stared at the wake. It was as straight as a plow furrow and as distinct as a missile track, even through those violent waters. The ship tore on. I turned to her main hull again, and knew she was a fighter.

She tore on, with the same desperate-seeming haste as had propelled her all day and all night—it was our second day—in the wildness of the angry morning, under a low, hurrying heaven and over leaping seas that showed green under the gray clouds and rose before us with a roar, then slipped away aft mute. The ship careered forward with an aching straining from every inch of her, aloft and below. Her shrouds strained and whined—a high-pitched whistle—and sang when the wind briefly reeled from her onslaught, then the wind boomed in her sails, the sheet-blocks beat. Again and again she heaved herself up, and surged and descended and swayed, smashing the seas white, boring into and up and out of the watery hills and hollows and singing as she did it, singing to herself and to us, too, and making us sing with her. Again and again she threw up her bows to the seas driven in by the northeast trade, all against her, and the ocean wind streamed into her sails and drove her, and *Outward Leg* laid her tough cheeks against the Equatorial Current and flayed it alive.

We ate supper early, to avoid cooking in the dark. We showed no lights off Colombia. The last thing we wanted to do was advertise our presence.

On the third day, with 470 miles under our belts, 150 of them gained directly into the eye of the trade wind, we sighted another vessel. It was about two in the afternoon, and she was on our southwestern horizon in the direction of the Gulf of Urabá. I sighted her first. Even though I must wear spectacles now to read, my distance vision is far better than either of my crewmen's; Wally has poor distance vision. At first she was a mere suspicion on the heaving horizon, a discoloration under the blue-gray of the sky. I broke out the binoculars and inspected her. She was not a big ship, which put her immediately under suspicion. She was about the size of a minesweeper, or a tug, and she was painted, it seemed, gray, although at that distance—about seven miles—it was impossible to see for sure. She was well hull down, but steaming straight for what would be our patch if we held our course. I decided to take no chances and sheered off the wind a couple of points. That was the first and only time the whole way from Panama to Santa Marta when we were not close hauled to the wind and sea. What a difference!

The eternal spray eased off right away as we eased off the sheets and headed her at a greater angle across the seas, so she was not now pounding directly into them at right angles. Now the lee ama bit deeply into the seas while the windward ama rose a foot above the heaving waters in the hollows and sliced through the humps. The log, for once registering, showed over ten knots. We were fairly flying. I stared back at the strange ship. She had changed course in our direction. I could not be sure at first, and I stared through the binoculars for a good fifteen minutes before I was absolutely sure. She was definitely heading right for us, and closing the distance between us slowly but steadily.

"We'd better clap on the staysail, too," I said to Wally. "Do you think we can shake out the reef in the main while we're still running on a broad reach?"

"What do we want to do that for? We've thirty knots of wind. . . ."

The boat was shaking and pounding, plunging and crashing with effort in the wild seas. The shrouds were howling, the sails juddering. There was still an hour and a half until dusk could hide us.

"Because that boat out there looks very suspicious to me, and I think we've got some bloody *bandido* chasing us."

Now both the crew are preparing the boat for the move to Tacanga on Wednesday. We've decided to sail a day sooner. A month in a remote anchorage is enough for two feisty young men, and a bored crew is a bad crew. It will be a short sail, but a voyage is a voyage, no matter what the distance, and so the ship must be made ready just as if it were five hundred miles instead of a mere fifteen or so.

Don Jesús has lent us a fiberglass dinghy shaped like a dugout canoe. This is to temporarily replace our own dinghy, stolen, as we shall see. The locally built boat is very tender, as she has no keel, and she tends to roll right over. Normally this would be acceptable, but with only one leg I must be a little careful about dinghies. We are going to choose a suitable piece of timber here and take it to Tacanga with us. There we will shape it into a keel for the small boat, and fix it in place. A keel should make the craft steadier by imparting a damping effect against the roll. Anyway, it's worth a try.

19

The Chase

On the fourteenth day of Febru'ry we sailed from the
 land,
In the bold *Princess Royal* bound out for Newfoundland,
We had forty-five seamen for our ship's company,
The wind from the eastward, to the westward steered we.

We'd hardly been sailing but a day, two or three,
When the man from the masthead strange sail did he see,
She came bearing down upon us with her topsail so high,
And under her mizzen peak black colours she did fly.

He chased us to windward and through the long day,
And he chased us to loo'ard but could not gain way,
And he fired long-shot after us, but he could not prevail,
And the bold *Princess Royal* soon showed a clean tail.

Go down on your grog, me lads, go down every man,
Go down on your grog, me lads, go down one and all,
Go down on your grog, me lads, and be of good cheer,
For as long as we've sea room, we've nothing to fear!

"The Princess Royal," a nonworking shanty, or forebitter,
probably of sixteenth-century origin

I must be more careful and less ambitious in my attempts to live a "normal" life. This morning at Conchita, while the crew were working on
board, I went into the house kitchen to make myself a cup of coffee.
The water here is brought in big fifteen-gallon containers. The one in
current use was standing on a waist-high shelf, full. I tried to tip it over
slightly to pour water into the kettle—and it fell right on top of me,
flinging me against the far wall of the kitchen. Apart from a bruised
elbow and a knock on the head I seem to be all right, and after feeling
sick for a few minutes I recovered. I am actually safer on board the boat
than ashore. There are no big empty spaces to fall across. On board I

can be flung only a few inches at the most; I made sure of that when I drew up the modifications during the outfitting. Here, Cotes, hearing the crash of the water container, ran to my rescue and helped me recover my footing. I decided I'd be safer afloat.

Yesterday before Don Jesús left, he told me that Bahía Concha is, in fact, a national park, and that was the reason the villas behind the beach are in ruins—the builders had to abandon them when the government stepped in and stopped any further construction. Here in Colombia there always seem to be two explanations for everything! The one from the common people, the poor, and the one from others, who probably are better informed. Now I feel much better about Bahía Concha; it is so beautiful that it deserves to be protected from "developers." Don Jesús is lucky—he built Conchita twenty years ago, before Bahía Concha was declared a national park. Now, nothing else can be built anywhere near.

When Wally came to lunch he looked more pleased with himself than usual, and quiet, too. Eventually Ivan asked me if I had seen "the surprise." He seemed excited.

"Where?" I asked him.

"On the boat's side," he replied.

I turned from my lunch and stared over the wall to where the boat swings to her three anchors. There on the port side, gleaming with teak oil, was a brand-new boarding ladder.

"Bloody well done, Wally!" I exclaimed.

He looked up modestly from his vegetable stew. "I decided to make it when we arrived here, but I didn't have the wood or the time until yesterday," he said.

"I wondered what you'd been up to, hidden below," I observed.

"I thought it would make life a bit easier for you," he muttered, and shyly returned to spooning his stew. He's like that, our Wally.

The bottom of the rubber tip of my cane has worn through, so the rubber works its way up the cane and leaves the wooden tip exposed and slippery. Such little things as this, in an isolated place like Conchita, make life much more difficult than it would be back in urban "civilization," but that is the price I must pay for doing what I am doing. Somehow we will find a way to cure that problem, too. It's all part of Operation Star, after all.

By dusk on the third of January, our pursuer was about two miles away from *Outward Leg* astern, and we could plainly see her as she, too, plowed and crashed into the rough seas all around. With all our plain sail up, including the staysail, we were making a good twelve knots in a welter of spray, with everything battened down tight but seawater still pouring into the boat, and the crew bailing out every twenty minutes or so. The scene below was chaotic, with food and stores flung everywhere, so that the bailers could reach the bilges. I stayed at the wheel, grimly hanging on, while seas rolled over and over the whole length of the boat, over the windward ama, right over the main hull—what did not sluice into the cockpit—and so away back into the ocean over the lee ama.

As blessed darkness fell around us—it was cloudy with no moon—I found myself hoping that our pursuer did not have radar. Outward Leg's mast is foam filled and packed with aluminum foil, so that it is one huge radar reflector. I knew how good its reflection was, because I'd spoken by radio with a ship up near Costa Rica, which had reported a good big fat blob showing from us on her radar set. Here I found the one disadvantage of this method of reflecting radar—it cannot be stopped, as it could have been with the usual type of reflector, which is hoisted aloft. Still we crashed on and on in the night, due north. I sought the pursuer in the darkness astern, but she was showing no lights. This made me all the more worried, because if she was not chasing us, why was she showing no lights? Or was it a coincidence that she had changed course, and was her skipper, too, wary of pirates?

At about nine o'clock I sighted two ships, both with their lights showing, on the northern horizon. They were on opposite, but parallel, courses. For the first and only time in a lifetime at sea, I headed straight for the point where the two ships would pass each other. Wally was in the cockpit with me while Ivan bailed out the cabin. We were all wet through and becoming cold now. Even in the southern Caribbean the night wind can be quite chilly, especially when it's blowing at thirty knots or so. Above the roar of the wind and the scream in the shrouds and stays, and the juddering of the jibs and the main, I shouted to Wally what I intended to try to do, "Confuse him! Get between those two ships and then change course. That way he won't know which of the radar reflections—if he's still chasing us and if he has radar—is us!"

That's what I did. I stuck at the wheel and raced Outward Leg straight between the two approaching ships, and she crashed and battered her screaming road through and over the whipping seas, with torrents of water pouring over her and spray whizzing over the dodger and great thumps as dollops of seawater flung themselves at us. Ever outward she plunged and wallowed, rose and fell, and always pushing forward, closer and closer to the ships. We passed ahead of one ship so close that it seemed she was only a hundred yards away from us, and then so close to the stern of the other ship that I could plainly see, squinting through the spray, someone standing on her afterdeck dressed in white overalls. I could even see, I'm sure, the expression on his face as he gawped at this ghostly apparition racing under his stern in the darkness of the night. A couple of minutes later one of the ships blew her siren, and I'm sure that it was the one with the white-dressed man on her stern. He was probably one of her engineers in his overalls.

Once clear of the second ship, I headed very close to the wind again—northeast by north—and held that course, close hauled, all the night, sleepless for us all. Wally and I relieved each other at hourly intervals through the night, until at four in the morning, an hour before dawn, we put the Aries back into gear and let our boat sail herself, left her to crash and bash against the strongest current in the whole of the Caribbean Sea.

At dawn I was awake, to search the horizon for any sign of our erstwhile pursuer, but the wind-whipped blue sea and the pale gray horizon were empty of anything but a couple of wild squalls in the north, and a leaping school of dolphins in the south. We were free, and *Outward Leg* smashed her way forward still, to even more freedom. As I told the crew over a jerky breakfast of cold porridge, "I know that what I did is against the rules of seamanship and common sense in normal times, but in the circumstances, in these waters, I'm sure that we did the right thing to try to confuse the bastard if he was still on our tail."

While Wally was a bit reserved about the matter—he'd pulled a face when we passed before the bow of one ship and under the stern of another so close it almost seemed that we could have reached out and touched her side—Ivan, with very little experience at sea, agreed with me. A good skipper in a crew of three should always make sure that one of them is not too much experienced—then he always has someone to agree with him when postmortems take place after a dire event. As I explained to them, "I'm not saying categorically that I was right, because we'll never know if the *bandido* was pursuing us or not, but as she did not catch up with us, and as she did not follow us all night, then no one can say that I did wrong!"

By dawn of the fourth day—the fourth of January—*Outward Leg* was about fifty miles to the northwest of Cartagena. The seas and the wind were still very wild. To the west of us was Nicaragua, to the north, Cuba, ahead to the east, Colombia, while seawater was gushing ever more into the boat as she plunged on. I suppose I could have considered

a return to Colón, but you don't throw away 250 miles directly to windward, hard gained. Not in the Caribbean, you don't, unless you're dying.
I don't, anyway, and I wasn't dying, nor about to either.

About noon I saw a curious thing through the wind-driven spray.
There were bits of pumice stone floating on the sea. I squinted and peered
at them for several seconds before I realized that they must be the relics
of some underwater volcanic explosion somewhere, and my guess is that
it must have been somewhere quite close, because the whole surface of
the sea was littered with pumice. If I hadn't been beating to windward
I would have hove to and collected a few pieces of pumice, just so that
people would believe what I had seen, but I would not give the Equatorial Current any opportunity to send *Outward Leg* back west one inch.

Also in the current we saw millions of Portuguese men-of-war. These
brave little souls, too, were being blown almost horizontal by the wind.
Some people say they sail to windward, but I don't think so. I think
that they are hove to and drifting to leeward.

All that day, the fourth day out of Isla Grande, and the fifth day,
and the sixth, and the nights too, we crashed and bashed our way against
winds of thirty knots minimum and fifty knots maximum in gusts. *Outward Leg* bit and chomped into the leaping seas ahead, and groaned and
dived, and steadfastly shot from one sea to the next, and farther and
farther into the gleaming dawn and the blackness of the night, and
scornfully, willingly, champed the white bone in her mouth—in her three
mouths—and viciously spat round her on all sides. She was queen of
this sea, and she let the Caribbean know it, with seeming scorn. Every
hour or so the boat was bailed out by one or the other of us. There was
nothing wrong at all with the hull—it is a beautiful piece of design work,
fast and strong. It was all because of shortsighted skimping on finishing
the forward hatch, and obstinacy on leaving in the large windows in
the foredeck above the crew's berths. All the long hours of damp misery
and hard work, very awkward for me on one leg, could have been avoided
with only a few hours, hardly that, of very easy adjustments in San Diego.
It's hell on earth to have to contemplate warnings you have given and
which have been avoided or turned aside, and then have to pay the
price yourself.

At dawn on the sixth day the whole horizon in the east was one
blood-red glow, and far down to the southeast over the wild moving
hills, white-topped and frenzied, it gradually formed a blood-red background for a faint shadow, like a blue pencil line drawn for a short way
along the edge of the sea, where it met the sky. Land! South America!

A new continent! Colombia! I tried to see it through Wally's eyes, and Ivan's, with the freshness of youth seeing something for the very first time, as I had done myself, so long, long ago.

All that morning and forenoon we smashed our way through chaotic seas toward the offing of Barranquilla and the mouth of the mighty River Magdalena. By the time we were thirty miles west from off the river mouth, the sea had turned cocoa-colored, and the current against us was now a good four knots. On we smashed at ten, eleven, twelve knots, sacrificing the knots stolen by the current for the little lee from the wind afforded by the river delta, which pokes north well out to sea. Then, toward noon, as we neared the river mouth we lost the lee and the wind came at us bawling its head off and hammering us down, so that we were forced to make out for the offing to the north, and the full spate of the gale and the Equatorial Current in all its power. By dusk we had again lost the thin line of the land, and were on our own lonely way, plunging and diving, wallowing and spitting, smashing and crashing, wailing and bailing. But when we tacked at eight o'clock I knew that we had the mastery of this bloody wind and current, for we could close reach, all sails in taut, drawing like steam engines, all the way into the long, high lee of Santa Marta Bay, thirty miles still to our east.

As *Outward Leg* drew herself against the weather more and more into the lee of Santa Marta, and into less and less steep seas, so she moved faster and faster forward, and by eleven P.M. we were making a good fifteen knots, and sending spray right up over the masthead. When Wally told me this, after he had peered out into the pitch-black wetness, I doubted him, and peered out myself, aloft, where our navigation lights gleamed. It was true. Sheets of water were being driven right over the masthead by the onward force of the boat and the wind, now howling at forty-five knots in a full storm.

I tried to imagine what the boat must have looked like from outside her, and realized that with these sheets of water flying over her, she would have been hardly visible.

By the time we were three miles off the port of Santa Marta, and heading straight for the town lights, the sea was comparatively flat, and I eased her speed down. I had lit the navigation lamps because I remembered that some of the local fishermen do not carry lights, and it might at least give them a chance to get out of our way. Closer and closer to the port we sped, until at last, about two miles out, I hove to, first with all sail up, and then we handed the jibs, but kept the main aloft; in case we should need to clear off in a hurry during the night. Then we let her drift, set the watches, and turned in, with only one of us on deck at a time, to watch for strangers and to give the alarm should any craft approach us. Thus we arrived in Colombian waters and, two at a time, slept the sleep of the justly exhausted.

The bilges were four or five inches deep in seawater, but we were all too weary to even think of bailing out. We had reached our destination–six hundred miles directly into the eye of the wind—almost a thousand miles through the water, in just over six days. That's not bad going, I thought, as I threw the navigation pencil down, and crept into my berth. That's not bad going at all.

The crew finished making two weatherboards today. Each one is simply two four-inch planks, made from scrap timber we found here at Conchita, screwed together with battens. These are now lashed in place, between the after-pulpit stanchions and the lower-shroud turnbuckles on each side of the main hull. Later, when we have some spare money, we'll varnish or paint them, so that they do not look so raw. Although I did not have it in mind when I designed them, now that they are in place they remind me of the weatherboards that are shipped in Arab dhows. They are there simply to increase the freeboard forward on each side, where the seas, when we go heavily to windward, break on board or even roll right over the foredeck and into the cockpit. I doubt if they will make the cockpit completely dry when beating, but I think they will probably lessen the amount of seawater that comes on board.

We are also testing out the new spitfire jib pendant, which we made yesterday. The former one, of stainless steel, snapped like a cotton thread on the way into Santa Marta.

Ivan is cleaning the hulls, just below the waterlines. In three weeks here at Conchita, three inches of green grass has grown on them, and the barnacles, while they are repulsed by the bottom paint, have grabbed on to the blue waterline just above water level so that there is a necklace of black shells all around the boat.

Now that I know I am leaving Conchita very soon, I look at every familiar thing, so that I shall recall it properly when we are at sea. I listen more closely to the *carpinteros* singing in the morning, and to the sound of the surf on the pebbles, which seemed so sinister to me when we first arrived here and now sounds like a fond mother's lullaby. I find myself staring at the shattered tree stump with its young green sprig growing out of it, and every time I do it reminds me of the purpose of my voyage.

Years ago I used to leave places with little thought about them. I knew that a sailor's life is full of goodbyes, and I accepted it more easily then. But now, as I grow older, it becomes harder, most times but by no means all, to leave a place that has my fondness. I suppose that's why I stare about me so these days, quietly ruminating and fixing everything in my memory, so that I may take some of it with me when I leave. Mario looks gloomy. He seems to know we are leaving, though, so far as I know, no one has told him.

I suppose that I shall forget the things I am trying so hard to remember: the coolness of the patio of the villa with its tiled floor, the soft morning breeze blowing through the dining hall, the absolute tranquillity of Conchita; and instead I shall probably remember Mario, a little deaf-and-dumb brown boy with sad eyes, sitting in the dust chawing on a hunk of melon and trying to remember the alphabet we have taught him. It seems to me that memory is like that; it's not like a series of photographs filed away but more like a collection of paintings, each one of which changes according to the circumstances in which it is brought forth; a slight change of lighting or color each time, yet the subject remains absolutely the same, fixed forever, until the day we die. When I recall a visit to the Louvre, it is not the *Mona Lisa* that comes to my mind, but the image of the face of a young woman in the crowd of people viewing the picture. She expressed all that *La Gioconda* was trying to, only she was alive.

20

The Pirate Coast

Oh, Stormy he is dead and gone,
To me way, you Stormalong!
Old Stormy he is dead and gone,
Ay ay, Mister Stormalong!

Of all the skippers he was best,
But now he's dead and gone to rest.

We'll dig his grave with a silver spade,
His shroud of finest silk was made.

We lowered him down with a golden chain,
Our eyes all dim with more than rain.

Old Stormy loved a sailor's song,
His voice was rough and tough and strong.

For fifty years he sailed the seas,
In winter gale and summer breeze.

Old Stormy was a seaman bold,
A Grand Old Man of the days of old.

From "Stormalong." Halyard shanty,
mid-ninteenth century. There are hundreds
of verses to this hard-work song.

Don Jesús is away on business in Bogotá for three more days. Until he
returns, I hope with a copy of the London *Times* for me, we will anchor
off Tacanga, a small fishing village about five miles north of Santa Marta.
The place has a bad name, so far, for thievery and drug-smuggling skull-
duggery, but I think we are pretty well honed against that kind of thing
by now, and will be wary.

We have very little money on board; February and March are always
bad months for writers, so instead of a tip we are going to give Cotes a

week's supply of the dried natural food we carry in the boat. We can ill afford it, as we do not know what is in store for us in Venezuela and the Antilles, and there are another six—probably eight—weeks more to last over until any earnings can be sent out to me. But Cotes has been good to us, and kept watch on the boat every night until midnight for all the time we have been here at Conchita. We shall also search round the boat and see if there is any length of line we can do without. Fishermen always appreciate rope, and the locally made hemp line is very tatty.

On the morning of our arrival, on the sixth of January, Ivan fell asleep just as dawn lightened the eastern sky while *Outward Leg* was hove to off Santa Marta. For once, I didn't blame a crewman for sleeping when he was supposed to be on watch. It could have been dangerous off the coast of Colombia, but we were all so bone weary when we reached the shelter of Santa Marta that to expect anyone to stay awake for more than an hour would have been asking the impossible and a good skipper should never do that.

I was flaked out in the after cabin, dead to the world, when the sound of a loud engine woke me. I sprang up, bleary-eyed, and stuck my head through the after companionway; I always sleep with my leg on at sea. There, heaving in the swell only feet away from *Outward Leg*, was a high-speed powerboat, open, about thirty feet long, with two big outboard engines, each eighty horsepower, on its stern, and two men on board. One, of Indian aspect and sulky-looking, was driving the boat. The other was a big man, stout, with black hair and eyes and a large moustache, and a sallow complexion. He was standing in the boat, maintaining his balance with some difficulty as it rose and fell in the swell.

Ivan was shaking himself awake. The big man shouted something at Ivan in Spanish, but too fast for me to understand.

I called out, *"Qué quieres, señor?"* ("What do you want?")

Ivan turned to me and explained, "He wants to know if you know Jorge Dingo."

"Dingo?" I shouted at the man in the boat.

"Conoces Dingo?" he yelled at me.

"?" Conversationally I'm never at my best when I've woken from a deep sleep.

"Dingo!" The big man shouted again. "You know Jorge Dingo?" This time in English, but with a very poor pronunciation.

By now I had scrambled onto the foredeck, so that I could look down into the powerboat. In its bilge there was a canvas awning folded over something. I wondered if it was arms.

I was wide awake by now. "No, señor, what . . . where is he from?"

"California—Jorge Dingo!" he shouted in reply.

"The boat's from California," I explained, feeling confused, "but we're not."

"Where you from?" he exclaimed.

"I'm British!" I yelled back. I thought that if he did have arms under that awning, and if he did open fire on us, he might as well know he was getting his money's worth.

"Dingo!" he shouted again.

I shook my head. By this time Wally was on deck, and I felt a bit safer.

The big man turned briefly to stare at Wally, then he signaled the driver, and the powerboat took off at an enormous rate of knots.

"What was all that about?" asked Wally. His eyes were red with sleep.

"Search me," I replied. Then, after breakfast, we hoisted the jibs and set sail again, but not for the port. I was still wary. It was a couple of weeks before I found out that the name *Dingo* was the password used by local drug smugglers. I think it was a highly suitable word—the Australian name of a scavenging, scrounging wild dog.

About seven miles to the north of Santa Marta is Cabo Agaja, and off the cape is the island of Agaja. My plan was to anchor in the lee of the island, in full sight of everyone and everything to the south, east and west of us, and there dry out the boat and wait for the authorities to come to us. In strange or suspicious circumstances, never give the locals the idea that you are dependent on them, and always try to meet them on your own ground. Always demonstrate that you have an option of actions; that you can stay or you can leave. Generally remember that what to you might be a safer haven is to them the last refuge before the wild world beyond. That is a lesson I have learned over and over again, and it still stands. Let them come to where their surroundings are strange to them, but at the same time, if at all possible, do not hide the boat in some remote spot. This had been in my mind ever since I had chosen Santa Marta as the place of arrival in Colombia. I remembered full well passing Isla Agaja in 1973.

We sailed quite close to the town of Santa Marta, in full view of the port, on our way north to Isla Agaja. *Outward Leg* slid smoothly over the flat blue sea until she was within a hundred yards of the rocky shores of that hot, weatherbeaten islet. There were fishermen with their boats offshore. One of them waved us off. "Anchoring forbidden!" he yelled. We sheered off. The fisherman followed us in his dugout. He was an old man, as we saw when he laid alongside. He was as brown as a berry, his face creased like a walnut from years of squinting in the sun. "If you follow me," he said, "I will show you where you can find a good anchorage." He spoke very fast, and as *costeños* do, he swallowed his vowels, so it was impossible for Wally or me to understand him, but Ivan managed to make out what he was saying, and translated for us. So it has been the whole time we have been here, whenever we talk with *costeños;* Ivan translates from Spanish into Spanish.

The anchorage the old man showed us was behind Cabo Agaja itself, on its south side, and it was good, with deep soft sand and only a slight, soft relic of the hard wind blowing north of the cape. There we gave the old man a length of line and a pack of cigarettes. It occurred to me at the time to wonder how many of the people who have encountered difficulties with locals in Colombia are nonsmokers—of tobacco, that is?

We set to, in the hot sunshine, dragging out everything that was wet through from inside the boat: sleeping bags, towels, carpets (carpets!), half my books and notepaper, clothes—all the clothes from all the lockers below, soggy bags of food, and a dozen charts. Soon the topsides looked like a refugee encampment, with steam rising everywhere, and we enjoyed, for the first time in a week, being *dry.*

After a couple of hours, as we kept watch, waiting for them, the patrol craft appeared, loaded to the gunwales with armed men. All except one, the captain, a slight man, were in civilian clothes, and one big man carried a submachine gun under his arm. As I watched them approach I considered that the civilian clothes were more scary than uniforms would have been. Before I scrambled onto the foredeck—always an awkward job with my street leg—I waited until the patrol craft was alongside *Outward Leg.* I did this intentionally. I did not want to appear too anxious or eager. When in danger or in doubt *be methodical.*

The captain was the first to step on board from the patrol craft. I offered him my hand, and he greeted me courteously. I told him where we had sailed from, and told him that we wished to make tight the hatch and the windows. It was obvious to all that seawater had been entering the boat.

"It would be better for you in the port, señor," suggested the captain. By this time four more patrolmen were on board, and the big man with the submachine gun was standing on the afterdeck, watching everything.

"I intended to enter the port," I replied, "but I did not want to go in with the boat looking like this, señor."

The captain smiled.

"Would you like to look around down below?" I asked. That was the key.

"Thank you," said the captain, and hardly before the word left him, the four patrolmen were down below, with the crew hard after them, to make sure nothing was planted on board.

Down below, from the looks on the faces of the patrolmen, it was obvious that our rude way of life quite impressed them. They were at first puzzled by our food bags, and amazed at the quantity of dried food we carried. But what impressed them most was when, searching through the library, they found three of my books, with my picture on the covers. One of the patrolmen rushed up top and showed one of the books to the captain. Silently he inspected the book, then he said, "And are you writing a book about this voyage?"

"Yes."

"What do you write about?"

"Oh, you know, what places are like, how we find people, how the officials receive us, that kind of thing."

"*Bueno*," said the captain. "When we get back into Santa Marta we will tell the port police about your problems. They will help you find anything you might need to repair your boat, and anything else."

Then, still as courteous as ever, the patrolmen left us. An hour later, with everything dried in the hot sunshine, we hauled the hook and entered the port. It was late afternoon, but the port-police captain was waiting for us, with six men and three motorcycles, and before dusk we had everything we needed—wood and glue—and with the help of two police mechanics, we repaired the hatch and applied silicone all around the deck windows.

Because of all the police activity around the boat upon our arrival, word got around among the port stevedores that we were drug smugglers under arrest, and they kept clear of the boat for a while. Then, after we were seen having our photos taken with the port police and drinking coffee with them in our cockpit, the word was that we had paid off the police, and so the stevedores gazed upon us with new respect, and addressed us all as "señor."

There was a bad surge alongside the wall to which we were tied, right in front of the Port Police Office, but we were not allowed to go to anchor until we had cleared the boat into Santa Marta at the Port Captain's Office, and this was closed until the morning. We spent the night feeling the sudden shock every time the mooring lines, alternately fore and aft, took the strain, and listening to them groan. We all slept, because the police captain had detailed off two of his men to guard the boat with their machine guns. At the cost of two or three cups of coffee each, a supper for one of the guards and a breakfast for the other, it was a good bargain, to get a full night's peaceful sleep, but one of us kept wakeful watch on the guards all night. This is Colombia.

The next day, bright and early, I started off to the Port Captain's Office. But before I did that, I had to go to the Port Police Office to get a written permit to leave the port and to get back in again. But before I could go to the Port Police Office I had to go to the office of the jetty superintendent to get permission to leave the jetty and return to it. But it was the jetty superintendent's day off. It was noon before I finally persuaded the friendly police captain from the previous day to accompany me to the port gates and instruct the guards to let me back in again.

The Port Captain's Office was in a palatial building in the middle of town, a mile or so away from the port gates. I had to hobble there, as I had no Colombian money for a taxi. After waiting in air-conditioned comfort for an hour or so, I was finally ushered into the port captain's luxuriously appointed office, right atop the building, with a fine view over the town, the bay and the port. To one side of the office there was a couch, and on the couch lounged a very elegant young lady, I supposed in her mid-twenties.

The port captain was a smooth-looking man of about my age, at a guess, wearing civilian clothes, and elegant. He had an unctuous air about him. I decided to play the simple seaman. I introduced myself and told him that *Outward Leg* had called at Santa Marta to repair storm damage.

"Ah, then you will need a ship's agent," he said, and started to leaf through a list of, I suppose, agents.

"What for, señor?"

"Every vessel that comes here from abroad must have a ship's agent," he replied.

I told him that it was not usual for private pleasure vessels to engage an agent, anywhere.

The port captain looked disappointed for a few seconds, then he said,

"Ah, then you must have a surveyor come on board to assess the damage." His English was good, but halting.

"But we've already repaired the damage, señor."

"Ah, but a surveyor must come on board to write a report about the damage."

"But I can write that myself," I told him. "It was merely a leaking forehatch and two windows. It's all repaired now."

The port captain was now thinking hard. There must be some way he could squeeze money out of this gringo, he seemed to be telling himself. I waited for his next move.

"Well, all right," he said, hesitantly, "but you have to pay for being alongside in the port." He leafed through another book of files.

"How much?" My heart fell.

"How long have you been in Santa Marta?"

"One night. We arrived at four P.M. yesterday evening."

"Then, that's—let's see—yes—sixty dollars, señor."

"But we have been in only one night, señor!"

"But that's the charge. Every ship pays sixty dollars—for every twenty-four hours or part of twenty-four hours."

"Then I will go out to anchor. The surge is very bad where my boat is moored."

"Ah, then you must pay to be at anchor, too. You must pay for the security offered by the port police." He searched again through his files. "Here we are—five dollars and forty cents a day."

"But I have very little money on board, señor, only enough to pay for food for my crew, and a few other things we need for the boat." This was true; there was no more than a hundred dollars on board my boat. I was thinking fast but steadily. "However, if you will accept it, I can pay you with a check drawn on my London bank—in pounds—"

At this the port captain started, then he burst out laughing. The woman on the couch asked him what he was laughing at, in clear, well-pronounced Castilian Spanish. He told her what I had suggested.

"Which bank is it?" the woman asked the port captain.

I barged in, in my best Spanish. "Lloyd's of London. It's a good bank; I know the managing director." That was a lie, but I was desperate to keep the cash in hand on board.

The woman ignored me, but with a straight face nodded at the port captain. "All right," she said, "but he must make out the check to María Beserra."

Now I'm not saying that anything illegal or corrupt was going on; but in over thirty years of small-craft sailing, and calling in at ports all over the face of the globe, never before have I been asked to pay harbor dues with a check made out to a private individual. When that had happened in the past the check was always made out to the harbor authority. I'm not saying that the port captain was going to have the check cashed by María Beserra and then pocket the cash, but I am saying that it as sure as hell smelled like it to me.

The port captain explained to me, unnecessarily, how I should make out the check, and that I should pay for five days at anchor in advance, and that I should add "five dollars or so" to make up for the trouble he would have in cashing the check. As I stared down at my false leg I could smell the woman's perfume behind me, in that luxurious office with its expensive furniture. Inside me I could hear a thousand Welsh miners singing. I quelled my rising blood, made out a check for the equivalent of a hundred dollars, and handed it to him. Then I asked him if I could take a handful of bay-bottom sand back home with me.

"Why would you want to do that?" he asked, fingering the check.

"Because I want to frame it in a glass case, so I can sit and stare at the most expensive handful of sea-bottom sand anywhere on earth!" I told him.

His expression of unctuous satisfaction did not change. I suppose I spoke too fast for him to understand what I said. He ushered me out of his office, and I hobbled down the stairs.

Capitán de Fregata Gaviria, of the Colombian navy, gave me the only real difficulty, the only hard time, I received from anyone in an official position, from the lowliest police patrolman up, the whole time I have been in Colombia. He is the main reason that yachtsmen should avoid Santa Marta. His name should be written in the pilot books as an obstruction to navigation, a hazard to mariners.

There was no money—or very little—in the Lloyd's Bank account. I make no apology for having passed the check; the bank would allow an overdraft. I was still fuming when I returned to Outward Leg, still angry when we dropped anchor in the bay of Santa Marta, and still glaring at the building atop which is the eyrie of one of the most vulturous, avaricious officials it has been my misfortune to encounter in almost fifty years at sea.

The night following my encounter with the port captain, our rubber dinghy and four-horsepower outboard motor were stolen from on top of the port wing deck while Wally was sleeping only a foot or so away from them. No one, including me, heard anything at all, nor felt any movement on board the boat. The theft was carried out with incredible skill. When Wally broke the news to me in the morning I could only say, "Thank God it was only the dinghy; we could have all been mur-dered in our berths. The loss of our transport to shore is bad enough, and doubly bad for me—I can't sw im. But from now on we all must take turns to stay awake the whole time the boat is in Colombia."

But there was another thing I thought, too: Thank God I didn't have a gun, and that I didn't wake. I would surely have used it—and that is very dangerous in places where there would most probably be no sup-port from the local police. Colombia is a country of vengeance. If I had shot a thief, his brother or cousin would be honor-bound to shoot me.

There will be some who will say that I was asking to be robbed by visiting Colombia. But I will reply that on my lawful occasions I have every right to navigate wherever I choose, and I also, by the interna-tionally recognized Laws of the Sea, have the right to expect the pro-tection of the law of the country my vessel is visiting. That is not a privilege—it is a *right*. And I am here, at great risk, to stress that and to prove that it is so.

There is an attitude among the foreign services of advanced coun-tries these days that if a yachtsman visits a "developing" country, he or she does it at their own risk, and that they are in no way committed to any responsibility for the welfare of vessels of their own nation. That is, by all usage and tradition, from time immemorial, wrong and unjust. All private boat owners and skippers should tell their lawmakers that the protection of the state does not and should not stop at the two-hundred-mile limit, when it is protection from violence. . . .

Outside the main gate of the port in Santa Marta, there is a vertical rock cliff, three hundred feet high. That afternoon Wally climbed it in full view of the gate police, the army, the Customs and all the rest. It was a hard climb as the rock is crumbly, but he made it in about an hour, and all the strutting *machos* were struck dumb and visibly deflated as they viewed true courage and skill. I watched him; concerned for his safety, but inwardly smiling and very proud of my crewman. Only one policeman congratulated Wally when he descended, red and sweating but calm. The rest were too amazed to do anything but stare at him. It was all done without any fuss, almost silently. It was our gesture to the port captain.

A couple of days later Don Jesús turned up. He remembered *Sea Dart* from eleven years before, and invited me to stay and write at Con-chita—and there I stayed, until we sailed for Tacanga, where the port captain wouldn't, I hoped, be able to see us from his eyrie.

21

Smugglers

At first I was a waiter-man that lived at home at ease,
But now I am a mariner that ploughs the angry seas,
I always liked seafaring life and bid my love adieu,
I shipped as steward and cook, my boys, onboard the *Kangaroo*.
Oh, I never thought she would prove false or either prove untrue,
Till we sailed away through Milford Bay,
Onboard the Kangaroo.

Our vessel she was homeward bound from many a foreign shore,
And many a foreign present unto my love I bore,
I brought tortoises from Tenerife and ties from Timbuctoo,
A China rat, a Bengal cat, and a Bombay cockatoo.

My true love she's not a foolish girl, her age it is two score,
My love she's not a spinster, she was married twice before,
I cannot say it was her wealth that stole my heart away,
She's a starcher and a laundress at eighteen pence a day.

"The *Kangaroo*." Capstan shanty, late nineteenth century.
Milford Bay is in south Wales. Many sailors' wives worked as
laundresses to earn extra money when their husbands were
away at sea.

It took a good hour to dig up our anchors at Conchita: a small Bruce,
a very suspect Danforth and a big plow anchor given to us by Don Jesús. Cotes was pleased indeed with the sack of food we gave him, and
his son Juan Carlos hitched a ride with us to Tacanga. He was surprised
at the ease with which we got under sail and in full voyaging trim. By
the time *Outward Leg* was out from the lee of Bahía Concha we were
ready for anything. We had sailed around Cabo Agaja too many times
to take the matter lightly. It is a hell's broth of hard wind and fierce
currents.

But on St. Valentine's Day fate smiled on us, and we sailed around
the cape sedately, right off the wind, in brilliant sunshine with a fif-
teen-knot breeze. The distance from Conchita to Tacanga is eight miles,
and we made it in just over an hour. It was not a long trip, to be sure,
but at least it got *Outward Leg* on the move again—and shifting a boat
after three weeks at anchor in the tropics is a bit like extracting a tooth.
From being a mere vehicle awaiting use she was again a home, a base,
the center of all our activities, and around her from now on our little
world of blue sea would pass by, intruded upon only now and again by
such things as shorelines, anchorages and officials.

Tacanga turned out to be a small fishing village strung along the
inner shore of a mile-deep bay, only one mile as the crow flies from
Santa Marta. But between Tacanga and the town a small sierra juts out
into the sea, so the distance by the winding road that passes over it is
increased to five miles.

On arrival at Tacanga the prospect was pleasant—a postcard vista
of small, neatly kept houses along a palm-tree-lined beach, fronted by
dozens of fishing vessels large and small. Some of these fishing boats,
called *bongos,* have a most curious construction, with a boxlike hull ta-
pered off to the bow and a flat bottom like a canal barge. They are anything up to seventy feet long and usually painted red.

At the south end of Tacanga beach is a small hotel, the Balena Azul,
and the best anchorage is right in front of this establishment. There is
eight foot of water until only fifty feet from the sea's edge on the sandy
beach; we anchored with the Bruce dug in only twenty feet from the
beach, and the Danforth set astern on a long rode so that we could pull
oruselves farther away from the beach at night as an extra precaution
against unwanted, uninvited boarders. The crew also arranged to sleep
on deck.

A meal for all three of us at the hotel was expensive, but the crew
had worked hard and long in Conchita—a semi-refit, in fact—and so
we celebrated being back on board and ready for sea again. The food
was not special; the French owner entertained us, his only customers,
by hovering over the cash register and fingering a hand computer as he
totted up each item brought to our table. Later he told Ivan that he
had sailed from France to the West Indies, and finally settled down here
in Tacanga. I said it was a pity he'd brought French prices with him.
However, the view over the bay as the sun set behind the boat as she
lounged lazily at anchor was worth half the cost of the dinner, so that
was a consolation, if you are happy to pay for what God gives us freely.

After dinner Wally and I walked northward along the beach to look more closely at the curiously built fishing vessels drawn up along the strand. Ivan stayed behind to watch Don Jesús's dinghy and *Outward Leg*, only yards away in the moonlight.

Wally and I poked around outside a few *bongos*, remarking on the roughness of construction; the bottoms of the craft are merely platforms nailed on to the hull, and all the frames inside are square and of the same size for their own particular hull, so that the sides of the boat are absolutely parallel. The stern, too, is slabs of wood nailed on to the ends of the side planks. But all the bows have a graceful rise, as if the builders felt guilty about knocking together such otherwise boxy, un-graceful hulls and felt the need to add something nautical as a finishing touch.

If these boats had been built for use in calm port or canal waters I suppose they could be considered fit for their job, but what amazed us is that they are employed here, where most of the time, a mile out, the seas are rough indeed. Our only conclusion was that these box-boats must be used only in inshore waters, hugging the coasts, right under the lee of the mountains and cliffs, as close as they can get to the shore, and the flat bottoms are for beaching them if the wind changes and blows onshore.

After we had looked at a few other vessels, we wandered along the beach a little farther until we came to a concrete pathway crowded with people—the local *paseo*. It was lined with concrete seats, and feeling the need to rest my leg, I sat down to watch the moon over the bay and smoke a cigarette. Smoking tobacco is the only vice I have that I really enjoy; the others I think of as social duties.

No sooner had we sat down that all hell broke loose. Most of the younger people along the beach and the promenade started running fast toward the north end of the beach, harum-scarum. I thanked my stars that I had sat down; if I hadn't I'm sure I should have been knocked down in the rush. For a second my mind flashed back to the scenes in Horta on the island of Faial in the Azores, when a whale is sighted out at sea and the bells toll and everyone in the town capable of standing upright on two feet runs like mad to man the whaling boats. Even as I stared at the running crowd my memory was knocked sideways, for from one or two lads and lasses came the loud cry, *"Los marijuanistas llega-ron!"* ("The marijuana people are arriving!"); and from others, *"Vamos a ganar dinero!"* ("We're going to earn money!").

On the seat next to ours a lad about eighteen was sitting. He looked tidy, a steady kind of youngster, the kind that helps old ladies to cross busy streets. "What's happening?" I asked him.

As I spoke there was a loud rumbling roar, which rose to a crescendo of noise and dust as a huge truck, a tractor hauling a great enclosed van, raced along the beach road at about fifty miles an hour. The cloud of dust was so thick that I instinctively bent my head down between my knees to protect my eyes. Then, when the truck had passed, I looked in the direction of its roaring progress. Both its back doors were already open, and dimly I could see figures standing behind a load of bales, ready to off-load them.

When the uproar died down somewhat the young lad said, quite casually, "Oh, it's the marijuana truck. They come here to discharge into boats, to export it abroad."

By now the truck, in the semidarkness at the north end of the town beach, had backed up with its lights out, but I could plainly see the truck in the light of an electric lamp above it halfway up a low cliff, and people running back and forth: back with nothing, forth with a bale either on their heads or carried in front of them. As we stared at this sight I said to Wally, "They're never going to believe this, mate, never in a hundred years. Look, there's a bale every three seconds leaving that truck; there must be at least ten tons of pot going out of it—." Then I counted off the loaded runners, "One, two, three, four . . ."

"I do, and so would my dad," Wally said, "after five years in Mexico."

By the time I'd counted thirty bales leaving the truck, I thought it time for us to remove ourselves from the sight. We had seen enough. It would be dangerous to stay too long staring at the north end of the beach and the shadows under the electric light. I stood up to go just as a pickup truck, loaded with men in the back and front, sped past in the direction of the truck.

"Mafia," explained the boy. "Come to see that everything is in order."

"What about the police?" I asked him. While we had been eating at the hotel restaurant the beach had been crawling with both antinarcotic police, in their Australian-type bush hats, toting rifles and submachine guns, and also National Police in their saloon car. Now there was no trace of police, anywhere.

The young lad made a gesture with his finger and thumb, rubbing them together, as if he were riffling notes.

"They're all paid off," suggested Wally.

"Why won't you go and help them and earn some money?" I asked the youngster.

He shook his head. "If they get caught, if police come that are not paid off by the mafia, they get at least a year in prison," he explained. "That's why these few people that you see, who didn't go, are still sitting here. They don't want to go to jail."

"But no one ever reports this?" I asked the boy.

He passed one hand over his throat, wordlessly.

"Good, then we shall return to the hotel and pretend we have seen nothing," I told him.

"Good idea," he replied, and wished us a good night.

Even as Wally and I regained the beach, the truck came roaring past again, I suppose empty, and sped up the road, which, like a scar, is slashed around the face of the bluff on the south side of Tacanga. All its lights were on, and I could plainly see the red tractor and the dirty aluminum color of its monstrously big trailer, as it pounded up the road around the headland.

"They'll never believe this," I repeated to Wally as we made our way back to the beach before the hotel. "Was it a coincidence, that load going out tonight—Jesus Christ, there must have been at least ten tons of the stuff on that truck!"

"It's got to be well organized," Wally reflected. "Look, it's a full moon, fair weather, not much wind tonight, sea pretty calm; it just has to be all thought out and planned before they can send that stuff down from the fields. All the cops along the route must be paid off. It would be the simplest thing in the world for the police to erect and man a road-block on that bluff—it's the only road into Tacanga. It's got to be very well organized. Look, they come here, where there're people, because they need the truck off-loaded in minutes. How long did it take them?"

"No more than five minutes," I replied, guessing.

"It looks like this happens regularly, Tris," Wally observed. "Those kids were watching the road on the bluff, for that truck. They were ready to run as soon as it appeared. The whole town is involved, the whole goddam town."

"It looks like we stumbled onto the main outlet of marijuana on this part of the coast," I replied. "And, who knows, maybe cocaine too."

"They can't send it out of Santa Marta docks," murmured Wally.

"And this is only a few miles up the road," I added.

"And the port authorities must know about it," said Wally.

"And the port captain, too," I said.

Wally added, "Unless he's blind, deaf and has a hole in the head!"

Then we met up with Ivan and the three of us returned on board, in the borrowed dinghy.

We set up the night watches and I turned in, but before I went to sleep I decided not to have this particular chapter of this book copied in Colombia. It could wait until we were well clear.

I was tempted to weigh anchor and clear off that night, but that would have aroused notice and perhaps suspicion that we were clearing out because of what had happened in Tacanga earlier on. Besides, I owe Don Jesús a debt of honor, and so we will hang on here until he returns from Bogotá. Also, in potentially dangerous places, one of the best strategies is to become part of the furniture, to appear to belong so much that the nasties hardly notice you. Like a chameleon or a stick insect, we shall become part of Tacanga in the next three days, and then leave quietly and innocently as I myself nowadays would hobble silently out of a bar where a roughhouse barney was threatening. . . .

Now Ivan has gone on the bus into Santa Marta, fifteen pesos from here, to check the mail and buy small items for the galley; and Wally is fitting up one of the running poles to use it as a derrick for hoisting on board our borrowed dinghy. Later he is going to fit a wooden keel to it, to try to reduce its nervous wobble. One thing is sure—we shall never be able to use it safely in any kind of seaway. I hope to get another rubber dinghy in some yachting center in the next few weeks, if I can find the money to buy it. Meanwhile I must step gingerly into the plastic "dugout" and sit with my knees close together, hardly daring to breathe until the thing reaches the beach.

Wally and I discussed our voyage last night after dinner. We agreed that while it was a pity in some ways that we could not stick to the original intention—of heading down to Chile—our present itinerary, and the things we are experiencing, seeing, exploring and reporting on, are of far more interest to the average yachtsman and to many other people besides, than some derring-do hell-bent saga of continual ocean sailing in the southern ocean. We also agreed that it is probably more dangerous, from a survival point of view, and much more worth doing and, apart from that, it *needs* doing. . . .

Now in the morning at Tacanga, as I write in the after cabin of *Outward Leg*, the scene ashore is one of busy indolence. Fishermen are dragging their nets onto the beach to dry, others are paddling their dugouts slowly out to the offing. From the direction of the village main street comes the continual thrum of *costeño* music, with its steady African undertones, and people idle along the beach under the trees. There is no sign of the rush and bustle of last night, when the marijuana truck burst into town and roared along the beach. Tacanga in the morning makes me wonder if I dreamed it all, but Wally is still talking about it, and so I know it was no dream. No wonder the yacht marina planned for Santa Marta is to be built at Rodadero, even though the wind at Rodadero blows hard and strong, while at Tacanga the bay is very well protected from the weather.

Until we leave Colombia we shall be guarded in all we say ashore, and the boat will be guarded day and night until we have done what we can for Don Jesús. Then we shall make our way east again, beating against the trade in the strong Equatorial Current of the Caribbean, to Aruba and Venezuela. We wonder what is in store for us on the way there.

Last night I told Wally that one of these days I really must get down to working out more ways to make voyaging easier for handicapped people. It will make a change from working out how to keep the boat dry, or how to outwit or fend off marauders and pirates.

We guard the anchors carefully at night. I should have brought some barbed wire to wrap them with, and the rodes, too. This morning, very early, two men came to the beach right in front of the boat; one carried an empty sack, the other a machete. They turned and left when they saw Ivan on watch, idly aiming an arrow at a passing pelican.

My shore contact told me that the pot-truck crew paid the town youngsters 2,500 pesos between them for off-loading the drug on to a *bongo*. That's about $30 among about thirty kids. Thirty dollars for thirty kids to risk a year in prison, each one of them. He also told me that the *bongo* crew will probably receive $100 each; there are three of them. That means that the income of Tacanga, at least that of the ordinary folk, will be about $330 for handling tons of illegal cargo for the drug mafia. Good people, those, they really look after their own.

The whole town knows about it now. When Ivan took the bus to Santa Marta the talk was of nothing else. Everyone knows that the police and Customs are paid off by the *narcotistas*. No one believes that anything can be done about it.

We are keeping very quiet about it all. We cannot tell the folk here that we believe that yachtsmen are discouraged from calling here because the mafia and the *narcopolíticos*—the officials who are involved in aiding and abetting the mafia—do not want yachts here because it would give the people an alternative means of income, and a much more remunerative one. The average cruising-vacation sailing yacht carries a crew of four; each one costs about $25 per day—that is the amount spent per head, say, all inclusive. That's $100 per sailboat per day, and we can easily calculate how much it would be if there were, say, ten yachts in Tacanga at any one time, as there very well could be. The mafia simply does not want that. It's in their interest for any honest endeavor to stay out of the area. It's in their interest for kids to starve and families to fall apart. They are the real exploiters of the poor. Now they are dealing in arms for the guerrillas—who are supposed to be struggling for the poor! The poor, of course, cannot see that the mafia gets the commission on the sale of the pot or cocaine; the poor think that the mafia is doing all this out of the disinterested goodness of its heart.

On the evening of the sixteenth of February the wind offshore rose to its customary strength. Ivan was cooking supper; Wally was helping him; I was below writing. It was the only time in the whole of the period that we have been in Tacanga when no one was on deck. Just before supper was ready, Wally stuck his head up through the galley companion and saw, or thought he saw, that the bow anchor was dragging. He raised the alarm and we gave the bow anchor more scope. It was the Bruce, small but very dependable. Then we brought the stern anchor line to the bow, so that the boat would be swinging on the two anchors from the bow, safely enough in the offshore breeze, as she had moved away from the beach about fifty yards.

While Ivan was untying the after anchor line, he inadvertently also untied Don Jesús' dinghy line but didn't notice it until the dinghy had drifted a hundred feet astern in the darkness. Then he raised the alarm, and Wally dived into the bay to try to retrieve the dinghy. It was a dangerous thing to do as the breeze by then was strong, about thirty knots. I searched for the boat and Wally in the night, and saw only the faint shadow of the dinghy, a very light plastic hull, heading fast out to sea. I called Wally back and dressed him down for risking his life for a dinghy. Then we squared away the anchor lines and set to watching them all night between us.

This morning, the seventeenth of February, we weighed the anchors to head for Santa Marta. I had the idea that we can raft alongside Don Jesús' boat *Amorua,* and the bigger boat would hide most of *Outward Leg* from the view of the port captain in his lofty eyrie.

First we weighed the stern anchor, then the bow. And found that the Bruce had not dragged—a fisherman's four-pronged iron mudhook, very old and worn, had been substituted for it, secured to the bow anchor line by a length of tatty string.

I was almost speechless with anger and frustration as we made our way to Santa Marta. I cursed Tacanga and its denizens up hill and down dale. Then I decided that I must not let this kind of thing affect my health. I must instead go alongside *Amorua* for the weekend, carry out my commitments to Don Jesús, and then get out of Colombia while the going was good as soon as possible.

But I also wondered if the mafia had ordered this; if they knew that we had witnessed the events on the evening of St. Valentine's Day on Tacanga beach; or if we hadn't, did they want me to spread the word that Tacanga is a hazardous place for yachts, anyway?

We will slip quietly away from Santa Marta deep in the night and be over the horizon before the dawn and get well away from the coast before turning east against wind and current.

22

Escape

Oh, have you heard the news, my Johnny?
One more day!
We're homeward bound tomorrow,
One more day!
Only one more day, my Johnny,
One more day!
Oh, rock and roll me over,
One more day!

Don't you hear the Old Man growling?
Don't you hear the Mate a-howling?

Don't you hear the capstan pawling?
Don't you hear the pilot bawling?

Only one more day a-howling,
Can't you hear the girls a-calling?

Only one more day a-furling,
Only one more day a-cursing.

Only one more day a-pumping,
Only one more day a-bracing.

Only one more day a-working,
Oh, come and rock and roll me over!

"One More Day." Windlass and pump
shanty, mid-nineteenth century. It originated in Mobile, Alabama, as a cotton-
hoosier's chant.

Outward Leg crept around the headland of Punta Betin early in the
morning to head into Santa Marta and, keeping the long black hull and
the rigging of *Amorua* between us and the Port Captain's Office, we crept

in and moored ourselves alongside Don Jesús' schooner. Now, unless he stares very hard, the port captain cannot see us. Here we shall hide away until the very early morning of the twenty-fourth of February, when we shall head out once more into the headwinds and the Equatorial Current to beat 250 miles east in a direct line to Aruba. Don Jesús is coming with us on that leg to gain experience. I don't usually take guest crew along, but I feel that we owe him so much for his help to *Outward Leg* during difficult times. Don Jesús is not young by any means, but I doubt he'll be a burden.

Ivan is keeping *Outward Leg* shipshape, cleaning and squaring away for the forthcoming heavy beat to Aruba. Three months is not a long time to learn the routine of an ocean boat, and language differences make it more difficult for him than it would be for an English speaker, but he is doing well enough, and although he is reluctant to speak English in public, we know that he is progressing well. By the time we reach the English-speaking lands he will be able to make his way all right, at least for the ordinary tasks of finding his way around a port and shopping.

Ms. Brimstone the cat has worked out her own routine, too, while we have been in Colombia. Mainly, she stays down below out of the heat of the day, emerges at dawn for her ablutions and in the early evening to gaze at the dramatic sunsets in Santa Marta Bay and glare at seabirds on a nearby ship-channel buoy. She is now about five months old, very much bigger than when we arrived here, sleek, very black and very beautiful. I fear we are going to have some serenading from Curaçaan and Venezuelan toms when we are alongside in some port farther east.

Wally and I went ashore last night in Santa Marta. Compared to the crowded streets when we arrived here in early January, the town is almost deserted, except for street vendors. Under the floodlit palms on the Avenida Bastida we were offered: twelve pseudo-Indian stone artifacts, six choices of sun hat, although it was well after sunset, four choices of sunglasses, eight offerings of sandals, fifteen of cigarettes, five of perfume, three previous morning's newspapers, four offers to change dollars, seventeen offerings of potato balls—greasy, in battered aluminum dishes—tiny oysters wrapped in plastic bags tied with dirty string, and the sexual services of eight ladies, all wearing tight pants that did nothing to hide either their tropical languor or the weight gained during the high tourist season, now past. We were asked for money sixteen times, mostly by small ragged boys. When we ate a small snack of fried chicken at the Pico Rico, at a pavement table—the inside tables were full—we were surrounded by four sly dogs, six small ragged boys, and a middle-aged man in a filthy suit, with no shoes, who had trailed us the whole length of the waterfront, and who pretended to be crazy. The chicken bones, when we'd finished eating, were collected by the small boys, who then disappeared up a side street. The middle-aged man roundly cursed us for not giving him the bones, and the dogs were kicked away, whining, by the waiter.

Over everything, ashore or afloat, lies a patina of fine brown dust. This is blown over the town by the prevailing wind from the grain-off-loading silos in the port.

On our way back to the boat we were offered an anchor, which shows that news of the theft of our Bruce anchor quickly flew around, even though we have not told anyone. It was an old, badly distorted and poorly welded copy of a twenty-pound Danforth anchor. The man selling it, well dressed and portly, wanted fifty dollars. I offered him ten, and he went off in a huff. Don Jesús is lending us a fairly decent copy of a forty-five-pound CQR, and I have promised to replace it for him with a genuine one of the same weight as soon as I can. That will be expensive, but I would much sooner do that than give the thieves or their friends here any satisfaction.

On the last day of our sojourn in Colombia, Wally and I went ashore to the Immigration Officer, at the DAS secret police headquarters. Again we were met civilly by Mario Torres and although Wally's visa has expired and its renewal is two weeks' overdue, nothing was said about it. I was so struck by the chief officer's attitude (he is probably the most helpful immigration official I have encountered anywhere) that we presented him with one of my sail mobiles, suitably inscribed.

From the DAS office we wended our way through the hot streets to the Port Captain's Office, to obtain a crew list for Aruba. Although that worthy enticed me into his office, no mention was made of any payment. I told him that Don Jesús is accompanying us to Aruba, and he kept quiet. He told his secretary to fix us up, and that was that. Captain Gaviria did not even wish us goodbye. That suited me fine, and I left his office with a great feeling of relief. At least we were free of Colombian officialdom, and if we can get out of the port and 250 miles east without being attacked, *Outward Leg* will be safe at last—at least comparatively safe, apart from the usual exigencies of the ocean.

A long procession of workers was marching through town all shouting their heads off in protest at the cost of living and low wages. The riot police were also out in force, wearing crash helmets and toting riot shields, batons and rifles.

A crowd of about fifty Indians from the Sierra Santa Marta mountains were passing through the town on foot. A picturesque but dirty lot, they were dressed in homemade cotton trousers and ponchos and most wore ancient fedora hats over their long, bright, glossy hair. The faces of the older men seemed to have been carved out of mahogany. A woman told us that they were in the city to look for food because they were starving in the mountains and were afraid of guerrilla or army attacks. She said that they would receive nothing from the Indian Agency here, because there was not enough money for the Santa Martans, anyway. The Indians stopped to stare into the plate-glass window of a tourist shop, where Indian-made artifacts were on sale. They pointed and gestured excitedly as if they were amused or astonished. I imagine the latter is more the case. On their feet they wore flat soles made out of truck tires and tied with leather thongs. All their women and children carried huge sacks, also homemade by the look of them.

Wally and I ate lunch at the Molino restaurant—beef, rice and yucca and beans, with cola. The total cost was $1.50 each.

Meanwhile Ivan, on board, has washed all the clothing, so that we shall sail away clean, and with clean bedding and pillows.

The gunboat, which had called on us in Conchita, sailed into port this morning just before lunchtime. There was no sign of any ensign. Wally said he thought someone might have stolen it, as he made ready the yankee jib, and then sorted out the remaining anchor lines.

I sent letters off to the manufacturers of the three electronic gadgets that are now defective—the Weatherfax, the Tillermaster electric self-steerer control, and the Impulse speed and distance log. I asked them where I might get them fixed in the Antilles, and also if there was any chance of replacing them. I am hoping for a reply in Curaçao.

Apart from those three items, everything on board *Outward Leg* was ready and prepared for another hard bash to windward by the twenty-fourth of February. All we had to wait for before leaving was Don Jesús, with six cans of corned beef and perhaps a recent London *Times*, for me to read on the way to Aruba. . . .

Before we sailed from Santa Marta, I knew full well that the most difficult part of the whole of the north coast of the South American leg of our voyage would be from there to Aruba. Of that leg the worst, from a point of view of making progress east, would be getting around the Guajira peninsula. We would be literally between the devil and the deep blue sea. The Equatorial Current sweeps westerly across the central Atlantic Ocean, all the way from the Bight of Benguela off the West African coast. Out in the ocean it runs at between one and one and a half knots. As it flows past the long shores of Brazil and Guyana it picks up speed over the—comparative—shoal waters, and when it is obstructed by the southern West Indies, the Windward Islands, it is forced into the gap between Trinidad and Tobago. The speed of the ocean river then increases to three knots and often more, with the same effect as when you put your thumb over the spout of a high-pressure water hose, except here we are dealing with trillions of tons of water to the square mile, all pushing west. This water then fans out gradually until it is again obstructed, by the islands of Curaçao and Aruba. Much of the stream is diverted to the south of Curaçao, onto the shoal shelf between Aruba and Venezuela. Because the water cannot expand sideways or downward its speed increases again, and all the strength of the current is directed due west, right around the Guajira Peninsula, driven by the trade wind, which in the northern spring blows at anything up to forty-five knots, also due west.

On the western side of Punta Gallinas, the northernmost point of South America, there are no havens at all. It is a dead lee shore littered with wrecks, backed by eternal sand dunes and the high mountains in the middle of the peninsula. It is one of the driest places on the face of the earth, and when the sun has warmed up the desert for a couple of hours, the hot air that rises from it is replaced by sudden, vicious gusts of wind from the Caribbean Sea, blowing up to sixty knots for short periods during the daytime, close to the shore. Ashore, the land is inhabited by Indians more than dirt poor who will, and do, kill strangers for the sake of a day's food. There is no lack of danger off the weather side of Guajira until you are well south of it, inside the Gulf of Maracaibo, in Bahía de Calabozo (Jail Bay). There you will be comparatively safe from marauders or pirates, but you will still be on a dead lee shore, even though it will be thirty miles to your lee. The waters of the gulf are very boisterous, so if your vessel cannot claw to windward and it blows hard, you are in an embarrassing predicament.

Also on the western side of Punta Gallinas, the wind increases in strength, as it often does on the lee side of hot, ovenlike landmasses of desert, and can blow up to sixty knots for gusts lasting up to five minutes. The rest of the time, in the day, it is around thirty-five knots and drops to about twenty-five knots at night. All the time the Equatorial Current marches past, setting up a huge sea, with waves up to forty feet high and close together. These conditions can prevail up to fifty miles out from the coast of Guajira. The only way to avoid them to an extent is to stand out north for over fifty miles into the Caribbean. But if we did that we would be swept back to the west thirty miles, and would still have a two-knot westerly current to deal with. To the west of Punta Gallinas there are two indentations in the coast—Bahía Honda and El Portete. In "normal" countries these could be used to shelter in, to await best conditions for rounding Punta Gallinas, but this is Colombia, and the two bays are the known haunts of drugs and arms smugglers, and are very dangerous places indeed for small, unarmed vessels. The only safe shelter, or reasonably safe, is in the lee of Cabo de la Vela, about thirty miles to the west of Punta Gallinas, and then only at night, hove to five miles offshore with no lights and a guard watch set up.

Between us and Cabo de la Vela there was a mere two-knot con-trary current and the trade wind, blowing eternally from the east right on our noses, and an unlit shore inhabited by semisavage Indians, much of it controlled by the drug mafia or the guerrillas. On board *Outward Leg* we were four now, with Don Jesús. Our complement was one gentleman of advanced age and very little seagoing experience, one young man with a smattering of experience but only a week in hard, wind-ward-going conditions, one young man experienced and able but with poor long-distance eyesight, and one elderly man with much experi-ence, very good eyesight, but physically severely handicapped. Such was our prospect when *Outward Leg* slipped her berth alongside *Amorua* in Santa Marta on February 23, 1984.

We left the port an hour after dusk, so as to escape the attentions of the port captain and anyone else who might have designs on our vir-tue before we got clear of Santa Marta, and sailed off under full working rig into the blackness of the windy night. We soon found what a bumpy ride we would have. No sooner had we cleared the port than the wind grabbed us and the sea flayed us. Spray flew everywhere and seas rolled right over the amas. This time the boat was shut up as tight as a drum, with all hatches closed, but still the forward hatch leaked, and still we bailed out every couple of hours. Don Jesús tried his best to keep a watch and to aid with the strenuous winchwork, but it was obvious that here was a classic case of the spirit being willing . . . By midnight I had decided that apart from keeping watch for shipping it would be best if Don Jesús just enjoyed the ride and perhaps learned what he could from us by observing.

All the night of the twenty-fourth of February we pounded away, going ahead on one tack for four hours, then the other for four hours, close hauled, as close as we could while still keeping the boat moving at from four to five knots in the twenty-five-knot wind and steep seas. . . .

Imagine *Outward Leg* pointing to within about fifty degrees of the direction from which the wind is blowing hard, and from which the seas are rolling, one after the other, hour after hour, in the starlit night. The boat is a gray ghost outlined in phosphorescence from the spray that pours over her bows. Her mast and sails weave and jerk violently as she mounts each successive sea, then bows to it, and each time she thrusts violently forward she sends another cloud of spray streaming aft right over the top of her dodger. Inside the dodger, in the darkness relieved only by the pale pink light from the binnacle and the wind instrument panel, I hold on, balancing as best I can on the cockpit seat. In order to have a mite of comfort, a bit less pain, I have to lay my false leg along the seat to keep it as horizontal as possible. As we are tacking back and forth along the coast, I have to keep a close eye on the dead reckoning. That means that every few minutes I must stand up, crouching, open the door to the after cabin, watching for sudden spurts of spray on the dodger windshield, then swing myself bodily into the hatchway, hanging on to the hatch cover with my arms. I suspend in space for a moment or two, to find the dark cabin sole with my good foot, then swing myself aft so that I land on the sole without banging my false foot on the deck, so bruising my stump. Then, when I have my balance and can hold on to something solid in the bouncing cabin, I find the seat in the dark, manage to sit down, and am reasonably safe once more from falling.

Then I work on the chart, plotting in the latest estimate of speed and course direction, depth and rate of current, all the many bits of information that make up the multifaceted matter of coastal pilotage. In the pink light over the chart table, the after cabin appears warm and cozy, as though it were lit by a blazing hearth fire. Over the tape system Bach's Variations are playing softly, a blessed relief from the screech of the wind in the rigging wires aloft and the drumming of the sails, the crash and sluice of the seas as they try to board the bows. But the apparent coziness is deceiving. Everything is damp or wet through. We have to push the boat so hard that there is no avoiding the tons of water that every minute encounter the three bows, and the cataracts of spray that stream against the dodger. In a center-cockpit boat, some water will always find its way through the small gaps in the dodger canvas, and so into the after cabin. Fortunately though, the chart table is out of the way of the hatch door, and it is about the only dry place in the cabin most of the time, except when an extra big sea rolls up the main hull bow and floods the cockpit. Then a great dollop might get a few drops on to the chart and make me curse again as I hold on.

Once I have worked out what I think, what I feel, is our position, it is then a matter of getting back up into the cockpit. First I find my feet, the good one and the false, and steady myself against the heavy jerks. Then I open the cabin door. Immediately a rush of cold air enters, and the noise of the rigging screeching and the sails thrumming and the seas crashing. Then I haul myself up the after-cabin companionway stairs. These are awkward; they were built into the boat while I was away. They are angled, and so I have support for only one foot, and I have to haul myself up the ladder by hanging on to the hatch cover and dragging myself up. Once at cockpit level, it is a matter of keeping my balance against the jerking, plunging boat, and regaining my seat in the cockpit, on the wet cushions. This process I repeat four times an hour, a hundred times a day, beating to windward on an ill-charted, unlit shore. All the while the top of my stump, in my groin, is red raw where the skin has chafed away with the friction of the rim of my false leg.

In the cockpit I mainly think about the progress of the boat against the wind and current. There is no romantic daydreaming when beating to windward. Only the skipper's whole mind, and body and soul, thrown into the fray will serve to fight the weather and grab the distance. I think of how the very fact of a boat's sailing to windward is against all man's intuitive considerations of logical activity. It must seem miraculous, to a landsman, that an entity weighing several tons can be made to move in the direction from whence comes mighty wind and weather. As opposed to sailing downwind, with the wind and current, it must seem like an impossibility to expect a boat to progress directly against the elements. I think of the forces at work as we are beating: the *sideforce*, pushing at right angles from the direction of wind and sea; the *dragforce*, pushing directly against us; and the *resultant force*, which is the sum effect of the first two that pushes us, against all sane expectations, at an angle against the strength of nature. It is something like an apple seed being squeezed between thumb and finger—the two digits push in opposing directions, more or less, but the seed shoots forward. For us the thumb is the sea, and the finger is the wind. I think, too, how the ratio of sideforces to dragforces must be maximum—the thumb and finger must both squeeze hard—so that we get the best hydrodynamic forces from the sea, and aerodynamic forces from the wind, so that the sideforces will balance the dragforces, and thus move the boat forward. This balance, between the wind and the sea forces, must be kept, and the skipper must make it so and keep it so, and make sure it is so. There can be little sleep for a skipper beating along a wild shore, and especially when beating against a current, because all the time the current is treacherously taking away the thumb, making the apple seed move sideways instead of forward. Put simply, and yet complexly, the drag angle of the sail (E) and the drag angle of the hull (d) must each be as small as possible because the angle of sailing into the wind is the sum of E and d. Dragforce is the result of fluid particles of water being slowed by the boat itself as it moves forward against the fluid. Sideforce is similar, to a degree, to the lift of an airplane wing. It is an expression of Newton's Law of the reaction to the deflection of fluid particles, with greater momentum toward one side of the hull than to the other, due to the hull's being aligned asymmetrically to the water flow. Bernoulli's equation shows that the static pressure is lower on the side that has the higher water velocity past it. Thus a hull is essentially sucked sideways by the leeside static pressure being lower than the mean value due to its higher streaming speed, assisted to a lesser degree by the excess pressure of slower streaming speed on the windward side of the hull. But however small the drag angles can be made for sails and hulls, there would be no good result if the opposing aerodynamic and hydrodynamic sideforces caused such heeling that the sideforce would be seriously reduced. In a monohull this means reefing down when the lee rail is under. In a multihull it means being sure to shorten sail before she capsizes. In short, for good windward work we need *righting stability*: low center of gravity, lightweight spars and topsides, and a high center of buoyancy. In *Outward Leg* the righting stability is provided by the amas and the keel. Additional righting stability is afforded by the *cool-tubes*. For those reasons, as a voyaging multihull loaded down with stores and water, *Outward Leg* is, I think, unbeatable at going to windward, but it is still enervating work and sustained effort, and my skinned, chafed groin gives me pain and stings as salt water gets to it.

Sailors call it "beating the shit out of her."

23

Into the Lion's Den . . . and Out

Little Sally Rackett,
Haul her away!
She shipped in a packet,
Haul her away!
And she never did regret it,
Haul her away!
With a hauley high oh!
Haul her away!

Up my fighting cocks, boys,
Up and split her blocks now,
And we'll stretch her luff, boys.

From: "Haul Her Away." A
hauling shanty. The tune is
very similar to "The Banana
Boat Song" and is probably of
West Indian origin.

All day on the twenty-fifth of February we beat against the hammering seas and the screaming wind, with the cockpit continually wet through, under a brazen, cloudless sky. Ivan, somehow, with the boat jerking and pounding continually hour after hour, put up meals on time: breakfast of Eden Foods oatmeal, lunch, tea, and dinner: a yurika preprepared Salisbury steak each. By now even as thorough an American as Wally has become accustomed to and fond of a cup of tea and biscuits at five in the afternoon. It is a cheering brew, a great morale booster before sunset and yet another night of wild movement and peering into the darkness. Tea, unlike coffee, does not interfere with the ability to doze when we are off watch. As for me, there can be very little "off watch" going to windward against wind and current. I must be awake and available at all times. In this area, shipping uses a channel about ten miles offshore to gain advantage of any weaker spots in the current. With the spray beating against our cockpit-dodger windows, visibility is severely reduced at night. We have the radar alarm but there is so much shipping, and so many offshore fishing vessels, and others no doubt, that using it would only lead to utter confusion. Radar alarms are very useful off the shipping lanes, out in the wide-open ocean, but offshore they are nowhere near as good as eyes peeping from gaps in the dodger. Only in the offshore boards, when the boat is heading out away from the land, can I doze, and even then I am aware that we are crossing the shipping lane and I have one eye open.

Daylight on the twenty-sixth brings the same scene. A wild sea and a howling wind. There are no birds in this part of the Caribbean. Even the sight of a gull would be cheering and would remind us that the world is not wholly composed of roaring wind and water off a deadly desert coast.

About eleven in the forenoon we suddenly became aware of being followed by another craft. Alarmed at first, we watched as her gray hull crashed through the seas astern, overtaking us. Then we recognized her as our old friend the Colombian Customs vessel that had sent over the officials to search the boat in Conchita a couple of weeks before. Nevertheless, even as she drew up astern, her siren blew and a loud voice demanded over her loudspeaker, *"Baja la vela!"* ("Hand your sails!").

Ivan had scrambled to mount the stern ensign as soon as it was obvious we were being overtaken. Now I told Wally to hand the yankee so that I could heave to. This took a minute or so while the gunboat placed herself between us and the wind. Then two officials clambered down into a rubber dinghy that had been lowered over the gunboat's side, and a minute or two later they were scrambling on board. They were not the same officials who had inspected us at Conchita, and so, with the boat heaving and pitching in the seas, they again gave us another thorough going-over. Don Jesús spoke with them in rapid Colombian Spanish, and introduced himself. I think that impressed them enough to cut short their visit on board, and they left us courteously, after ten minutes rummaging down below, wishing us a good trip. Then, when they were back on board the gunboat she wallowed and crashed off at high speed in the direction of Río Hacha, a small port just to the west of the Guajira Peninsula, which is about as attractive a haven for small craft as Chicago would have been to a religious convention in the mid-1920s.

Again, there was no ensign on the Customs gunboat. There was no sign that she was a government vessel except for a small badge below the bridge with the insignia on it of the Colombian Customs Service. I have no doubt that if we had not known the vessel, and if we had been armed, we would have been tempted to fire at least warning shots in her direction as she approached us. None of the officials on board, nor the sailors, wore any kind of uniform. I have no doubt that more inexperienced yatties, inexperienced in the ways of Colombia, might have been scared out of their wits and perhaps even opened fire on the gunboat.

As it was, all I did the whole time the search officers were on board was curse the waste of time, while the boat was hove to in a three-knot current and drifting back west toward Santa Marta.

After noon the eternal trade wind woke from his half doze; he had been lazing along at twenty-five knots since dawn; now he tightened up his belt, hefted his braces, pulled his cap down over his eyes, lifted his hobnailed boots and kicked us right in the teeth. In minutes the wind was up to forty-five knots; in minutes Wally and I had reefed down the main two hands, rolled up the staysail, dowsed the yankee and hoisted the spitfire jib. Then, of course, reefed down, I had to lay *Outward Leg* off the wind a few degrees so that she would maintain maximum forward speed at the optimum angle against wind and weather. Now that means that for every thirty miles sailed—fifteen miles out to sea, fifteen miles back toward the shore—we gain only *eight* miles to windward. Back and forth, back and forth. Beating is an exercise not only in stamina but also in determination and, above all, patience. You must be strongminded, and even ambitious to grab as much as you can, but at the same time you must be very careful not to pinch the boat too close to the wind, not to be too ambitious.

All the leg from Santa Marta to Cabo de la Vela, I was using both celestial and sat-nav navigation. This was necessary, because sat-nav reception in the area was very erratic. At times I was waiting up to ten hours for a satisfactory satellite pass and so an acceptable position reading. That is good enough out on the wide ocean but offshore, against wind and current, sat-nav alone will not serve. The only kind of satellite navigation that would be acceptable to me in those circumstances would be continual reception of positions from a fixed satellite. I understand that may be a possibility by the end of the eighties. Meanwhile, off unlit and featureless shores like the Guajira Peninsula, good old-fashioned celestial and dead-reckoning navigation must be used, and so these arts should be practiced and well honed by any kind of navigator who intends to stray off the well-beaten track and away from the hamburger stands.

After two sleepless nights in heavy weather I decided to heave to in the lee of Cabo de la Vela. The geography of the cape is such that the Equatorial Current sweeps right by it and misses the large bay to the southwest of the cape. The water is shoal enough up to five miles from the shores for large ships to anchor there in shelter from the hard winds. But the coast itself is the haunt of all kinds of riffraff; piracy, drug running and arms smuggling are the main occupations of practically everyone not in an official capacity in Guajira. The main activity of those in an official capacity seems to be, from all accounts, taking bribes to be absent from the scene of the other activities. We kept well offshore, and hove to at a point exactly five miles offshore, with the staysail backed, the mainsail still hoisted, reefed, and the wheel hard over to weather. In this stance we were ready to run should we sight any small craft approaching during the night. As added precautions, the bows and arrows, the flare pistol and the Molotov cocktails were all placed in the cockpit ready for use. A guard watch was set by the crew of Don Jesús, while I grabbed a few hours' sleep, or something approaching it, and arranged to be awakened an hour before dawn.

Morning showed that the wind had drifted us four miles southwest during the six hours *Outward Leg* was hove to. It took only a minute to hoist the yankee, yank the wheel over, and be away out to the offing once again, to jerk and bounce, crash and bash, burrow and bore, drum and pummel, flog and flay, our way east, east, east. Northeast, southeast, northeast, southeast, but always *east*.

By midnight, after sixty-eight miles sailed through the water, we were exactly fifteen miles northeast of where we had been hove to the night before. We stood out to the heaving sea once more, knowing that if patience was a virtue, then we must be the most virtuous men alive; or that we had better be, unless we were to turn back and run again for Santa Marta, 120 miles to the southwest, and lose all the hard-gained ground of the past three days and nights. The following dawn showed that we were twenty miles from where we had heaved to, and this after pushing the boat as hard as she could possibly go, at five and six knots against a thirty-knot wind and a three-knot current. It was as if the whole world was wind and water flung against us on the one hand, and a murderously dangerous, unmoving and glowering shore on the other. I knew that we must go on. To have returned defeated to Santa Marta would have meant displaying a weakness and that, in Colombia, could be fatal.

All day on the twenty-seventh we beat out to sea and again back in, just in sight of the coast, a menacing yellow line on the southern heaving horizon. By now the seas were at least twenty-five feet high from crest to halfway down their steep slopes, and no more than a hundred feet apart. Every sea was topped by blowing spume. The color of the water was a sickly green. Close to the shore, about four miles out, it was a light brown. We stood out yet again at dusk, with the sky blood-red in the west and darkness descending like doom in the east.

I remember that while we were eating supper as best we could in the cockpit, Don Jesús asked if I would put some classical music on the tape recorder that evening. A discussion on the power drain by the tape player followed, but no one was quite sure of the amperage drain. Finally Don Jesús and I agreed that while Vivaldi or Beethoven tapes probably used only a milli-amp each, rock and roll used three amp-hours per tape, so rock and roll was out, at which Wally pulled a face. The soothing effect of classical music at sea should not be underestimated. I find that the best type of music in storm or gale conditions, to cut out the sounds from above when in the cabin, is violin or flute concertos by Mendelssohn or Haydn. Modern classical music is, to me, unsuitable for such circumstances. The whole scene outside the boat is discordant. Adding discord to discord is, I think, bad for the nerves. Bach, too, with his precise mathematical progressions, is the perfect music for beating to windward and calculating against leeway and current. He shows that with patience and persistence we will arrive eventually. Bach teaches faith, hope and compassion, and with these we can overcome anything. With good music playing down below, the best thing in that noisy world is to be able to relax physically. There is little mental relaxation, of course, but the important thing is to rest the body. The mind has much more stamina than the body. Rest the body, soothe the mind. It should be the watchword in any small craft beating heavily. But be ready at all times to spring into fast action. When something gives, it gives fast and usually without any warning.

Just after dusk, when Wally changed the yankee for the spitfire, he found that the starboard forestay deck fitting, of quarter-inch stainless steel, was being torn apart by the tremendous forces transmitted from the yankee sail through the stay every time the boat smashed into a sea—about four times a minute. I decided to hoist the spitfire on the port forestay, so that we could keep the boat moving. Then, an hour after we had found the fault on the starboard forestay fitting, the stay-sail halyard block, the pulley that hauls it up the mast, parted with a crack like a pistol shot, in the darkness, in the roar of the rigging, and the staysail came clattering down on to the foredeck. There was no chance of trying to rehoist the sail in the dark in that kind of sea with the boat thrusting around like a fighting bull. The crew tied up the sail as best they could in a lumpy bundle and we left it there until daylight, and pressed on, pounding away in the roaring darkness of the night. I went below to think things out. *When in danger or in doubt—go below and think things out.*

If the port forestay fitting went altogether, as well as the starboard one, we would probably lose the upper half of the mast. That would mean an enforced return all the way to Colón in Panama, six hundred miles to leeward with a jury rig. Therefore, using the big yankee sail on that stay was out of the question from then on. For safety's sake, to keep the mast, we would have to use only the much smaller spitfire jib. Getting the staysail block back up the mast was going to be a hazardous task for Wally in that kind of sea. He was our only experienced, and also able-bodied, hand. To risk losing him, or wounding him, swinging around aloft in thirty-foot seas, would be foolish if there were any alternative.

The chart showed that there was a possible alternative, although a dangerous one. It was to enter Bahía Honda, where there would be much flatter water, even in this storm, and so Wally might fix the staysail block much more safely. In the civilized world this would be the perfectly obvious thing to do, without hesitation. But Bahía Honda sits slap-bang in the middle of the Guajira Peninsula; it is a notoriously risky place, much used by drugs and arms smugglers who are reputed to attack any intruders, and to murder them, or at least rob them of everything they have. That is apart from semisavage Indians.

I usually insist in making decisions myself in all circumstances except *in extremis* where there are several alternatives, and where any particular one might spell extra danger or even death. In the false dawn of the twenty-eighth I gathered all the hands on board together in the bouncing, jerky cockpit, and put the situation and the alternative actions to them as they listened, red-eyed. But first I put my own case, gleaned from many previous occasions where life and death have been matters for consideration, and especially where there might be a risk of human aggression: to go into Bahía Honda, stay long enough to repair the staysail block, and get out again as quickly as possible. But, further than that, to enter the bay on the side where no one would expect us to—on the leeward side, onto which the weather was beating with all its might. This would probably increase our element of surprise arrival a good deal, and so diminish the opportunity for hostilities to gather their force, or even their wits.

I must have put my case more convincingly to the crew than I did to myself. Everyone else thought it a good plan, and so we bashed our way toward the western side of the entrance to Bahía Honda. From ashore, I knew, if there was anyone watching on that barren, treeless coast, it would appear that we were heading past the bay, southwest. Right by the western tip of the bay, on a godforsaken headland, we suddenly headed up into the wind and screeched our way, and scraped with God's aid past the point, missing the outlying rocks by only yards under our lee. As we rushed into the yellow-watered bay under all working sail less the yankee, plus the engine, I glued my eyes first to the lee side ahead, then to the depth-sounder. Less and less the depths went; I had no chart of the bay beyond a ten-mile-to-the-inch section on my main chart, but the Red Sea had taught me hard lessons about bays on desert shores—that the lee side is usually steeper-to than the weather side. Suddenly the world turned to one of windy desert, gold under the sun, and orange bay water.

Finally, with my heart in my mouth, we beat up the bay to the weather side and anchored there in nine feet, sandy bottom. Already, as we went to anchor, the mainsail flapping, an Indian was running along the shore. Minutes later he was alongside the boat in a dugout that had been concealed on the beach, hanging on to *Outward Leg* in a forty-knot wind. He was dressed much like a desert Arab, in flowing robe and a turban.

In conversation with Don Jesús, the Indian said that it was very dangerous to stay at the eastern end of Bahía Honda, as that was used much by the *marijuanistas*. He said we should go to the south end of the big bay, where there was a safer anchorage behind a low cliff, and where there was a "government station." He wanted to come with us in our boat, but I did not want him on board. I was very wary. As he had along with him his grinning "nephew," I said that he had better help the youngster reach the shore again in that heavy dugout against the strong wind, otherwise the lad might be blown out to sea and lost. The Indian agreed finally with this argument and took off with his grinning "nephew." Then we weighed our anchor and motored—practically sailed under bare poles at six knots—around the point and under the low cliff.

The scenery was the most desolate I have seen in years. It was as if the world had died. The land was low sandy hills, bare of all but a very few stumpy trees, writhing and bent over at an acute angle by the wind.

The waters of the bay were bright orange, and so was the air, with the fine sand being blown off the desert right out over the boat. (As I write two weeks later the fine sand is still in the halyards and sheets.) The "government station" turned out to be a small hut with three radio aerials sticking out of the roof. The wind blew so hard, often reaching fifty knots in the afternoon, that a steep brown sea was set up only a hundred yards from the shore. There, in a sandstorm, working fast so as not to give the Indian time to catch up with us on foot over the desert, Wally replaced the staysail block, while Ivan and I kept watch with the few puny weapons we had to hand. The scenery ashore seemed to be that of a strange planet, utterly dead.

After a short while, another dugout approached us from the shore below the "government station" and sitting in it, with three other Indians, I saw to my utter surprise the first Indian's grinning "nephew." How he could have managed to get from our first anchorage to where we now were, eight miles across a sand-blown desert, defies my imagination. He could not have done it in any other way but on foot. There were no animals and no bicycles. The four Indians in the dugout asked to come aboard, but I told them that "the other three crewmen were asleep below." This was a white lie, of course. There was only Don Jesús below. Wally was up the mast, and Ivan was on deck with me. But I thought it best to make them think we were six men on board. Villains understand being outnumbered. Then they asked me for cigarettes, but I told them we were all nonsmokers. I wanted them to have no excuse for laying a hand on *Outward Leg,* much less coming on board. All the while their dugout strained at her anchor alongside *Outward Leg.* They asked how long we were staying. I said overnight. Another lie, but it was best to let them think they had time to organize an assault, if that was in their minds. By now dusk was falling, and after staring hard at the boat and at us three on deck, the Indians got out their punting pole and paddles and thrashed and shoved their boat back against the gale toward the shore. There they seemed to hold a conference on the beach.

After supper, about two hours after sunset, we quietly hoisted sail and in the hard, sandy wind, which blinded our eyes unless we covered them, slid away into the darkness over the shallow yellow waters of Bahía Honda, and were soon haring off over the flattish water, depths unknown, with a thirty-knot wind, for the offing. Now we had the staysail to push us again, and with that and the spitfire, *Outward Leg* would pretty much point fifty degrees off the wind. Out into the darkness and the heaving seas off Punta Gallinas we shoved, crashing and bashing, heaving and plunging, rinsing and pickling, tossing and pitching, sluicing and sloshing, sliding and yawing, all night, all day and all night again, until at long weary last we found we had Punta Gallinas to the southwest of our boat, and we could turn for longer boards along the wreck-littered shore of the Guajira Peninsula. But it was another day and a night, too, before we found that no longer did we have land on our lee bow, that we were free from the iron manacles of the Equatorial Current right ahead of us, with land to our lee, and could turn a little more off the wind and head down into the Gulf of Maracaibo, to seek the shelter of the eastern shore of that huge stretch of water, half the size of Britain.

From the Gulf of Maracaibo to Aruba was simple, straightforward upwind sailing. We kept close hauled, but the seas in the gulf were much less steep. The wind was still thirty knots or so, but we did not feel the full effects of the heavier gusts until we were out in the Aruba channel. Then the wind and sea, piling over the shoals between Aruba Island and the mainland, let us have it again but this was only a short hop of twenty-odd miles, a mere spit to windward. Finally, on the first of March, six days after we departed from Santa Marta, and after sailing through the water 780 miles to cover 260 direct to windward, we fetched up in the harbor of Oranjestad, Aruba, and laid *Outward Leg* alongside the market jetty.

"Where have you come from?" asked the Aruba Customs officer.

"Santa Marta, Colombia."

"Good grief! The last two boats that went to Colombia from here were both attacked," he observed as he clambered aboard. "One of them was stripped of everything on board. That man was lucky to get back here alive. The other one was attacked off Rodadero. All the people on board were murdered."

"When was that?" I asked him. What a pleasure to speak English.

"Last year and the year before. Only crazies go to Colombia now."

"Yes, only crazies." I looked at Wally as I said this. He grinned . . .

That night, after a thorough search of the boat by the Aruba Customs naturally, we all ate *rijstaffel* ashore with Don Jesús as host. That night, too, for the first time since New Year's Eve, I slept at long last fully and deeply, with no concern about sudden attack or the safety of the boat and her crew. For the first time in over two months we were safe from storm or disaster, theft or murder.

Don Jesús left us the following morning. He said he had learned much, and especially that he would be able to handle *Amorua* only with an experienced and efficient crew. I only hoped that we had afforded him sufficient repayment for his help while *Outward Leg* was in Santa Marta and Conchita, and for the replacement anchor.

The beat from Aruba to Curaçao Island was a heavy one, too, with steep seas, a three-knot current and a twenty-five-knot wind dead against us. But it was much easier on my mind. At least now I knew that should anything go seriously wrong we had a friendly port under our lee, where we would not be attacked, robbed or murdered. It's a good feeling to know that you do have a line of retreat, which is reasonably safe from human bastardy. . . .

Now *Outward Leg* sits at anchor in little St. Kuris Bay, on the western end of Curaçao Island, while I finish writing this part of the account of her voyage. Tomorrow we will head into the port of Willemstad, to repair the breaking forestay deck fitting and, I hope, to find letters and money awaiting us so that we can press on, first east along the Venezuelan coast, and then north and east across the Atlantic to Europe, on our way east around the world.

Now *Outward Leg* rests for a while, in calm blue water with the trade-wind clouds streaming west overhead. There is a rocky headland to each side of our anchorage off a sandy bay. Pelicans and other seabirds hover overhead and perch on the rocks. Goats climb the low cliffs. Above them cactus and cypress trees lend sweet greenery to the scene, and landbirds sing in the low bushes, as we thank God we are not stuck in Bahía Honda. People come to the little beach to sunbathe and swim, and fishermen wave to us as they pass out to the offing in their boats. It is a blessed relief to be able to wave back, and not be afraid of them. I would like to stretch my leg on the beach, but we have no dinghy. That is something else to solve in Willemstad. I need all the exercise I can get when the boat is near the shore. But I must be content for now with stomping up and down the wing decks on top of the amas. I only hope I do not look too anachronistic to the courting couples who come down to the rocky shore below the headland in the evening. My chafed stump is healing, but slowly.

There are lobsters under the cliffs. We caught two last night, and we are feasting on them, with rice and onions, today. Ivan has washed all the clothes so that we shall, as usual, go into port clean.

Tonight I shall break out my charts—those and I have—of the Venezuelan coast and the Windward Islands. I rejoice quietly that we will soon be home again, or at least I will be, back in the Western Ocean.

PART TWO

To London

24

The Treasure Coast

1 Oh! Sally Brown she's the gal for me, boys,
  Roll, boys, roll, boys, roll!
  Sally Brown she's the gal for me,
  Way hi, Miss Sally Brown!
2 We're bound away down south, boys,
3 We're rolling down the Trinidad to see Miss Lucy Loo,
4 She's lovely at the foreyards—she's lovely down below,
5 She's lovely 'cos she loves me, boys, that's all I want to know.
6 Forty fathoms and more below, boys,
7 Oh, way hey ya! and up she rises!
8 One more pull—don't you hear the mate a-bawling?
9 One more pull, boys—that's the end of our hauling!

Halyard shanty, nineteenth century. It was very popular in
Caribbean ships, which had one watch of white sailors, one of
black. These were called "Checkerboard ships." The number was
always called out as the verses were started.

I suppose most yatties who wish to visit the coast of Venezuela and the
islands of Aruba and Curaçao should read this chapter backward. By far
the majority of cruising vessels that visit this area approach it either
from the northeast, from the Windward Islands, which is a quartering
run, or from the east, from the wide Central Atlantic Ocean on their
way around the world, which is a dead run downwind. But the way to
really get to know a coast with reasonable intimacy is to beat along it,
dead to windward. Then the skipper finds himself scrutinizing the charts
minutely, and every foible of the wind and current is cosseted, curried
and digested, so as to gain every yard of the passage, and to waste not
one yard to the wind.

In *Outward Leg*, in any case, heading east to the Venezuelan island
of Margarita was always part of the planned voyage, after the long beat

from Panama, along the coast of Colombia to Aruba. There were several great advantages to gain: to get our easting, so as to make the leg to St. Thomas and Puerto Rico with as commanding a wind as possible, a treat after the long wet beat of two thousand miles through the water from Panama; to test the windward ability of the boat in the lighter winds of the eastern part of the southern Caribbean—they work up to only twenty-five knots or so hereabouts; to see the coast of Venezuela— a well worthwhile ambition by any standards; and to cruise for a month in a country where the cost of living is about two thirds below that of the United States, and there stock up for our forthcoming Atlantic passage at a duty-free island. If anyone can fault these objectives I hereby challenge him or her to a duel with bottles of Drambuie at three bucks a bottle, or a heaving match with cans of corned beef at forty cents a twelve-ounce can, to be fought in shirts at fifty cents each and pants at fifty cents, too. The loser to pay for a tasty, sustaining dinner at an average cost of two and a half dollars a head.

All the Dutch islands of Aruba, Curaçao and Bonaire are spoiled, from a sailing point of view, by oil tanks grouped along the shores. Huge oil refineries, too, on Aruba and Curaçao, shoot noxious fumes up into the otherwise blue sky, where they are picked up by the wind and taken swiftly God knows where. Off the coasts of both those islands, fleets of oil tankers lie at anchor, unemployed and laid up for the present. Some people would find this sight, too, depressing, but not I. The more tankers laid up the fewer to run *Outward Leg* down in midocean, I say.

But all the industrial litter apart, the beat down the coasts of the islands is glorious, and if you stay well inshore, the seas are much less steep; in between the oil camps there are picturesque vistas of tidy Dutch houses with flowery gardens on the beaches, and sun-lit cliffs.

One of the problems with short hops under sail, even beating, with two lusty lads on board and beautiful lassies ashore, is that the crew start tarting up for arrival practically the moment the boat weighs her anchor. I've never had such a clean, smart, well-dressed and eager crew as I've had since Aruba. In the back reaches of the Colombian coast they had been most of the time unkempt and unshaven, but here, with brunettes, blondes and redheads all along the shore, you would have thought we were on our way to a Buckingham Palace garden party. They should have waited.

Although I recalled it from my last visit to Willemstad, the capital of Curaçao, in 1973, I didn't say anything about the small pedestrian footbridge that spans the harbor entrance most of the time. There they were, both Wally and Ivan, all toffed up and ready to step ashore as soon as we tied up. I, of course, was still in my sailing gear, i.e., the soiled one of my two changes of clothes. I steered close to the shore to keep as much as possible out of the current, so that the harbor entrance was out of sight until we rounded up hard by the old Dutch fort—and there, right across our patch, was this low bridge, no more than eight feet or so above water level, and crowded with people going to and from both sides of the harbor, all carrying shopping bags and briefcases and looking very Manhattan and West End-ish indeed. The look of the faces of our two Lotharios was a sight to behold. You never saw a headsail come down so fast, nor scrabbled down by such a good-looking crew in your life, unless it was in an advertisement for fashionable sports clothing in one of the more élitist magazines. You would have thought you were in Spillsborough Sound or off the yacht clubs in Cowes. With my two deckhands prancing about like Monte Carlo beach boys on the foredeck, and me trying to figure out how I could patch my corduroy trousers, thick for the tropics but at least presentable, I felt like Quasimodo in Studio 54.

The bridge kept us waiting for ninety minutes, it being lunch hour for the office workers, and we found ourselves hove to only yards from casually gazing tourists on the promenade of a great hotel that now overwhelms the old Dutch fort by the harbor entrance. The architecture of the hotel is not too bad, as modern hotels go, but I still found myself thinking that whoever put it there, where it completely cancels out the fort's solid Dutch lines from the Age of Reason, should have been rammed down into one of the old cannons and fired out to sea in the general direction of the Gulf of Maracaibo, preferably to the music of Tchaikovsky's "1812" Overture.

Once inside the harbor of Willemstad it's all fairly straightforward going to moor alongside the Handelskade, but there's a hefty surge there most of the time, so the best thing to do is to put out an anchor to hold the boat off the jetty walls, which are none too smooth. This surge is reinforced by the wash from passing tugs and ships, and also exacerbated by the wash from the cross-harbor ferries that operate when the bridge is opened to allow sea traffic. These ferries are about the noisiest small craft anywhere in the Caribbean, so between them and the car traffic scooting along the Handelskade, a noisy racket prevails most of the day and night. The best antidote here is a good pair of earplugs or some loud music tapes. But circumstances are always in balance, and there are one or two advantages to being in Willemstad; you can admire the old Dutch houses, buy consumer items on your credit card just about anywhere if you're well-heeled, or if not, buy fruit, vegetables, fish and meat cheaply at the marketplaces just around the corner. The Venezuelan small craft moored up in the market canal are straight out of a Brueghel painting, except for the build of the boats. Loose awnings to protect the good ladies of Curaçao from the sun as they buy their day's food flap in the wind, and the Venezuelan sailors lounging on deck, a perfect picture of tropical indolence, are a complete contrast to the busy hustle and bustle of the passing traffic and people on the street.

Willemstad is geared to, and exists for, service industries to tourism and shipping. Service is its only livelihood, apart from some oil refinery, and so it is expensive. Postal rates are about as high as anywhere on earth. Phone calls abroad are expensive, and so are telegrams. Bank charges, for transfers and such, are also high. The main thing that Willemstad has going for it, as far as yachtsmen are concerned, is that these services are dependable, in contrast to similar services in Latin American lands nearby, and in the main the people are helpful, honest and trustworthy at all levels. Punctuality and dependability are great assets, friendliness and courtesy even greater.

In Willemstad, beware of any temptation to get out of the sea surge and tug wakes by mooring in the market canal; there is very shallow water there, and it is not easy to extricate your keel from the soft mud in the crowded basin under the amused stares of hundreds of Venezuelan bumboat men and boys all grinning to loud *salsa* music.

Without a doubt, the best place to anchor in Curaçao is in Spanish Waters, about six miles to the east of Willemstad. There, inside an enchanting entrance of blue water in the narrow channel between dazzling white sand beaches, there are several yacht clubs. The best ones to aim for are the Asiento Club, in the northwestern waters of the extensive fjord, or the Dutch Naval Families Club, hard by. The snag at Spanish Waters—there is always a snag somewhere; there will probably be one at the Pearly Gates—is that it is remote from any shops or services, and taxis in Curaçao are expensive. But yacht-club members are helpful and afforded us lifts into Willemstad. The Asiento Club, hearing about the theft of our dinghy in Colombia, presented me with a heavy nine-foot wooden jolly boat, which is much more stable and so easier for me to enter and leave with my handicap. The sailors on duty at the Dutch Naval Families Club presented us with a gallon of light gray paint with which to paint the dinghy and the as yet unpainted bulkheads in our engine compartment. I shall name the dinghy *Dutch Treat*, of course. What else?

Despite the idyllic conditions at Spanish Water: blue, blue waters, splendid scenery, charming and helpful people all around us, Venezuela was calling and so, after six days of relaxation we secured a couple of days' fresh food and set off for La Guaira, which I had last visited over thirty years before in a British frigate.

We had a slogging beat to the coast of Bonaire, then a broad reach, swift, down the coast of that island, and after that a broad reach all night and most of the next day. We sighted the mountains of Venezuela at about two in the afternoon, when we were still sixty miles from the port of La Guaira. For the first time since leaving Panama, seventeen hundred miles astern, we were not on a beat. For the first time we were sailing without the cockpit windows up. For the first time we were dry. We had money in the boat and all the inexpensive riches of Venezuela ahead of us. Dry, drooling and on a reach—that's the way to sail . . . !

Steering *Outward Leg* into the dusk-moonrise and away from the setting sun, the horizon blood-red astern and mauve indigo ahead, our sails pregnant with anticipation and the northeast trade breeze, La Guaira was now only ten miles away. We were no longer reaching La Guaira. We were fetching the main port of Venezuela to us.

On the western half of the Venezuelan coast, around the peninsula of Paraguana and off the Gulf of Maracaibo, winds are generally stiff and the westerly-running current sets up unkind seas for a windward passage; but we had left all that behind us now. On the eastern half of the coast, close inshore, the Equatorial Current is muted by the off-lying islands and reefs with magic names like Aves Barlovento (Windward Bird) and Aves Sotovento (Leeward Bird), Orchila and Blanquilla, Testigos and Tortuga, a whole chain of them, about two hundred and fifty miles in extent, all sitting at sixty to eighty miles off the coast. They stave off the sweep of the three-knot current and keep it well out to sea. Inside the islets and reefs the current, much subdued, even reverts on itself in a countercurrent, at lucky times, along the mountainous, steep-to shore.

The mountains behind the central Venezuelan shore rear up to around nine thousand feet only a few miles from the littoral. Around them in the mornings a light mist hovers so that their peaks gleam above it, blue and ghostly, mysterious, like an undiscovered land, Shangri-La. This is what our first sight of the land had been like, around early afternoon on the seventeenth of March. We were following the track of Columbus on his first voyage along the coast of South America. I tried to imagine what was in the Genoan's mind when these mountains, one of the sacramental sights of the Caribbean Sea, showed themselves before him. The scene would not look out of place in an ancient Japanese or Chinese painting. He must have imagined that at last he had reached his long-searched-for Cathay or Cipangu.

Usually, from a small craft in clear weather, a landfall is discovered from the deck in a curious, dreamlike sequence. Usually the land does not reveal itself gently, but appears like a coy wraith, a mirage. There was none of that about the Sierra Miranda. One minute there was nothing on the southern horizon; the next minute the whole range of peaks burst into bloom from the sea with Latin drama.

Airlines do two good things for mariners; they get us from A to B quickly though unromantically when we need to be consigned like biscuits in a box from one place to another; and even more usefully, they provide airports and beacons to guide us into places where we might not have the proper large-scale charts. They do this very well at La Guaira, and their green and white beacons show up brilliantly in the cobalt evening mist. The airplane industry has stolen much of the romance from the ships and ports in the past thirty years or so. Practically every airport observation deck is crowded with sightseers watching the big lumbering jumbos take off. But a poor old port like La Guaira, even though it has an overhead sightseers' walkway right through the main dock area, is deserted, except for the usual guards and watchmen. As we crept in among the ships from Greece and Yugoslavia, Holland and Japan, there was no one on the platforms to stare and wave at the seamen, as there once was. This is a pity, for the ships and shipping still shift more loads than the airports ever could. But there are even now Conradian dreams in the shadows under the cranes for those with the right eyes.

Large ports have always fascinated me. But the most fascinating ones are those close to the capital city of their country; ports like Callao, in Peru; Valdivia, in Chile; Puntarenas, in Costa Rica; Belém, in Portugal; and even more so where the capital city is high in the mountains, hidden from the port. La Guaira is a classic. From the port there is no sign of Caracas, a city of six million people, hidden behind the mountains that rise above the port. And yet Caracas is only ten miles away as the proverbial crow flies.

The jetties of La Guaira are high—about fourteen feet above the water. There are no ladders. Now to the normal one-legged sailor this might present problems. But in Outward Leg we had foreseen this particular little snag. The running poles can be stepped on deck or on the mast. Ours, stepped on deck, made a very handy derrick for hoisting me ashore and neatly onto the cobbles of the quayside. It also helped Ivan, the Spanish playboy, to keep his short togs clean and neat. Being landed on the jetty like a Toyota car or a prize bull adds a touch of airiness to one's arrival.

As mentioned before, most yachts enter Venezuela in the eastern part of the coast, and head west. That our route was unusual was shown by the utter surprise with which we were received. The entering facilities are rudimentary indeed in La Guaira. You walk to the end of a jetty, into a narrow, litter-strewn shed and up very rickety stairs in almost complete darkness. I put my walking stick several times through the gaps left by missing planks in the stairway. We were all together, me and my crew, so between them they managed to save my life half a dozen times each on the way into the Customs shed. Again, as I said before, there are always snags, everywhere. The main thing is to find them as soon as you can, then enjoy the rest.

The next snag was that Ivan, being Spanish, was not allowed into Venezuela without a visa. We had been to the Venezuelan consul in Willemstad to get one, but they could not issue him a visa because he did not live in Curaçao—it was one of those Catch 22 situations that most bureaucracy is set up to bring about. The minions in the Customs office of course reveled in raising an obstacle before us. That's what most bureaucracy is about—to stop people from doing things. We would have to await the arrival of the Immigration chief. That worthy showed up eventually and turned out to be that rarity of rarities, a bureaucrat with a heart, that joy of man's desiring, a human being. He heard me out for a few minutes, as I told him how I once was an instructor to the Venezuelan navy, and how Ivan had been with us since Costa Rica, and how he was part of our crew and how if he wasn't allowed in, right, I'd slip my lines immediately and head out of Venezuela, and so on. The chief looked me in the eye, nodded his head and gestured at his minions. "Let him in," was all he said.

La Guaira has everything needed for a cruising boat: ice, cheap food at a market just outside the dock gates, and easy transportation anywhere at very cheap prices. But it also has rats, dirt and noise. We had done the right thing, entering there. Having been where we had, in Colombia, it was the best place for us to enter. Having bits of paper, stamped, on board from La Guaira, would protect us from too much prying anywhere else in Venezuela. That was the thought behind our entering there, and as it turned out, we were absolutely correct.

La Guaira has little to offer in the way of shore attractions, apart from a few seamen's bars and cheap restaurants, but we found a charm-ing place, Macuto, a dollar taxi ride along the coast. There, on the trafficless seafront, is a tree-shaded promenade lined with restaurants and bars. A full dinner there for three cost us all of eight dollars. There is a lively crowd of people in Macuto, of all ages and states, fit for the *boulevardier* or the rocker alike. You can see an inshore fisherman, bare-foot, bronzed, traipse his catch in the night direct from his boat drawn up on the sandy beach in among the well-dressed diners sitting at the outside tables, and hardly help but watch overwrought Latin lovers beating up their lady loves with an intensity undreamed of in cooler climes.

From La Guaira cast along the coast is a series of shortish hops, none longer than sixty miles, all the way to Isla Margarita, about two hundred miles all told. Immediately to the east of La Guaira there are many crowded beaches. These have groynes or seawalls poking out to protect the sandy beaches from the depredations of the Caribbean swells. You can get behind one of these for a lunch stop as we did, and watch the antics of the locals as they frisk in the sea and each other. The bathing apparel in these parts is so skimpy as to be in many cases almost non-existent. Ornithologists (genuine bird watchers), too, will find these stops interesting, as the wild life along the shore does not seem to be at all discouraged by the presence of thousands of brown, seminaked humans. As in most parts of Venezuela *Outward Leg* visited, there is a colorful line of seeming jetsam along the sand at high-water mark. This is gar-bage in the form of beer and soft-drink cans and plastic bags. There must be at least a million tons of garbage lying around in Venezuela. It exists wherever humans tread, along that shore.

The first real stop for *Outward Leg* was at the Club Puerto Azul, at Naiguatá (pronounced Nygwat*ah*), about fifteen miles or so from La Guaira. If Columbus had landed here now, he would have really thought he was at the court of the great Khan of Cathay. There is no word for Puerto Azul but opulence. I have been in probably a thousand yacht clubs in my lifetime of roving, from tiny backyard sheds to the New York Yacht Club, but never, not even at the Costa Smeralda in Sardi-nia, have I ever seen anything to match Puerto Azul in grandness, in luxury, smartness, efficiency and in the variety of its amenities. There is everything there, including ten tennis courts, a huge shopping cen-ter, cinema, theater, restaurants, four different types of beaches, three swimming pools, one half a mile long, and other facilities for every other type of sport or pastime imaginable. It is a resort of the Caracas rich, and so is guarded day and night and impregnably fenced off from the real world outside.

I have been in many prison camps of the rich, too, in many lands, but this one is again different from most of the rest, where the reception of wandering visitors, arriving casually, is concerned. At Puerto Azul we in *Outward Leg* were treated with every courtesy and kindness, and invited to stay for as long as need be. As soon as I met the manager, he provided the boat with an alongside berth to make things easier for me to get to and from the boat. We were offered access to all the amenities of the club. There was no sign that the manager knew who we were, apart from the fact that we were foreign visitors.

In the midst of all this luxury and opulence, a lunch in the club cafeteria cost $2.30 each, and there was so much food provided that we took on board a kitty bag for Ms. Brimstone the cat that fed her for the next two days.

At Puerto Azul there are a chandler's (imported items expensive), hauling facilities for boats up to about forty feet, and good cheap transportation to anywhere along the coast.

Outside the club, about half a mile away, lies the town of Naiguatá, which reminded me of George Orwell's *Road to Wigan Pier*, but set in the tropics. The only attractions in the town are a bottled butane-gas depot, a Laundromat, soccer field and two shabby cafés. Traffic is dense and fast. So are the drivers, as it seems they are practically everywhere in Venezuela. Local people are more standoffish than in other Latin American countries, but friendly and helpful if approached. They bring to my mind, in their attitude to strangers from abroad, good English butlers. The lasses, so Wally and Ivan agree, are a bit like the mountains that back the coast—very, very obvious, inviting, but difficult of access on a short visit. Like any worthwhile project, climbing the Venezuelan mountains needs planning, foresight, care and *time*. The approach cannot be made direct, but has to be by a devious route, to avoid a swift and deadly fall. If you see what I mean. And, as Wally finally agreed, once you've climbed the mountain, what do you see? Why, other mountains, of course—it's one bloody mountain after another.

25

A Sailor's Heaven

Oh blow, my boys, I long to hear you,
Oh blow, my boys, I can't get near you.

A Yankee ship came down the river,
Her masts all bent, her sails a-shiver.

How d'you know she's a Yankee clipper?
By the Stars and Bars that fly above her.

Who d'you think was the skipper in her?
Why, Bully Forbes was the skipper in her.

Who d'you think was First Mate in her?
Why, Boss-Eyed Bill, the Bowery Bastard.

Who d'you think's the second greaser?
Why, Santander Jim, the Frisco Bludger.

The Third was Sam, the Rocket from Hell, boys,
He'll ride you down like you ride a spanker.

The Bosun was a big buck nigger,
His handle was Joe, the Mobile Digger.

The sails was just a jobbing tailor,
The chips was not a Blackball sailor.

The cook was Jack the Boston bugger,
He chased the steward up the bunt lines.

Her sides was old and her sails were rotten,
His charts the skipper had forgotten.

Irish pendants in her rigging,
Oh, can you hear the banjos pinging?

The crew was anything but frisky,
The times they'd crossed the Bay of Biscay.

She sailed away for Kingston City,
Never got there, more's the pity.

Blow today and blow tomorrow,
Blow for that old ship in her sorrow!

Tops'l halyard shanty. Mainly sung in British
ships in the nineteenth century, it is a sardonic
comment on the Yankee "blood-boats," where
sparkling decks, shining topsides and hard, violent discipline were the rule.

A sailor's life is one of goodbyes. When you are as sorry as hell to leave
a place is when you know you are really happy. Paradoxes, paradoxes,
what would we do without them? But on the Venezuelan coast the sorrow at leaving one place is leavened by the anticipation of arriving at
the next, and of the voyage in between, short as it is. Along this mag-
ical coast it is one sailor's delight after another; as we leave each place
in turn I imagine in my mind's eye the cruisers farther north, among
the hot dog stands and smoldering resentment of the West Indies in
general, as I remember them, and I wonder how it is that there are so
few yachts on the Venezuelan shores of the Caribbean. Is it the voyage
across a few hundred miles of sea that keeps them away? Is it the thought
of a bit of a beat back that puts them off? Is it the language difference?
Good God, to learn enough Spanish to make one's way around a marina
is the application of only a few days' diligence to the reasonably intelligent person. Is it a suspicion that perhaps the Venezuelans in general
are a bit like the Colombians in general? Let there be no doubt about
it, there are no two nationalities on the face of the earth who could be
more different. There are no people in the whole of the Caribbean—in
the whole of the tropics indeed—who are, on the whole, more honest
and trustworthy than the average Venezuelan. There can be a very few
tropical countries better policed, nor more incorrupt. There is no reason why anyone should not sail for Venezuela and cruise her coast with
the utmost confidence in others, as long as he has the right charts and
goes about it in a seamanlike manner, and *pays his way.*

That's where we come to a sticky point. I'll keep it short. From Aruba
on to Isla Margarita I came across instances where yachtsmen had in-
curred expenses and sailed away without paying them, and where they
had simply left their boat at a berth or a mooring and flown away without saying anything to the person in charge of the berth, and without

making any arrangement for overseeing the safety of the vessel, and without leaving any kind of payment. Now it may be a coincidence as far as the instances I was told about, but in every case it was a French yacht that had offended in one way or the other. Out of eight cases I was told of, all were French. I can only come to the thought that if yachtspeople become unwelcome in Venezuela—what a sad day that will be—it will be mainly Frenchmen to blame. I know that some people may dismiss this point as a reflection of my own Francophobia, but let me assure you that it is not, and that I am reporting things exactly as I found them, or as close to the truth about them as my memory will allow. If anyone doubts me, I will provide names, chapter and verse on all eight instances of yachts not paying debts in Venezuela, Aruba and Curaçao. Behavior such as these French people displayed can only bring cruising yachts into disrepute in yet one more, so far welcoming, area. Elegance and flair are all very well, but paying your dues is far more important.

On another forty miles east along the coast to Carenero. Here a word about the wind and sea off the eastern part of Venezuela. The effect of the mountains heating up in the daytime is to bring about an increase in the wind strength from about noon to around dusk, when the land cools. During the night the wind drops, and around three A.M. it is just about flat and calm. If you have a good engine, then is the time to get out and motor on dead east. That way you arrive at your destination during the daylight hours. If you don't have an engine, then the time to leave is around eleven A.M., tack all afternoon, lie to off the destination all night, and sail in on the light morning breeze.

Carenero is tucked in on the windward side of Cabo Cadera, and so the sea rolls right into the natural harbor entrance. But the shallows wear down the rollers, and by the time you reach the harbor it's practically flat calm. Incidentally, the beacon that Don Street shows in his guide to Venezuelan waters, at the entrance to Carenero harbor, is missing. We found that out when *Outward Leg* touched the reef. Fortunately and wisely as it turned out, I was making only one knot at the time, creeping in simply because I could not locate the beacon. There was no harm done. *Outward Leg*'s cool-tubes are built like the bulge of a battlewagon. I was later told by Miguel Vasti (about whom more later) that there was a marker buoy on the reef, but the Caracas weekenders kept shooting it out of the water or stealing it, and so the authorities gave up replacing it.

Like Puerto Azul, Carenero is a seaside outlet for the people of Caracas. In Puerto Azul it's the very rich that congregate; in Carenero it's the middle class. Let no one ever tell you that republics don't have class systems. The Puerto Azul crowd are mostly staid people. In Carenero they are jolly and lively and everyone wears their sex like I wear my hats. Dickens would have had a field day in Carenero. There is no theater stage that I know that could put on a show like Carenero at weekends. All of humanity is there. It's fun. Noisy, but fun. In the Varadero, that is. That's a sort of public wharf, where everyone lets their hair down. In the Yacht Club Varadero, around the point, it's a different kettle of fish. There, after we tied up alongside the jetty, and before I had a chance to hobble around to the office, an armed guard told us that foreign-flag yachts were not welcome, and would we please leave? One thing about having a choice or two—it saves arguing or pleading, explaining or protesting. Having choices is the only saving grace of democracy. Having choices of other places to berth, we promptly left the Carenero Yacht Club to sizzle in the sun. I never stay where I'm not welcome.

Our choice of a place to take refuge from the wrath of the Carenero Yacht Club turned out to be serendipitously happy. At the Varadero we were made welcome by Miguel Vasti, of pure Italian descent, a true son of Michelangelo. He sold us a boatload of diesel oil, forty-eight gallons, at $9.20.

Carenero is about a mile from the nearest town, a place called (and it looks like) Higuerote. This has several advantages. A good telephone office for cheap calls abroad, a marketplace and a fair choice of shops of all kinds. It also has restaurants. The one we ate dinner at, for a total of six dollars for three, while not a candidate for the Michelin Guide where the food was concerned, was interesting. The waitresses were local ladies of the night, and our fellow diners were Portuguese fishermen. The music played there, over the radio or the tape, was so loud that by the time we left I had earache. I told Wally that I have a theory that people of Latin descent must have a hearing problem. Their music always blasts and they are always shouting at each other. There is, however, nothing wrong with their eyes. They notice everything about you, down to the minutest detail. Within minutes of our sitting down to dinner the café was almost chockablock with small children staring wide-eyed at the ankle of my false leg: I cannot wear socks in the tropics. I have a trick for making the leg move, just like a normal leg. This proved a wow with the kids, and we were soon the talk of the town. None of this kind of socializing goes down very well with Don Ivan, the playboy of the bounding main, of course, so he gazed moonfaced at the ladies of the night while Wally and I had a ball making the kids roll with laughter.

From Carenero to the island of Tortuga is about forty miles, and we made an overnight beat in lightish winds. Here I should point out that very few trimarans indeed, it seems, have visited the Venezuelan coast. Everywhere we went *Outward Leg* was the object of much curiosity. In Carenero alone over fifty yachtsmen from Caracas visited the boat and looked over her. She is obviously a new breed to them. It was difficult at first to explain the function of the outriggers, and the capsize-preventing cool-tubes. It isn't easy in English to get such a simple idea over at first; in Spanish it is even more difficult. But once the Venezuelans seized the idea, their enthusiasm was almost tangible. To say in English "I think—I believe that we have developed a multihull vessel which, besides being faster than a monohull of the same length, is also *safer*" is one thing. It can be expressed in English with soft nuances, almost whispered, so as not to sound too outlandish and boastful. In Spanish it can only be explained as a proclamation. Yet it is truly what I believe, after the performance of *Outward Leg* off the Guajira Peninsula of Colombia in very high seas indeed.

The islets of Tortuguillas, off the western end of Tortuga island, are gems. They are probably among the most unspoiled and certainly among the most beautiful, in all aspects, of the islands of the Caribbean sea, if not of the world. Clear water, blue and green; good holding ground, sand; white, clean, dazzling sandy beaches, and shady low trees and bushes ashore. Our only company here was birds and a dozen Venezuelan fishermen harvesting the waters around the reefs nearby. Surf and silence. Incidentally, television is everywhere in Venezuela—in the shabbiest shack, the sleaziest bar. Here, at Tortuguillas, it was on board the otherwise quaint and ancient-looking fisherman's "mother-vessel"—a nineteen-inch color TV! As they spend two months at a time at the reefs, it helps to while away the idle hours. They had two or three young lads with them, who spent hours, I was told, watching the goggle box. It brought to my mind the hours I spent as a lad on board a sailing barge, where what idle hours I had were spent reading the *Oxford Book of English Verse.* I wonder which will foster better minds, TV or good literature? It might be intriguing to live another fifty years and find out.

The fishermen asked us if we had fresh water to spare, so we afforded them twenty gallons. So often the boot is on the other foot, and so often have fishermen helped me out with a drop of water or fuel. In return they presented us with a baby turtle. Ivan fell in love with the turtle, which I named Somerset, because he looked like Somerset Maugham. But I can't stand to see wild things kept captive—I've been inside too many prisons—and so a couple of days later I persuaded Ivan, tearfully, to let Somerset free in the sea.

Our next passage, from Tortuguillas to Puerto La Cruz, was about seventy-two miles, and this we made in a daylight leg for a change, the wind being fair. Seventy-two miles on a broad reach in ten hours, with a voyage-loaded vessel, is not bad going, especially with the wind at no more than eighteen knots maximum. The sea was so small and the boat so steady that I became bored to an extent, so went below and reread some of Sir John Barrow's *Mutiny of the Bounty*. It's a pity Nordhoff and Hall didn't go deeper into the story of that sad episode in the history of the Royal Navy. They might not have been so eager to make a hero out of a roguish wretch like Fletcher Christian, nor such a big tyrant out of such a fine and humane seaman as William Bligh. Humane for his time and circumstances, that is.

La Cruz is my favorite among the ports of Venezuela. There is a new, half-finished marina to the north of the port, but it is simply a mere convenience set among building-sitelike eyesores. Modern architects and planners have been at work, raising great big hen-batterylike apartment blocks (I think it's a plot to reduce population by increasing the incidence of suicide) and razing precious old Spanish colonial buildings to make way for concrete strips along which metal boxes proceed with insane, inane velocity. In other words, depending on your taste of course, you either feel at home there, in which case God help you, or you hate it. I hated it and wished it the same fate as Gomorrah. *Outward Leg* wended her way out of the dusty marina and sought a better place. This is off the town beach, at the northern end, where we anchored in eight feet, sand, just in the lee of the short harbor wall. Getting ashore was easy with our wooden dinghy. It could be left safely on the beach with no fear of theft. Friendly kiosk owners guarded the oars for us, and immediately we were right in the middle of town.

La Cruz is a delightful mixture of seaside resort and market town. The seafront promenade, at early evening, is a parade of people of all ages and conditions, and no doubt to suit all tastes, even the most jaded. Among the people we met on our evening perambulation, were: a Lebanese popcorn seller who was studying to be a doctor and who spoke good English but no Spanish; several young lady students, highly amused at Wally's attempts at gallantry in Spanish; an ex-sergeant from the Republican army of Spain during the Civil War of 1936–40, also with one leg; a young man who was learning English at a local college and was attempting to delve into the difference between "may" and "might"; and a couple of Venezuelan navy sailors who heard with awe that I was at the commissioning of their ship, *Arugua*, in Barrow-in-Furness, England, in 1951.

As the moon descended over the palms and the silvery beach, they mostly waved us goodbye as I clambered into our dinghy, *Outward Leg* anchored ghostly and gray in the cobalt night only yards offshore.

The next port of call was Mochima, about twenty miles east, and at the end of a long, winding fjord among the coastal hills. Don Street, I am told, said he thinks this is the best anchorage along the Venezuelan shore. I don't agree with him, but for one reason only: There are mosquitoes. I correct myself—there is at least one mosquito, and that little bugger found me, of course. But in every other respect Mochima is a safe, good spot. We found anchorage only twenty yards from the Club Marina Restaurant Viejo, in very good holding ground, sand. The grandiloquent name of the establishment disguises, at first sight, a simple fisherman's bar (with, of course, loud music) where we had our cheapest meal in Venezuela: fried parho fish, salad and soft drinks, and two beers each, for the sum total of $4.60. That is $1.53 each. The little *pueblo* has a street, a tiny park with the obligatory monument to Simón Bolivar, flowers galore, dingle-bobbing boats, a basketball court and very little else. The surrounding mountains hug the little town to their bosoms. There is no garbage on the streets. This makes Mochima exceptional in Venezuela. Over the door of one tiny restaurant there is the notice *Visitante Comportate* ("Visitor Behave Yourself"). A very good idea, I thought when I saw it. I behaved myself.

The scenery on this part of the Venezuelan coast, amid beautiful islands in the morning calm, with the mist hovering around them, makes me wonder if the name *Venezuela* ("Little Venice") came not from the native houses built over the water farther east in the old days of discovery, but because the coast reminded the explorers, among whom were many Italians, of the scenery on the Adriatic coasts, much of which was then the territory of Venice. You can very well imagine yourself on the shores of present-day Yugoslavia.

Some of the islands have cliffs that fall vertically for hundreds of feet straight down into the Caribbean Sea. They are so steep-to that I decided for once to combine Wally's two main activities, rock climbing and sailing, into one clear-cut episode, by laying the boat directly alongside the base of the cliff, and having Wally ascend the cliff from the deck.

This was on the island of Caracas Este. Doing this kind of thing could be considered foolhardy unless the skills involved in working the boat in under the cliff, bearing in mind breeze and tide, currents and surge, are exercised diligently and with great care. It is not every day that a two-hundred-foot vertical cliff is ascended directly from the deck of an oceangoing sailing craft. But for the sake of exploration we thought we would do it at least once, just to prove that it can be done. To marry two endeavors so alike as rock climbing and sailing is an achievement in itself. To do that was alone well worth the trip to Venezuela. Whether it has been done before I do not know. Bill Tilman combined sailing with mountaineering, but I don't think he ever scaled a cliff direct from his vessel, *Mischief*. Let history record that it has been done. I like to think that Bill was watching us from the Halls of Valhalla, and smiling as Wally somehow scaled that vertical rock, and I swore and sweated at keeping her off the cliff face. *Sport*. That's what it's all about. One thing we all three agreed on, hazardous as rock climbing from deck is, its's a thousand times better than sitting in some marina staring at the result of some Bauhaus-bred mad architect's rambling machinations.

The next project along the Venezuelan coast was to combine cruising with cave exploration, so far as possible. I managed to get *Outward Leg* hovering off a couple of caves, quite close, while my crew, a precocious pair, pried around at bats' nests and tested the echoes inside the caves. Again, this is not an exercise for the unwary. There are tide surges and sudden accelerations of the katabatic breezes. These, small as they are, can be dangerous when the vessel is right in among the rocks. The situation demands knifelike vigilance at all times.

Puerto Sucre is the port of the city of Cumana. Apart from the very Spanishness of Cumana, with its park of almost Gothic lushness and its cathedral, there is not much attraction here because the best anchorage, off the public ferry landing, is prone to much traffic and to youngsters swimming out and boarding the vessel while no one is on board. Otherwise, there is another unfinished marina around the headland to the northeast of Puerto Sucre, again where some "planner" has made a complete mess of what must have once been good potential parkland for the city. Instead there are now ugly square concrete egg-crates stood on end, surrounded by a brick-colored dusty desert, through which the usual concrete ribbons hurl people encased in metal boxes on their vital errands. The charge at the marina is only fifty cents a night, but it would take two dollars' worth of effort and cleaning gear to get rid of the dust. On the whole, Puerto Sucre is not very interesting. The port itself is little more than a sunny slum interrupted here and there by modern travesties like multilevel parking lots and supermarkets. I would miss Puerto Sucre on a visit to Venezuela, on a purely coastal visit, although Cumana is worth a visit. I had a "time warp" there. It was as if I were back in Barcelona, Spain, in the middle fifties, apart from the shapes of the cars. The standard of car driving in Cumana is on about the same level as a bumper-car ride in a fairground. The aim of most drivers seems to be to drive straight at the nearest object, moving or not, at as high a speed as possible. Venezuela has the highest rate of road accidents in the Americas, and no wonder.

From Puerto Sucre *Outward Leg* made her way, at last, to the island of Margarita. We had fine winds, although we were headed again, but by this time, after almost two thousand miles of beating all the way from Panama, we were accustomed to it. To us it was like water off a duck's back, as the saying goes. Forty-two miles brought us in the early afternoon to Punta Piedras, on the island of Margarita. As the wind was then at its strongest, we anchored under the lee of a seawall there and waited until dusk before heading three miles east to Punta Mangles, where we anchored again only yards from yet another fisherman's bar with loud music. There we celebrated, with forty-cent beer, our arrival in Margarita, and the end of our long beat against the trade winds all the way along the north coast of South America. From now onward, all the way to Europe, all the way to the southern half of the Red Sea, given the usual wind patterns, we should be mostly off the wind, with much easier going than we had been through in the past two thousand miles.

Margarita Island is a curious amalgam of peasantry, fishery and tourism. Until 1959, when the government provided an undersea aqueduct, there was very little fresh water here. Then a duty-free zone was established on the island, to encourage tourism. This means that practically everything sold here is cheaper than anywhere else. It also means that Porlamar, the main port, is crowded by day with visitors who flock in from the mainland to buy goods to take back to sell at a profit. At nighttime the town of ninety thousand souls, is almost dead. It is the only Latin town of any size that I have been in that is completely asleep by eight P.M. apart from a couple of small bar-restaurants.

There is a yacht "marina" to the northeast of Porlamar, where most visiting yachts (what few there are) congregate. This is because the holding ground in the tiny port right off the town market is not too good unless you anchor carefully, and also because there is not enough water for vessels drawing more than five feet. But if you are careful it is possible, as we have, to enter right in under the protection of the seawall, and be comfortable and secure. The surge will make monohulls roll somewhat, but of course in *Outward Leg* that is no problem. The racket from the marketplace, only a hundred yards or so away from the anchorage, has to be heard to be believed, at least in the mornings, but in the afternoons the tumult and the shouting die. Then the wind increases and we are left to do little chores in the cool wind and the silence, broken only by the low groaning of the kedge anchor and the flapping of the windscoop.

It took Wally three days to find a little oasis of peace and quiet ashore here. At first we completely missed it, yet it is only three cables from the boat, just past the little university college buildings on the seafront, a little café with outside tables, a wonderful view across the bay to seaward beyond the headland of El Morro, and meals at about two dollars a head.

In Porlamar I stocked the boat with canned food and dried victuals, enough for the next three months for three men. Total cost $210. I bought myself two pairs of trousers and two tropical shirts. It is rare for me to afford new clothes, but the nine dollars total they cost me did not disturb too much my conscience.

As a port of call for yachts, Porlamar has a couple of drawbacks. The waters are shoal in parts around, and night life is a bit puritanical, to put it mildly, at least outside the big hotels (and who wants to go there? Might as well be in Las Vegas or Monaco). But what it has going for it is of great interest to yachtspeople. Cheap prices for practically everything—at least two-thirds cheaper than in, say, Connecticut or California—good supplies, and honest people. But most of all, and an object lesson to every Caribbean state or island that wishes to attract cruising people to its shores: In Margarita the officials *leave us alone.* That, after all, is all we want.

26

Raves and Caves

Oh, the bully's boat's a-coming,
Don't you hear the paddles rolling?
Ranzo, Ranzo, hurray, hurray!
Oh the bully boat's coming,
Down the river she's hauling,
Ranzo, Ranzo, Ray!

Oh we're bound for Yokohama,
With a load of grand pianos!

Oh we're bound for Gibraltar,
And our cargos's bricks and mortar!

Oh we're bound for Valp'raiso,
And our load's old rusty razors!

Oh we're bound for Buenos Aires,
With a bunch of green canaries!

Oh we're bound for Santayana,
And our cargo's German lager!

Oh we'll tie her up in London,
And we'll all go on the ran-tan!

One version of "Ranzo Ray," capstan or halyard shanty, nineteenth
century. It originated on the Mis-
sissippi.

Sailing from the Pacific Ocean to the Windward Islands, and on to Europe, is a bit like opening a big heavy door by pushing at its hinges. At
first there is hardly any movement at all, then the door gives a low creak,
and gradually, progressively, it opens a little more easily, a little faster,

until at last centrifugal force takes over and it swings fully open. At Panama with the winds dead from the east, and the current too, progress is slow and arduous, but as the passage east is gained, and especially after the Aruba Banks, progress is better until at last, when the Isla Margarita—or Trinidad in safer days—is reached, the doorway to the whole of the Atlantic Ocean is open and fairly free. In other words the boat now is sailing along or across the weather systems of the world, and no longer beating against them.

I suppose a lot of landsmen (and probably some yachtsmen, too) find this difficult to understand. Why should you head for—why is your best route—as far east as you can get in the Caribbean, and then north for New York or Bermuda, in order to make easting across the Atlantic Ocean? One minute's study of the weather systems of the North Atlantic Ocean will clarify matters.

There is the Gulf Stream heading north and east, which turns, off the Nova Scotia Banks, into the easterly-running Atlantic Drift and which runs at anything from a knot to three knots eternally. There are the southeast winds of the Caribbean (at most times of the year), which will push you up to the Windward Passage or the Mona Passage and so out into the southwest North Atlantic. There the winds will be variable in strength and direction for a few hundred miles off the Bahamas, and then the westerlies are encountered, which will blow you over to Europe. This is the old sailing route from the heyday of working sail. It is the route used by the Spanish treasure galleons, the British and Dutch privateers chasing them, and the wool clippers and tea clippers on their way home from Australia and China. It is the reason that ports like Willemstad, Trinidad, and San Juan, Puerto Rico—and New York, too—were established in the first place. But the hardest part, from the western Caribbean, is getting that old, squeaky door open. Once it is open, all the sailing world, from Greenland to Gibraltar, from Canada to Cape Horn and the Cape of Good Hope, lies open before you. That's why the British seized Trinidad and Barbados, and the Dutch grabbed Curaçao, against the Spaniards in the old days. The frequent exchange in battle of the West Indies islands was not only a matter of sugar crops, but also of valuable sailing bases from which trade to and from the South Atlantic and South America, as well as North America, could be controlled, threatened or attacked.

Now, with *Outward Leg* at anchor in the pretty bay at Pampatar, just along the coast of the island of Margarita from Porlamar, our imagined door was wide open. After the long slog along the north coast of

South America, I felt as I imagine Balboa must have felt when he climbed a tree in Darién, atop a peak, and sighted the Pacific Ocean.

Now I could study a chart of the North Atlantic Ocean and know that I could reach any port marked on it—if not easily, then at least far, far more easily than I had reached Pampatar.

Somewhere in my makeup there lurks an incipient yachtsman. In the West Indies there are many yachting centers, such as Grenada, St. Vincent, Martinique, Guadaloupe, Antigua, and so forth. I remembered these islands from previous visits—their green lushness and good havens. But I also recalled the frequent occasions when I at least had been made to feel resented and unwelcome there. There's no point in my being anywhere where I feel this, and so I decided to miss the Windward Islands, and most of the Leeward Islands, too. Instead we would call at St. Croix and St. Thomas, both U.S. territories. That would mean over a four-hundred-mile run on a broad reach, across the wind. That prospect was mouth-watering after months of beating heavily to windward. There was another reason, too, for heading for U.S. territory, apart from simply not wanting to visit any other West Indies islands: Ivan had no United States visa. I knew that he would not be granted one there, in either St. Croix, or St. Thomas, because you cannot be granted a visa for the United States inside the United States. But I would pretend I didn't know. The aim was to get permission for Ivan to remain in U.S. territory on board a yacht, so as to establish a precedent for when we arrived in New York. As it was, it didn't work out that way, but we'll come to that later.

The Venezuelan Customs were supposed to give us a clearance certificate for the duty-free goods we had on board—mostly food—but it was a Saturday and the chief wouldn't be in the office until Monday—

When in the office the chief is out
Hoist the main and fuck off out. . . .

which is exactly what we did. The young duty guard didn't mind at all. He was busy with his lady friend on the veranda of the Customs House as we weighed anchor and slid out only yards away. His lady friend waved her fingers behind her back at someone on board *Outward Leg* but I'm not sure if it was Wally or Ivan. She'd been flirting with both of them, so it could have been either. I rather suspect it was Ivan though, because while Wally was grinning at her, Ivan kept his gaze off her and maintained a serious Spanish visage.

Soon we were haring past Punta Ballena. I recall very clearly the moment when we turned thirty degrees off the wind from beating. One minute it was the same old wet, pounding Panamanian plod, and the next—I can't say laid her cheeks fondly to the seas because trimarans don't do that, but had she been a monohull she would have—she gracefully picked up her skirts and started to *fly*. It took us some minutes to realize that at last, at long, long last, we had the wind slightly abaft the beam and there was a breathless moment of relief before, with hardly a word spoken, the silken genniker sail was dragged, silently worried and fondly handled, from its long-time stowage in the after cabin. Minutes later it was aloft, in all its green, white and red glory, and pulling like a champion. Oh, the elation of capturing, at last, the trade wind in a great big splonker, and spitting to leeward around its leech, just to make sure that none of that damned defeated wind is being wasted! Wally and I were quiet in our satisfied vengeance on the north equatorial trade. We had the bugger pinned down now. It was no longer our master. We were commanding the wind, and we were the masters of the Caribbean. Ivan stared in wonder at the huge sail heaving, full and pregnant, and at the wake as the hulls slid and slithered over the cross seas. Wonder and vast delight, for he had never seen the genniker in action like this. The only time we had hoisted it in the Pacific, there wasn't enough wind to shift a gnat and the genniker had just hung there, like a pair of whore's drawers, for an hour or two, before we had grudgingly handed it down again. That had been in the Gulf of Panama.

Our first day's run out of Pampatar was our best day's run to date on the whole voyage from San Diego—171 miles. That's over the twenty-four hours noon to noon. The second day's run beat it—174 miles. On the evening of the third day out we were at anchor in Frederiksted, on the island of St. Croix. That's 420 miles in sixty hours. That's the crossing of the Caribbean Sea, from south to north, in two and a half days. That's *flying*. Total fuel consumption—one pint of diesel oil to charge batteries. Breakages, nil; and that was a fully loaded trimaran—loaded to traditional, oceangoing monohull standards and more. There were, don't forget, three months' supplies of canned food for three men on board, plus the remaining dried and packaged food, say six weeks' supply, plus eighty-two gallons of cheap diesel fuel and eighty-two gallons of fresh water, plus all our personal effects, the three of us, together with the ship's equipment. That was a total payload of around *four tons*. I suggest that this is the most important statistic, besides the speed of the passage, in this account. I suggest that, together with the safety factors built

into *Outward Leg*—the self-righting system, and the cool-tubes to prevent capsize—we realized at St. Croix that what we had under our feet
was one of the fastest, and one of the safest, cruising vessels afloat under sail. Hitherto multihulls had been considered as either hair-shirt racing
craft, for speed-drunk masochists with tiny appetites, or boxy floating
sheds for short cruises and always downwind, because they were thought—
and quite rightly in most instances—to have the windward ability of
Carnegie Hall.

St. Croix is one of the multihull centers of the world—some would
say that along with San Francisco it is *the* multihull Mecca. There were
not many in Frederiksted, and if there had been we would not have
seen them for we entered in the dark on a moonless night. But we were
greeted from the pitch-black jetty by a voice shouting, "Is that you,
Tristan?"

This, when he arrived on board, turned out to belong to a local
diver for the U.S. navy submarine base. He was a multihuller, Brian
Friedman. He said he would herald our approach at Christiansted, just
around the corner, where the passage was a bit tricky but where the
majority of multihullers were based.

I said, "Whoa, Brian. I may be on board a multihull, but I don't
consider myself to be a multihuller. The last thing I joined was the Royal
Navy and that cured me of camps, thank you very much. I think of
myself more as a sort of enforced lodger in a multihull, and if I have
brought some of the old, traditional, deep-keel philosophy into multihulls, and if it does some good, and if I have caused some perhaps revolutionary ideas to be bandied around, and if some good things come
out of that, so much the better. But I want you to alert the monohullers
too. They are also my kind of folk. A boat is a boat—"

At that Brian laughed and nodded his head.

Of course, in Christiansted the racing multihull men were eager to
look over *Outward Leg,* and in every instance they pulled a face. Jack
Petit, a well-known ocean racer in trimarans, said we were far too deeply
loaded and that we should not carry so much food around with us but
buy it at our destinations en route.

"What, at thirty cents for a half-pound can of corned beef?" was my
succinct reply to that one.

There was no problem for me with Ivan's presence on board without
a U.S. visa. I always, where possible, sent Wally to deal with officials.
I have a good excuse for this nowadays, pleading a sore leg, but apart
from that the truth is I just can't stand the attitude of the vast majority

of bureaucrats, nor the cavalier way in which, for the most part, they treat sailors, and especially in the West Indies. They don't often make me angry anymore, just a mite sick. Anyway, the immigration officer in St. Croix was a decent stick and evidently said that Ivan could stay, but no longer than twenty-four hours, and that he could wander around ashore. At the same time he served a deportation notice on him, but that was a mere formality. Ivan was not the first sailor to be told by the United States, and many other countries, "Welcome and get out!"

All three of us in *Outward Leg* went ashore in Christiansted and enjoyed rambling round back in the twentieth century again. We had a couple of drinks in the Bilge Bar and then, at Brian's invitation, rolled off to eat at Captain Weeks restaurant, where the floor heels at an angle of about fifteen degrees, and that's *before* the cuba libres.

An interesting and curious encounter was with the lady commodore of the Seven Seas Cruising Club. She had been rambling around the San Blas Islands on her travels. She showed me some *molas*, the colorful embroidered garments of the Cuna Indians, which were decorated by the Indians' idea of modern technology. One showed the plumbing system of a yacht, complete with head and hull outlet, and the other a man—obviously a white man, his nose was so large—with a telephone. I decided there and then never to revisit the San Blas Islands, which I remember as one of the few completely unspoiled places in the Western Hemisphere. If phones and plumbing have reached there, mugging can't be far behind.

The next day, the twelfth of April, we weighed and wended our way out of the tricky passage to the offing, and headed for St. Thomas. That is probably one of the busiest charter-boat capitals of the world. My main intents were to visit two good friends: Don Street, who was there in his *Iolaire*, now about seventy years old, and also Charlie Peet, who swallowed the hook in St. Thomas after a circumnavigation of the world some years ago.

For one rare instance, the wind—I won't call it the trade wind in this area—the Charter-Wind—wasn't blowing steadily from the east at fifteen to twenty knots. Instead there was an almost flat calm, so we motored over and dropped the hook off the Yacht Haven Marina. This brought back a flood of memories. This was where I had handed *Barbara* back to her owners after the six-year argosy described in *The Incredible Voyage*. This, too, was the scene of my demise as the shortest-ever-employed charter skipper, as described in the book *Adrift*.

In St. Thomas I never got any farther ashore than the Bridge Bar at the Yacht Haven. My crew did not get much farther either in the five days *Outward Leg* was at the end jetty. The welcome from other sailors was so overwhelming that after five days we groggily slipped and made our way over to the shelter of Elephant Bay, on Water Island. I thought we would be remote and private there, but within minutes of our arrival we were hailed by the skipper and crew of an old, restored steam yacht and spent an hour with them reminiscing about bygone days, in the cockpit, under the moon. They were New Yorkers and had been in exile in the islands for some years. Conversing with them, it was obvious that they imagined that they were in a remote area, far from the hustle and bustle of the modern world. To us, though, St. Thomas was a sort of southeastern suburb of New York City, and to me, outside of the Yacht Haven, not a very pleasant one either from what I recalled. I can't stand any form of racism, and reverse racism even less.

It was still too early in the year to head direct for New York City— there the last pangs of winter were still hovering over the city—so I decided to make a diversion of around three hundred miles or so and visit Puerto Rico, to call on my old friend Russel Gurnee, the man who helped me haul *Sea Dart* up to the fourth story of the Waldorf Astoria Hotel in New York in 1977 for the Explorers' Club Annual Dinner. Well, if your best lady friend is in New York, where else are you going to take her for dinner? Even if she is a twenty-one-foot cutter?

Now Russel was, I knew, exploring and developing what must be the most extensive underground cave in the Western Hemisphere for the Puerto Rican tourist industry. A bit of cave exploring appealed to me, so we weighed the hook and took off, on our first dead down-wind run since the coast of Mexico months before. It was glorious. The wind was steady at twenty-five knots around noon, the boat was as steady as a Popemobile, and the scenery was lush and ever changing on the north coast of Puerto Rico. A one-and-a-half-knot current was with us, and we shot along to San Juan in no time at all. Sixty miles between nine A.M. and five P.M. A slower passage would have done no harm; when we tied up alongside the Customs house jetty in San Juan we realized that it was Good Friday and practically everyone had the day off, except the guards who were minding the various boats in the Customs' mooring that were under arrest for drug running. I was pleased to see that some of these scoundrels, at least, were collared and waiting to meet their just deserts.

After various telephone calls were made we were told that we could proceed along the coast to Arecibo, near Russel's caving base, and another dead run, next day, brought us to that tiny haven by noon.

Arecibo is now a big, sprawling, American-type city, but the fishing port is still the same, in a tiny corner of the big bay, under the lighthouse. There is plenty of anchoring room inside the reef, in sand, but the only alongside berth is by the fishing jetty, only feet away from a very noisy, but jolly, fisherman's bar. For ambitious sailors heading to and from the West Indies or wherever, just around the cliff face, about half a mile from the bar, is a tiny shop that sells bread and potatoes and such, so there's no real need to traipse into Arecibo, which to me seemed a bit dreary and dull, full of flashing neon, empty pavements and parking lots. We were better off at the jetty. Puerto Rican fishermen are "okay guys."

Russel was down to see us the next day and took me to see his cave, which is at first an immense hole in the ground, then a series of long tunnels, and all very beautiful and cathedrallike. As we approached the cave mouth to be dropped down hundreds of feet on a crane cradle, I saw a line of men outside the fence. These were unemployed searching diligently and waiting desperately for a chance to work. I thought about them as I painfully made my way in the caves. I didn't get very far, though, only a few yards of the seven miles of underground passages and streams. Still, for the first attempt at speleology on one leg, I thought it wasn't too bad. Wally and Ivan got much farther, of course.

Back at the jetty, at the weekend, the locals were curious to know if we were from New York City, the Promised Land.

"No, we are heading there."

"Oh, how long will it take to sail there?"

(Proudly) "About eight days—"

(Pulled face) "Ah—that's far too long. Much longer than a plane!"

From Arecibo Ivan and I made a side trip by land to see the Old City of San Juan (and to buy some charts). I was very disappointed to find that what a dozen years ago used to be one of the liveliest, truly Spanish Colonial, down-to-earth cities in the Americas has now been converted into yet one more tourist trap pure and simple. It is now full of jewelers' stores and chi-chi dress shops, where it used to be a hive of fishermen's stores, net makers, carpenters' workshops on the street, sailors' bars and good, honest, cheap restaurants. Now it brings to mind a sort of film set. It is a tropical Disneyland, without the much more genuine kitsch of the Florida and California originals. It is a place where tourists are led to stare at other tourists. It is as phony as can be on the streets, although the old Spanish ramparts and forts still stand, just as they did in the days of Drake. I returned to the jetty at Arecibo with relief at the thought that I shall not, probably, live to see all the other places I know that are genuinely themselves thus despoiled. I won't say where they are. Find them yourself.

The next place we headed for in Puerto Rico must be the second worst place, from a scenic and interest point of view, on the island. I know that there are many attractive places on Puerto Rico. I doubt if there could be a more unattractive place than the port of Mayagüez. After sailing all day along the dramatic northwest coast of the island, it is a complete anticlimax to enter Mayagüez port. It is remote, bleak, dusty, and there is a bad surge alongside the wall. One hour there was enough for me. I took the crew ashore in a friend's car for an ice cream, then we headed out into the gloaming of the Mona Strait, for the Dominican Republic, on the island of Hispaniola.

There was a strong tide and current running; there is an unlit islet sitting in the middle of the passage; there was no moon, little wind, and word on the radio, after we were well under way, with Hispaniola in clear view under our lea, that riots had broken out in Santo Domingo, the capital of the Dominican Republic. I had to head to Samaná, the nearest port, to pick up fresh victuals for the voyage to New York. So there was plenty to distract our minds from the memory of the singular ugliness of Mayagüez harbor as we made our way over the Mona Passage, dodging many fast steamers en route.

27

Another Bloody Revolt

Oh, the mountain's so high, and the river's so wide,
Poor Lucy Anna!
The mountain's so high and the river so wide,
I'm just going over the mountains!

"Poor Lucy Anna." Probably the shortest of all the
shanties, it has a haunting melody. Of Spanish-
American origin.

There was another reason for heading to the Dominican Republic: There
is a United States Embassy in Santo Domingo. I would go overland to
the capital and try to get a visa for Ivan, or at least some kind of note
from the consul to state that Ivan was employed in *Outward Leg,* and
not after any New Yorker's job. Our best plan, I thought, was to enter
the Dominican Republic at a port marked on the charts as Samaná and
travel overland by bus to the capital.

After a very dramatic approach to the Gulf of Samaná, misty mountains and shallows below us setting up heavy seas, the first thing we
found was that the port was not called Samaná at all, but Santa Bárbara.

Although it is as remote as it looks on the maps, 250 miles from the
capital, Santa Bárbara turned out not to be the scruffy little fishing port
we had expected, but instead a full-blown tourist town, with a model
town center, hotels, bars, beaches, fair shops—and that wonder of
wonders—no tourists. There was even a six-lane highway along the
waterfront, which either side of the town led from one hill track to another. The only traffic I ever saw on it were the bus that chunders off
to Santo Domingo once a day—and a donkey loaded down with ba-

nanas. It struck me, as I looked at the deserted beachfront and the empty road, that this is the way some town, miraculously spared, might look after a nuclear holocaust had wiped out the rest of the world.

Nearby Santa Bárbara are the foundations of the first fort that Columbus built in the West Indies, at Punta Flecha—Arrow Point. It is a great mistake to think that the Indians of the islands were passive victims of Spanish aggression. Some were, no doubt, but the battles on the shores were long and bloody. The ruins are hardly worth a long traipse over the coast track—especially on one leg—there are only traces of the foundation ditches. But the view is splendid out over the Gulf of Samaná, away across to the blue mountains of the Engaño range in the south. I walked along the magnificently empty six-lane highway, then precariously mounted a decrepit mare which jogged me up to Punta Flecha. Neither Wally nor Ivan came along— there was a disco on the waterfront.

On our arrival I had headed straight for the town jetty and berthed bows to. Of course, even in a remote place like Santa Bárbara, there is always an obstructionist, an unconscious objector, to try to prevent our tying up. I think that there is some kind of production belt or mold in some hellish backwater shed where these characters are stamped out; they seem to be cast from the same mold the world over, from Valparaiso to Vladivostok, Harwich to Hong Kong. I can always recognize them even before they open their mouths to start their whine. They are always in unsoiled clothing—that's the first clue that you have a walking picket fence facing you. They always have clean hands, clean shoes, neatly parted hair (they are very rarely bald), eyes too close together and a mouth that looks as if it had just clamped shut around two prunes. In this case he was dark brown, too, but he was still of that same brotherhood of worldwide jetty defenders, sworn to prevent the structure from being put to any useful purpose.

Wally was starting to argue with him when I espied farther along the jetty a Dominican sailor from the navy gunboat tied up there. I dashed down below, rifled the bookshelf, and came out with *Jane's Pocket Book of Major Warships*. A quick riffle through in the sweaty, hot confines of my lair and there it was. Yes, without doubt, page 90, LSM. Good! I dashed up top and over the pulpit (try that on one leg) and waved the booklet in front of the sailor's face. He was a noncommissioned officer of some sort, and although the handle of his six-shooter swung from his hip, he looked amiable. I showed him the picture of his ship. He beamed. Excitedly he grabbed it and ran on board the gunboat to show it to all and sundry; next minute we were surrounded like heroes by the crew of the navy vessel, officers and men alike, slapping our shoulders and grinning, their gold teeth glinting in their dark faces. From one corner of my eye I watched the jetty führer slink away fuming and speechless.

Ivan's respect for me has increased greatly lately, and especially since I developed my Speech Number Five for Contrary Latin Harbor Masters and Immigration Officers. It goes something like this: I hobble into the office, looking, I imagine, like some kind of eccentric Victorian butterfly collector. I don't wait for him to speak. I wade in, but politely, *"Buenos días, señor Capitán"* (or *Coronel* if he's Immigration; they like that touch). "We've arrived here in my sailing vessel (*velero*) to visit your country, but we don't have much time for messing about with papers. If you want us here, these are the ship's papers" (I tap the wallet under my arm) "and our passports. If you don't want us here, please say so now. My boat is ready to sail at a moment's notice and there is a big ocean out there waiting for us, and plenty of other countries. We shall have appreciated the beauty of your shores and the friendliness (*amistad*) of your people, and especially your sailors" (soldiers, police) "on our way to your office, and take fond, if short, memories out to sea with us immediately, so give the word, señor—"

Now, unlikely as it sounds, Speech Number Five works wonderfully. By the time I have got this far the officer is out of his chair, with his cigar discarded in his ashtray and his hands on my shoulders and generally tears starting in his limpid Latin eyes, and I find myself being gently led to a luxuriously padded chair, with reassurances of unquenched welcome for as long as we wish to stay, no matter about papers, because after all, what are papers between friends?

The next step is for me to shake my head and complain about what tardy and cavalier treatment I received in the last country we visited (wherever that was) and how much better things are here (wherever that is). This is always met with complete agreement and approval.

He picks up his cigar again and waves it generously into the office-fan air blast. "Ah, señor, but those people in (Colombia, Panama, Venezuela) are not, of course, as we are in (Dominica, Colombia, Panama); their . . . antecedents are not the same. . . . There is, of course, you understand, much more pure Castilian blood here in (Costa Rica, Panama, Colombia) than in (Costa Rica, Panama, Colombia)."

I light the cigar he has just passed me and agree entirely. "Of course, that is evident in even a short stroll, señor, from the boat to your office," and so on, in that vein, as the officer, smiling, riffles through our papers and passports and mechanically stamps any page that seems to need some sort of decoration.

When I first used this ploy, in Venezuela, Ivan had merely nodded his head in agreement, but now that I have refined Speech Number Five, he enthusiastically puts in little side comments, straightfaced of course, such as, "The captain (*El capitán*) is a most discriminating gentleman," or "*El capitán* is a great student of (Cervantes, for right-wing officers; Lorca in left-wing regimes)."

In Santa Bárbara this diplomacy par excellence worked wonderfully well, and the port captain—the most powerful man for a hundred miles around—even sent for coffee. Then Ivan, scanning his bookshelf, noticed a copy of *The Incredible Voyage* in Spanish (*El Viaje increíble*). Excitedly he grabbed it from the shelf and showed it to the port captain, with my mug on the cover. That did it. From then on there was not enough that the official could do for us, arrange for us, provide for us—everything except a means of transport to, or communication with, the U.S. Embassy in Santo Domingo (which is all I was really after).

He pursed his lips for a moment and frowned; then he explained, "The situation seems to be quietening down in the capital. A messenger arrived here this morning—but the phone lines are down—there was heavy wind last night."

This was the first I'd noticed of a heavy wind. In the Mona Passage we had ghosted as best we could in the strong currents in light breezes; but I said nothing about that—"When Caesar speaks . . ."

To cut a long story sideways, it was arranged that I would catch the first bus into the capital the next day. The chances were that the revolt would have been put down by then, entirely, and all would be back to "normal."

That evening I treated the crew to a meal ashore, at a brightly lit, wonderfully situated, tastefully appointed, otherwise completely empty Chinese restaurant on the hill overlooking the twinkling lights of the ghost-tourist center. The service was remarkable for its downright unfriendliness, surliness and tardiness. Otherwise the food was excellent. It was the only place in Santa Bárbara where this was so. The boss even flatly refused to change some dollars, and that's a wonder anywhere south of the Mexican border.

Traveling on a bus in the Dominican Republic is, as they say in those American travelogue films, a truly unforgettable experience. The fare is the equivalent of two dollars for the 250 miles. So in order to make the venture pay for itself, the bus drivers pack the vehicles rammed tight. In a bus with sixty seats there were about one hundred and fifty passengers, together with chickens, some piglets, a goat and numerous squalling babies. The Dominicans are naturally happy people, very lively and talkative. The noise on the bus, from blaring radios and a hundred voices all shouting over the racket was unbelievable. Every human activity except actual coition and warfare went on in its confines, but now and again things got pretty close to them. Someone even lit up a tiny charcoal stove on the seat next to me—about five and a half passengers away—and cooked a rice meal. I had gradually shoved and jostled my way to a window seat. The scenery, out of the stuck-fast-open gap alongside my ear, was amazing. Sometimes we passed through deep tropical forests, where all the world was tinged green, including us, with the light filtering through the mighty growth overhead; sometimes we were riding over the crests of mountain ridges a couple of thousand feet above sea level, staring down at a sea of green jungle, or extensive rice paddies that faded away into the distant blue horizon. Every now and then passengers would dismount or board the bus. Their dwellings, way in the outback, were nothing more than sheets of tree bark nailed to a rough wooden frame. Through the open doorways, above the heads of, every time, a huge family waving, laughing, weeping or just looking plain overawed, could be seen the roughly-knocked-together furniture, a plain box or two, and swinging hammocks over an earth floor. On the road there was sparse traffic until the outskirts of the city. A few trucks, loaded with rice or people, and a few donkeys, each lugging away at a seeming ton of load with its owner perched, stiff-backed or slouched fast asleep, atop the load.

In Santo Domingo, at the central bus depot, an open square surrounded by ancient, tumbling tenements under a scorching sun, all was chaos. On each corner of the square squads of soldiers, armed and ready to fire, glared at the crowds passing by. Most of the soldiers seemed to be about sixteen years old. Often they stopped people and inspected papers, but I hobbled past them undisturbed, and found a small hotel nearby that did not look too expensive. By that time I was very tired after eight hours crushed up in the bus, so I took a shower (cold water, no soap) and lay down for a siesta. I made sure the door was locked, the one letting out into the corridor, but forgot to lock the shower window, which opened out on to an outside veranda. When I awoke I found that practically all the money I'd had in my wallet had disappeared. I had only about three dollars in change. There was no sign that anyone had been in the room, and I had made sure my money was all right when I paid the hotel in advance.

By this time there was the noise of firing in the streets. There were other explosions close by, which I later learned were caused by hand grenades being thrown into people's homes by the soldiers just in case there were rebels inside. After I remonstrated with the hotel owner, who of course disclaimed any knowledge of the theft, I hobbled out into the street. No sooner had I emerged from the door at the bottom of the mean stairs, when a fusillade of bullets whizzed overhead. I found myself falling backward, along with about a dozen other bodies, into the hotel lobby. I stayed there for an hour or so, until the firing died down—or faded away into another quarter of the city.

Soon I was able to make my way, past civilians cowering in shop doorways and soldiers menacing me with their machine-pistols, to the Plaza Colón. I knew some people there—waiters and shoeshine boys and so on—from previous, more peaceful visits. Sure enough, good old faithful Enrique, the old waiter in the Café España, was sturdily maintaining his station in the otherwise almost deserted restaurant. The outside window was shattered on one side, and several tables overturned, but otherwise all was normal, except for a few regular customers all crowded behind the bar for some sort of ethereal protection.

No sooner did I greet Enrique (as if a revolution was a routine thing and beneath a British sailor's notice) than he sent word off somewhere for Antonio. As I waited, I recalled Antonio as a small, skinny kid I used to buy sandwiches for to keep him alive another day, but when he at last turned up, grinning all over his black face, I found he'd grown into a much younger version of Idi Amin, and he looked just as tough.

Minutes later Antonio was off on his way to Santa Bárbara with a note to Wally to send some money for my next night's hotel room and my fare back to Santa Bárbara. It would take Antonio at least twenty-four hours to make the round trip. Meanwhile Enrique extended me credit to eat in the Café España until Antonio returned.

He came back next day, sure enough, with Ivan in tow, pale and shaken. They had been fired on in the bus and had made their way to the Plaza Colón through a hail of bullets around the bus station. Now the word was that another army division had arrived from the north and had cleared the area of town around the main square, but it was still impossible to get to the new city, where lay, half beseiged, the American Embassy. I decided that we should give up all ideas of trying to get Ivan a visa and hare off back to Santa Bárbara and the boat as soon as we could.

When we finally arrived, by a very devious route to dodge fighting, at the main square, the scene brought to mind the films of the evacuation of Saigon, except in this case the transport was not helicopters but buses. Crowds of people were fighting and screaming their way on to the half-dozen buses in the square. One policeman became excited and fired a few shots right into one crowd of desperate families. No one stirred to lift the bodies out of the way. The rush continued right over them.

Antonio said, "Come on, Captain, there's a window," and with that he lifted me bodily—he was still only sixteen or so—and thrust me straight into an open bus window, where I landed upside down right on the laps of two tearful matrons. At first they screamed their heads off until they saw my plastic leg staring at them, then they were all condolences and care, and righted me vertical between their knees. By that time both Antonio and Ivan had somehow clambered through the window and were sitting on the top of the back of the matrons' seat. In no time at all they had cleared a space on the luggage rack over the matrons' heads and stuffed me horizontally onto the rack. Farther down the bus there were at least thirty small kids and babies stuck on the luggage racks, and at my head were three pecking hens with their heads stuck out of a richly reeking sack. And there I stayed for eight hours, as the bus roared out of Santo Domingo, zoomed past three road blocks with bullets flying, and so out over the now rainy mountains, with about two hundred scowling men, weeping women and screaming kids, and me, back to peaceful, quiet, forgotten Santa Bárbara.

There, the port captain let Antonio stay on board that night and he slept in the netting of the ama vent. The following day, at dawn, after making sure Antonio had enough to live on for a few days, we took off for the safety of New York City. The port captain gave me a beautifully inscribed Certificate of Departure, as he worried about the welfare of his family in strife-torn Santo Domingo. I later planted a tree outside his office.

The events told in this tale are, I think, unusual. It was a matter of time and circumstances. Also of lack of communication between the capital and Santa Bárbara. Normally sailors can expect a wonderful welcome in the Dominican Republic, cheap prices for victuals of all kinds, and a happy-go-lucky friendly people and easygoing officials. For those with language problems, there need be no hesitation about visiting Santa Bárbara. Many of the locals are descended from slaves who escaped from the USA and were shipwrecked in the Gulf of Samaná. They were completely isolated for over fifty years until discovered in the latter part of the last century by explorers. The English language remained pure and unsullied among those people, and their descendants are mostly fluent in both Spanish and English still. In fact, their English is, for the most part, more pure and distinct than that spoken on most of the West Indies islands, which were formally British. As a port of call, Santa Bárbara is thoroughly recommended for short stays at anchor, but not in the hurricane season as it is wide open to the east.

28

The Big Apple

Oh, now we are bound for old New York town,
Tiddey Hi Ho, Hi Hey,
Goodbye to them black gals, the yellows and
   browns,
Tiddey Hi Ho Hi Hey!

Oh, old Sally Rackett of Kingston Town,
I spent quite a packet on her new silk gown.

We loaded our packet with sugar and rum,
Goodbye to Jamaica, its gals and its sun.

We're bound to the nor'ard, its ice and its snow,
We're bound to the nor'ard, oh, Lord let her go!

And when we get back to old New York town,
'Tis there we will drink and our sorrows soon drown.

"Tiddey Hi Ho!" A halyard shanty, early nineteenth
century, of Caribbean origin

I had wanted to be in New York City for my sixtieth birthday. I don't
know why. Perhaps it was because in New York, two years earlier, I had
thought I'd never see my sixtieth birthday. As it was, the futile search
for a visa for Ivan, together with the political events in the Dominican
Republic, had delayed my voyaging itinerary somewhat. I'd intended to
sail direct for New York from Santa Bárbara on the thirtieth of April.
As it was, it was the second of May when we left the Weeping mountains of Hispaniola astern of us and shoved off on the twelve-hundred-
mile leg to New York.

If you look at the chart you will see that this direct sail took us straight
slap-bang through the very center of the so-called Devil's Triangle at
its longest extent, right from the base to the apex almost. For those

who still believe in little green men and things that go bump in the night, I can tell you that this sea area holds no fears over and above those we already encounter in the ocean. It all boils down to Jones's Law on Accidents at Sea: *The more people there are in any given sea area (or any other area, come to that), the more fools there will be as a percentage of the total, and therefore the more accidents there will be within that given area.* What exists is a tropical weather area carried north by the Gulf Stream's warm waters, impinging on a temperate weather area—the westerly winds from over the North American continent. A moment's sensible thought about the result of these climates clashing will render conclusions about the type of phenomena to be expected: sudden wind-and-rain squalls, with swiftly increasing local winds, sudden variations in barometric pressure, long, thin, "fingers" of swift current flowing between the steadier streams, and so on. There is nothing supernatural about these effects. The only real wonder about the Devil's Triangle is the number of novices who tackle that ocean area without bothering to learn anything at all about the conditions they are likely to encounter.

As it was, *Outward Leg* made the twelve-hundred-mile passage in ten days—and that was despite four days of dead flat calm in the very center of the notorious (mistakenly so) Devil's Triangle. It was so calm that if you had had floating balls, you could have played billiards on the ocean. It was so calm and peaceful that we could motor around sleeping whales only feet away from them. It was so calm that to counter the boredom I read my way through Boswell's *Life of Johnson* for the fifth time and still found myself twiddling my thumbs half the time. That lasted only until the electric steering motor gave up. Then it was back under the tyranny of the tiller.

One thing livened up this passage in its first stages, before we met the stormy weather off Cape Hatteras. Wally had taken the sat-nav antenna to bits in Santa Bárbara while I was away from the boat. This was because he had found corrosion on the bottom of the antenna mounting. It was understandable enough in his case. But my rule is: Always leave well enough alone when you are in remote places. If it works, leave it. Don't mess with it until you are back in so-called civilization. As it was, we went on to celestial navigation for the whole leg, and I showed Wally through the maze of calculations (as it seemed to us, after several months of being spoiled by the sat-nav) for noon sights, sights over the meridian, sights antemeridian, sights postmeridian, moon, star and planet sights and so on. Our standby sextant is a plastic Davis model, with an intrinsic error. I worked out an error on its scale of fifteen minutes, but once I knew that, we got pretty good results, and by the time we sighted the coast of North America off Atlantic City, New Jersey, Wally was getting a line of position no more than five miles off the true line. This might have had something to do with his decision to leave the boat in New York City. But youngsters, I suppose, find it very difficult to see what matters and what really doesn't.

Ivan had already told me, as soon as we got within earshot of U.S. radio stations, that he would be leaving the voyage. He had family problems of some sort back in Spain, so that was understandable enough.

The first of my erstwhile crew to disappear in New York was Ms. Brimstone, the cat. Next was Wally. He was an amateur undersea diver and thought that helping at a diving museum in New York was more attractive than more bouncing around the oceans in *Outward Leg*. I can't say that I blame him, but I would have appreciated a little more notice than I had. Here today and gone tomorrow is not exactly fair on such an immensely difficult project as the one we were engaged on. Besides, *Outward Leg* is only once in each place she visits on this voyage; the diving museum will, I presume, perhaps still be there in five years' time. Who knows?

As it was, soon after we entered New York Harbor through the Verrazano Channel and went to anchor stern to at the South Street Seaport, Wally disappeared and left me to fend for myself—on one leg, at a very difficult berth, with ladders to climb, and much gear to arrange and obtain, in a huge, thoughtless city—with the help, for a week or two, of an inexperienced, although loyal, Spaniard with hardly any English. A moment or two of thought by anyone who knows what was going on at the South Street Seaport—with piledrivers banging away, and chaos all around; the broken-down jetty I had to clamber over in the humid heat; the distance to the nearest telephone or the nearest taxi-halt; and the plain cussedness of New York City—will show what obstacles and frustrations I had to overcome. Anyone who knows the character of New York City—its uncaring eternal chase after the buck—will appreciate, I think, the difficulty of even finding a replacement crew there, let alone signing one on. When we arrived in New York I had exactly twenty dollars on board.

The skin damage under the wings had to be repaired. The engine oil had to be changed. Repairs had to be made to some mainsail seams. There were leaks in the netting fixtures to the main hull, caused by heavy hammering, that needed fixing. The underside needed cleaning. The log, the Weatherfax and the electric self-steerer all had to be dismounted and despatched to the manufacturers for repair and return. The rigging needed inspection and refurbishing where necessary. There were the thousand and one things to do that are generally needed when a vessel has covered ten thousand miles of hard going for the most part.

I had to earn enough, and quickly, to keep the voyage under way. In my role as an author, I had to make attempts to see my publishers and my agent and to attend functions and meet readers wherever I could. I also had to complete accounts of incidents and technical reports to date. On top of this I had to provide for Ivan, and keep both of us alive until he departed for Spain. Fortunately, Ivan promised that he would not abandon me until someone else turned up to take his place. For that I can never thank him enough. Earl Grey was right when he said that the Spaniards were "the last race of gentlemen."

But nature holds a balance, and in this instance she provided good friends for me at the North Star pub, just outside the gates of the South Street Seaport. There Devan Black, a Welsh American and one of the owners, arranged to take phone calls for me, and Steve the barman offered his help and his wheels when they might be needed. For three weeks the only things that kept the voyage alive were the encouragement and help of the North Star pub people, the assistance in obtaining some money quickly by Richard Curtis, my literary agent, and the help and moral encouragement of Joe Gribbins, the editor of *Nautical Quarterly*. Otherwise I might just as well have been in the middle of the Gobi Desert for all anyone else cared. Sure, people gathered around me and the boat to bask in, I suppose, reflected glory, but very, very few offered any kind of practical assistance. This was even more marked after Ivan had to leave me on the illness of his brother.

Anyway, it was no good moping, so I set to and planned the transatlantic passage. I found a scratch crew eventually and sailed the boat up to Glen Cove, in Long Island, where I knew there was a wall we could lean her against at low tide to clean the hull bottoms and fix the skin damage. We had a fine welcome from the Glen Cove Yacht Club members, and they mainly left us in peace to get on with the job, which we completed over one tide, working from dawn to dusk, as well as chasing around ashore for gear and materials. Then we headed back to the South Street Seaport, past the end-on canyons between the skyscrapers of midtown Manhattan.

Representatives of a British brewery company, eager to promote its beer in the USA, came on board. They brought three of their T-shirts with them, and promised three cases of their brew for the ocean voyage. Could they take photographs of myself and my crew, wearing the

T-shirts in New York, on our departure? They promised me a free berth alongside one of their riverside pubs when I reached London. As he looked around him, the representative obviously found it incredible that we would ever reach London.

I told them a big fat *No!* But if they liked to do it on our arrival in London, and if they provided a berth, then I would be only too willing. When would I arrive? the representative asked me, as if I were traveling by jumbo jet, as if there were no such things as gales, storms, calms, collisions, whales, gear failure, capsizes, fogs or groundings.

I thought for a few minutes, while he fidgeted with his briefcase. Then I told him, loud and clear, as Terry, a new crewman, listened, obviously fascinated, *"The thirty-first of August, at high tide in the afternoon."*

When the representative of the British brewery company left the boat, I felt a sort of misgiving. I felt as if I had, perhaps, given a part of myself away. Not exactly sold it, mind you. I mean, three cases of beer, three T-shirts and perhaps a berth in London isn't exactly what you might call Sinatra-standard recompense, but I still had this uncomfortable feeling and realized what it must be like, for anyone at all sensitive, to have to solicit sponsors. From what I could see and feel, these people had no more idea than the man in the moon as to what is involved in any kind of serious ocean voyaging. It only confirmed my previous opinion that in the main they are a menace to the continued existence of impressionable young dreamers.

But still, a free berth, even if it was only for a couple of weeks, would help me out enormously while I finished my book and planned the continuing voyage through Europe on my way east around the world—and after all, I didn't have to drink their beer. . . . By the time I'd paid for all the charts, food, fuel and odds and ends in New York, I was down to about $350. That was the bottom of the barrel, except for what bit of naval pension was lurking in my London bank account.

The scratch crew, three of them, were taken on a trial basis, to see how they would work out on the trip to Glen Cove and back. One of them, a native New Yorker, as soon as we weighed the anchor and set off upstream on the East River, lounged back in the netting and sunbathed all the way to Glen Cove. There, although it was obvious to any sailor's eye that he was an almost complete novice, he shouted orders at the other novice on board and in general gave him a bad time. It was the same on the return downstream. Then, back in South Street, he was missing ashore half the time.

The night before we sailed for Newport I told the Lounger that I didn't really think he was ready yet for an ocean crossing in a small craft, and gave him a hundred of my hard-earned and scarce dollars for his time and trouble of two days' work. That was in the North Star pub. He rushed out of the pub and down to the boat, waving a knife. Luckily we were alongside the very ocean-worthy sail craft *Sumunu* and their deck watch managed to restrain the knife wielder and coax him ashore, where the dock police quickly hustled him out of the gate. Outside the fence, he stamped up and down for a couple of hours, shouting and waving his fist, and only confirmed what I had suspected soon after he joined the boat: His open stare into the eyes of whomever he was conversing with was a mite too open, his anxious agreement with any statement was a little too anxious, his blustering in front of any audience, especially a female one, was too obvious. I thanked my lucky stars that he had shown his true nature in port and not in midocean. It only goes to prove that you must try out anyone for crew and get to know them fairly well before you set sail on any long-distance passage.

The new crew were now Terry Johansen, a New Yorker of Norwegian extraction, twenty-eight years of age, with no previous sailing experience. He had been a Russian history student in New York but lately had worked as a cook's assistant. He was of a helpful disposition, he obviously knew how to talk with people, and he could cook after a fashion then. His cooking has improved immensely in the three months he has been with me. The other crewman, for the transatlantic passage only, was Pat Quinn, a male nurse from Virginia. I had heard of him from the first mate of the *Sumunu,* and he turned out to be a good, ingenious hand, with plenty of energy. Pat has his own boat in Virginia, a twenty-six-foot sloop. He was also twenty-eight years old, and recently married.

So the situation on board *Outward Leg* when she set off to cross the North Atlantic via Newport and the Azores was that there was one semi-experienced hand with one trip to Bermuda in a monohull under his belt, one complete novice, and one cripple. Here was an acid test, indeed, of the dependability of a multihull vessel for ease of sailing and for a forgiving nature.

There was no fuss or palaver when we slid out of New York in forenoon of the seventeenth of July. To see us off, quietly, there was only the crew of *Sumunu* and Devan Black from the North Star pub. That suited me down to the ground. Play the bugles when the voyage is done, I always say. I was content to have managed to get back and to have replaced the log, the Weatherfax, and the electric self-steerer;

to have repaired the skin damage, to have cleaned the bottom, and to have replaced my "irreplaceable" crew. I was not sorry in the least to see the skyscrapers of Manhattan sinking lower on the western horizon as a skittered wing and wing along the north shore of Long Island. If that sounds a bit different from my paeans to the city at the start of this book, so be it. There was still tremendous hurt in me, brought about by the plain unthinking callousness of New York City. But I was determined, as we picked up speed and were cheered by other sail craft, to make the rest of this voyage a success, come what may, no matter what the difficulties might be that I would have to overcome to do it.

In fact the ambience on board *Outward Leg* was now, if anything, better than before; there was none of the silent, and sometimes vociferous, resentment that had been the general rule previously, whenever I had insisted on things being done my way. Now, with two new lads on board, my way was the only way, and so we had no mistakes and very few errors in the setting up of gear or in the settling down of the boat to her new crew and to her new passage across the western ocean. As the miles reeled by, through the sunshine and rain of Long Island Sound, and the fog of Block Island Passage, so I felt happier by the hour, and by the time Newport hove into view, in the dusk, I was positively singing at the wheel. I knew my crew were not very experienced, and not at all in multihull sailing, but on the other hand they were lively, pleasant company, and I was content that to a great degree I could depend on them to do their allotted tasks. It works both ways: a dependable crew means a happy skipper means a happy boat means a happy crew means a dependable crew.

The first evening in Newport we went to a mooring buoy. It's much cheaper, of course, than being alongside. Newport, the queen of the yachting centers in the States, couldn't care less where you go. She doesn't even care if you are there. She seems to think that if you are there, then it's only because you want to be, and can afford to be. She doesn't give a rap whether you are or not, because she can do very well indeed without you, whoever you are, no matter how much money you have. If you don't like Newport (and I do) then you can lump it or go away.

The next morning I went alongside the Newport Yachting Center pontoon. I thought it would be more convenient for the editor of a certain yachting magazine to come and chat. I'd sent a message that I was anxious to see him, but would find it difficult to get to his office—you must, it seems, walk a mile to get a taxi. But he must have been very busy as he didn't show up. Many of his (and my) readers showed up, mind, and I signed a lot of books. So perhaps it was worth paying exactly half the amount of dollars I had left in the world to stay alongside. For the curious, it was $130 for three days and nights. Actually, it was a little over half of my worldly fortune; the exact amount of money now on board was just $115. That, I would need to revictual the boat in the Azores with fresh food. It wouldn't leave much for the arrival in England, but then I'd left that country in my own craft last in 1964, with only five pounds of potatoes and seventeen shillings on board, so I hadn't lost much. Come to think of it, at the rate of inflation, I might return with about the same as I left. And a bit more, I thought wistfully, as I arranged the one copy of each of my ten books on their shelf, along with Conrad and Kipling, Shakespeare and Gerbault . . . just a bit more, as I sang out "goodnight" to Terry and Pat up forward in the "ghetto," and dismissed from my mind the thought of the three-thousand-mile ocean crossing ahead of us. I had to be in London by the thirty-first of August—the brewery company had a free berth waiting.

29

Across the Western Ocean

Oh, the times are hard and the wages low,
Amelia, where you bound to?
The Western Ocean is my home,
Across the Western Ocean!

A land of promise there you'll see,
I'm bound away across the sea.

To Liverpool I'll make my way,
To Liverpool that packet school.

There's London Pat with his tarpaulin hat,
And Frisco Jim the packet rat,

Beware them packet ships I pray,
They'll steal your gear and clothes away.

We are bound away from friends and home,
We're bound away to seek for gold,

Mothers and sweethearts don't you cry,
Sisters and brothers say goodbye.

"Across the Western Ocean." A brake-
pump shanty. *Packet* meant a sailing ship
that sailed between regular ports, usually
Liverpool and ports on the eastern seaboard
of North America.

The wooden dinghy that had been given to *Outward Leg* way back in
Curaçao weighed at least one hundred pounds. That was too much excess baggage, really, to have sitting out over one of the wing decks. It
was too late to try to sell it, so I donated it to a local organization in

Newport called Shake-a-Leg, which encourages and trains limbless youngsters in dinghy sailing. I would be dinghyless on our arrival in Europe, but God is good and looks after His own, so maybe He'd provide for Terry and Pat. I wasn't so sure about His view of me.

That was minutes before we sailed. There were very few people at the jetty—and I wouldn't have wanted it otherwise—just my good friend Henry Wagner of Sailor's Bookshelf in New Jersey, with whom I've shared many a hamburger and a beer in some of the most unlikely places in the USA, and his family. There are certain doubts that rankle your mind when setting on a transoceanic voyage at the start of the hurricane season with an almost untried crew, so I arranged that if I did not contact Henry before the twenty-fifth of August, he would call the Coast Guard in New York and inform them that something untoward might have happened to us. It was now the twenty-second of July. We were cutting it a bit fine. The hurricane incidence increases greatly at the end of July. But I had been severely delayed in New York by Wally's taking off and the search for a new crew, so there was no helping it. Care is needed in selecting shipmates. No one should take off into the blue with any Tom, Dick or Harry.

A last visit to the supermarket in Newport provided fresh bread (rye is the best keeping), apples (Granny Smiths—ours lasted until England), cabbages, carrots and forty pounds of Nevada potatoes (without doubt the best anywhere). And onions, too: nutritious, sustaining and tasty, cooked or raw. A last-minute recall to buy gas cigarette lighters, and we were off. There was very little wind, but it doesn't do to keep friends with their hands half hovering to wave farewell standing on a hot jetty, so on went the plonker and off motored we.

I was surprised to find that when we reached the offing we were approached and accompanied out for some distance by several other yachts, and very pleased indeed to see that they were all monohulls. Of course, once we got a breeze we could have walked away from them, but courtesy demanded restraint, so we held back and kept pace with the others until they tired of waving, and one by one, toward late afternoon, they dropped away, still waving, and headed back in to Newport.

Of course, as we had carefully checked all the rigging, sails and reefing gear, greased all the winches, reversed all the sheets and halyards and generally gone over the sailing gear like mother monkeys picking nits, the wind, for the first twenty-four hours, wafted weak and parsimonious. Had we just shoved off (as many landsmen seem to think we do) without a care in the world, it would probably have blown a gale and from the east, too. As it was, we motored with all working sail up out past Martha's Vineyard and an island that we hardly glimpsed in the night, with the curious name of No Mans Land.

It was back to my own chart and studying the distance between Newport and Horta, in the Azores—two thousand miles more or less. I might have taken the Great Circle Route, which would trim off about fifty miles from the distance, but we had just come up from the tropics—in my case the "official" tropics, in my crew's cases from New York and Virginia, which can both be said to be well and truly in the tropics, climatewise, in summer. In New York, probably even more tropical than the tropics. Walking through the streets there, in search of butane gas, had been like hobbling through a bath of warm engine-lubricating oil. I'd had to search for that, too, to no avail. We finally found the right type in Glen Cove.

Mentioning butane gas, on the second day out of Newport, one of the cylinders, filled in New York only a week before, expired its last whiff; on the sixth day out the second cylinder, also filled in New York, also emptied itself. They were supposed to last for at least three weeks each. Previously they had done so. It was obvious that we had been shortchanged in the Big Apple. Now we were left with one remaining cylinder, thank goodness, filled in Puerto Rico by an honest man, and a small emergency paraffin stove, which I carry for this very purpose.

By noon of the second day out we had covered only seventy-two miles. This was because I ran the engine at an economical speed, to cosset our diesel oil in case of later calms. Now we were on Georges Bank—and sure enough, down came the fog. At the same time the wind increased to fifteen knots or so, and we spent the next three days in a swirling mist, straining our eyes, day and night, for other vessels. This is a bit nerve-racking. If you're making six knots and a trawler is making ten, your combined speed is sixteen knots toward each other. That doesn't give much time for avoiding action when the visibility is down to ten yards or so.

But, on the other hand, you can carry only so much food and water, and fuel, too. You can't hang about on Georges Bank waiting for the fog to go away—it might last weeks. You simply have to push your way through the fog and get over the banks, and so into the deep ocean water of the Gulf Stream, where the wind is brisk and the air clear. Leaving New England, fog is an almost ever-present hazard, and the risk of maintaining way through it has to be taken. The only thing for it, of course, is strict lookout discipline. This is where single-handers come unstuck. They simply cannot keep a continual lookout for two or three days.

In *Outward Leg* I had a Watchman radar alarm fitted, which is supposed to give warning whenever the signals from a radar set, i.e., another vessel, pass through it. But our particular unit has a strong imagination, and even in clear, brilliant weather with never a ship in sight, it insisted on giving off burps and bleeps almost continually. When the flourescent lights were switched on, it went into transports of panic, practically playing the "Flight of the Bumble Bee" in electronic bleeps. The boat started to sound a bit like a Broadway slot-machine arcade. I switched it off soon after leaving San Diego. Every now and again some member of the electronic generation takes an interest in Beeping Bertie, as I call it, and fiddles around with it to make it operate correctly. Then it stays dead quiet for an hour or two and the new crewman smiles quietly in self-congratulation. But I know that Bertie is just waiting for him to be lulled into complacency, and sure enough, just as the fixer shifts his attention to something else, Bertie first gives a low whistle, then a bleep, then a hiccup, and then he's off, sounding a bit like a scared hen. In England I am determined to send Bertie to his makers for an appendectomy or tonsillectomy. But I'll bet that before we get more than twenty miles out in the next ocean he'll start his nonsense again. And this is the type of gear that the single-handed racers depend on to give them notice of ships in their vicinity, while they take a nap. A dog's a thousand times more dependable, and a Labrador especially. And they don't bleep. Well, maybe Pekinese, but not real dogs.

On the morning of the twenty-fourth of July—early morning; gales are no respecters of late sleepers—here it came, a full gale from the west. It was a precocious gale, a sudden gale, a playful gale, but it was a friendly gale, which swooped down on us shouting "GOING MY WAY?," made us dash for the headsail rolling gear and rut one reef in the mainsail, then carefully unroll the headsail again one third of its area, as the gale shoved us, hard, in the general direction of the Azores. At first, in a calmish sea, we were simply barreling along, at about ten knots steady, but as the seas set up we were soon surfing. Then the speed varied between about six knots in the troughs to sixteen on the waves as a sea picked up the ship and heaved her forward. I had only a rough guess at speed—our electronic log had packed up just after the land had dropped astern on the first day out.

I'd forseen this failure of the log, and carried a dinghy log, one of those plastic pipes where the end is shoved into the sea and water mounts the pipe and so gives you a rough estimate of speed through the water. But that registers only up to nine knots, so at speeds above that, it was all pure guesswork at first, until, after staring over the side and the stern a thousand times, it became an educated guess crossed with a calculating instinct. So much, up to now, for electronic logs. But give them their due, they do look terribly impressive on the cockpit bulkhead when the boat's sitting alongside in harbor.

Both Terry and Pat must have used that dinghy log, hanging over the side of the amas, hanging on for dear life, at least a thousand times. But at low speeds, under nine knots, it was more accurate, I found, than the chip log, where someone throws a piece of wood or garbage over the side and someone else times the travel to the stern, etc. That was fair enough for speeds over ten knots, but even then it was very rough measurement.

The sat-nav was handy for (suspiciously) confirming my position, but often in mid-Atlantic there were several hours between any kind of fix, and in many cases the fix was very wild off the mark, with no sign that it was a "duff" until, sooner or later, a fix would pop up and confirm my own reckoning. No one should trust a sat-nav too much until the day comes when we can get a continual fix. Then any error will be immediately obvious. Even greater care must be taken when coasting with a sat-nav, or you'll find yourself, in short order, banging into real estate.

Our Weatherfax machine worked beautifully all the way to the Azores, and I had a good view of the weather in the Atlantic, Indian Ocean and the Pacific, too. But in general, the Fax forecasts and analyses are far too general to be of much use. Local disturbances are hardly obvious. You can be, as we were, in a gale for a whole day, and the charts show no sign of it. I didn't complain, though. The first gale shoved us 185 miles on our way in twenty-four hours. That's an average speed of almost eight knots.

That's not bad for a very heavily loaded thirty-six-foot vessel. The payload at the start of the leg from Newport was around four tons. During the first gale I saw no sign of any tendency to broach, even though the seas were up to a good twenty feet from trough to crest. The Aries wind vane, with the boat slowed down under reefed main and one-third headsail, steered her within ten degrees each side of the course, and there was no hand steering at any time.

As the wind diminished on the twenty-fifth, I determined that when the boat was a little lighter—when we had used up some of our food, water and fuel supplies—I would put *Outward Leg*, for her first time, through what I consider the acid test for any craft: keep her running in a gale with all working sail up. In our case, that was the only way in which the cool-tubes could be really tested in a way that meant anything. I said nothing of this to the crew, because it would have given them time to think about it and perhaps object after some reflection, and always, to me, the happiness of my lads is a primary object. Least said, soonest mended, or, softly, softly, catchee monkee.

After the gale subsided, for twenty-four hours, we were under genniker and full main, with the wind in the northeast, haring along at about seven knots. By now both the lads were getting into their stride. Our watch system worked. It was the old Baltic watch bill, which goes, for three men, like this:

0800–noon   Skipper. So he can meet the morning weather and take morning and noon sights.
Noon–1600   Mate (Pat Quinn). So he can sail in the (usually) worked-up afternoon wind, and take the afternoon sights. He clears up midday meal.
1600–1800   Cook (Terry Johansen). He can cook supper in his watch.
1800–2000   Skipper. He can meet the night weather.
2000–2200   Cook. Usually a quiet, steady watch.
2200–2359   Skipper. Ditto
2359–0400   Mate. Weather change may come late in this watch.
0400–0800   Cook. Weather usually firm. He cooks breakfast and prepares midday meal.

A lot of people ask if watches need to be kept outside the ocean shipping lanes. The answer to that is, if there are the people to keep them, by all means, yes. We sighted six ships "outside" the lanes during nights. Also—and an important point—if three men are keeping night watches, then they must catch up on sleep during the day, and that means that they tend to keep out of each other's way much more than they would otherwise; at least one will be turned in at any one time, except during meals. This makes for a more "roomy" boat, and it means that everyone gets a change of company at regular intervals. In larger vessels, with perhaps martinet skippers, it prevents, to a great extent, "mutterings forward."

The tape cassette is played, when we are out of radio range, for only one hour a day. This serves two purposes: It saves battery power and it means that the selection is much "fresher" than if the thing were playing for long stretches. In *Outward Leg*, we play two pop tapes and two classical tapes per day, usually during "happy hour" (1700–1800). This serves two purposes: It makes the skipper thank God he's not younger, and it makes the crew turn off their speaker when it's the skipper's turn, and so makes for a quieter boat.

The next gale caught up with us on the twenty-seventh of July, in the skipper's watch, at 2300. (That's why the Baltic watch bill is the best for three people.) By early dawn it was blowing a stinker, and by forenoon up to a good thirty-five knots with mounting seas. I did not sleep that night, as here I made my running trial of the cool-tubes and the rig under all plain sail. The Aries vane gear, too. I just let her go, with all the mainsail up, the staysail and all the roller headsail. The wind was in the west-southwest, and by the forenoon it was gusting over forty-five knots. Still I kept all hoisted. While the other lads were on watch in the cockpit, I kept bobbing up from the after cabin where, most of the night and the next day, I listened to the roar of the sea catching up and rushing past our stern, and the alternate silence, the hovering pause, just before she was picked up, grabbed by some great growler and rushed forward, surfing at over twenty knots, with the Yanmar propeller, below the hull, screaming as it whizzed in the breathless forward motion. Then, as I bit my fingernails down to the elbows, sitting on the typist's chair below before my desk, I felt the hover, the silence, then the roar and the thrust. My chair would be moved a foot or so each time forward; then, when she slowed down again and pitched to await the next huge sea, the chair slid back a foot against the lockers. So it went on, for thirty hours. All the time I could see, in my mind's eye, the three hundred feet of drag warp stowed under the wing decks, and the emergency full-size parachute, and the smaller sea anchor, and in my memory inspected them all closely again and again, forever tempted to call it a day and order the sails to be shortened, but always telling myself to hold on. *Outward Leg* must be *proved* to be the safest, surest vessel afloat. It's no good merely saying it. It has to be proved, and this was the only way to do it. But even with two hands on board, it was a very lonely, frightening experience for me, as I sat quiet in the eerie red glow of my cabin lamp. They had neither of them ever sailed in a multihull. I knew that they imagined that this terrific speed, these panicky surges, these breathless pauses, were all part and parcel of the techniques, heretofore, of sailing multihulls. It was, in a way, a deception on my part, but on the other hand, I had versed them thoroughly in the procedures in the event of a capsize: that no one should attempt to get out of the boat—they were safer inside than out; that if they were on watch in the cockpit when she went over, they should somehow, anyhow, scramble inside the boat, and seek trapped air. The inside escape hatch had a screwdriver lashed under it, so if anyone was trapped outside the vessel, on the bottom of the hulls, he could open the hatch and get inside. The hammocks were ready for slinging in the air space of the boat's upturned bottom if she went over. The life-raft drill had been gone over time and again: that it should, under no circumstances, be cast free of the boat; that it was intended merely as a dry place to rest and sleep until the time came to right the vessel again and as a second point from which to fly a radar-reflecting balloon. All three of us knew how to get the emergency stove, in the trapped-air space, into operation, and how to get to food and first-aid gear and, above all, fresh water, if she did go over. We all knew exactly where the ringbolt on the bottom of the keel was, so that a lifeline could be secured to it in case we should have to move about on the bottom of *Outward Leg*. We all knew where the EPIRB (the Emergency Position Indicating Radio Beacon) was stowed, and how to get it into action, so that passing ships or planes might be alerted to our situation. But we also knew that if the worst happened and she did go over, there would be no "rescue" by ships, except in the direst emergency. We would wait, and for the first time in history, we hoped, self-right the vessel ourselves and then, with God's grace, navigate her somehow into the nearest port, wherever that might be. We also knew where the matches, candles, flashlights, safety pins, splints, vitamin tablets were, and where everything else was, exactly. So the next time anyone imagines that we take off into the blue without a care in the world, they'd better think twice.

The gale, the testing gale, lasted until the forenoon of the twenty-ninth of July. During it, we covered, according to the sat-nav and to my own reckoning, 223 miles. That was an average speed of nine and a quarter knots. The Aries steered the boat, with some small help from the helmsman to help her stay true, within fifteen degrees of our course—due east, true.

When the wind piped down a touch or two and we inspected the rig, we found that the mainsail (of course, as expected) had come apart for a foot or so along five different seams, and at the head was flapping about like a leaf in a gale. But otherwise all was well. The masthead blocks for the headsails, which had been my main concern, had held well and true. All the running gear was sound. We had taken in hardly any water at all through the hatches—a mere six buckets or so. We waited until the wind dropped to twenty-five knots, then handed the main and, in slashing rain, repaired the seams, putting in great half-inch mailbag stitches all along the parted seams and a bit to spare either side of the tear. Then we rehoisted the main at teatime, and again, let her go! All the time this was being done the twin headsails were swung out, wing and wing on the running poles, and the boat was running dead downwind, reducing the breeze, with her speed, to about fifteen knots. We all got a good soaking, but when fresh water is not available at the turn of the tap, rain provides a good shower. It may be a bit cold, but it also washes the clothes you're wearing, and a bit of late afternoon sunshine soon dries them off. Full laundry service in the ocean!

We were now halfway to the island of Flores, in the Azores, where Sir Richard Grenville in *Revenge* had taken on the whole of the Spanish fleet and finally blown up his own ship and all her crew after sinking many of the enemy. But I did not intend to call at Flores. Instead I wanted to make direct for Horta, where I had old friends, and also I wished to get to England and London as soon as possible, to restock, if possible, my almost empty coffers. I was down to just over one hundred dollars. The free berth from the brewery company looked even more attractive.

There was another reason for heading as soon as could be for London; I wanted to look into an idea I'd first had in New York: of including in my east-about circumnavigation of the world the first-ever crossing of Europe via the Rhine and the Danube by an ocean-going vessel.

As the Azores approached us, nearer and nearer each day, we were all happy but I was, I think, the most content. Now I knew that *Outward Leg* was what I had believed her to be: the first of a new breed of fast, safe, comfortable, easy, all-round ocean-cruising vessels.

I am not saying that anyone else should do what I did, and try their vessel beyond the ultimate seamanlike expectations. But I did what I had to do: I tried her so others would feel more safe and confident—especially those with youngsters on board in the future.

30

Old Friends, New Faces

We've ploughed the whole world over
And soon we'll be off Dover.
Ranzo, Ranzo, away, away!
We've ploughed the wide world over
Like a proper deep-sea rover,
Hilo Ranzo, away!

I'm shantyman of the Wild Goose nation,
Got a maid that I left on the old plantation!

From "Ranzo Ray," halyard shanty, early
nineteenth century

What can be written about the facts of ocean sailing that has not already been written? That the days passed, one after the other all too quickly? That books brought on board at Newport remained unread while I read again my old favorites like tales from Conrad and yet another account of the *Bounty* mutiny? That I never tired of looking at the changing faces of the sky and the sea? That, no matter what the vessel, life at sea is never as easy as it is ashore, that no matter what the type of vessel, she will still be thrown around, that every movement, and especially by me, has to be made with care? That I am always holding on, or braced between two objects, or wedged in a position where it is impossible to be flung by a sudden lurch of the boat as she slides off a sea? That on calmer days the gods that rule the sea tried to make up for past hardships when the gentle trade wind caressed our sails as we slipped mile after mile over a lazy ocean? That most of the days were blue, with white, fleeting clouds; that most of the nights were unforgettably lovely, with a crescent moon at first and weird flickering phosphorescent lights on the horizon? That one night, with a gentle thud *Outward Leg* touched some great fish—a sleeping whale perhaps? That nights in the after cabin were cozy, with the warm golden light of the oil lamp glowing on the chart of the North Atlantic Ocean, on which the thin penciled line drew inexorably closer and closer to the tiny dots that were the islands of Flores and Faial? That sometimes there was a fine drizzle of rain at night, and then we would curse softly as the wind played with us gustily, and kept us from our warm sleeping bags? That often in my sleep I was aware of increasing wind and sea, so that it is difficult for me to know whether I was asleep or not? That on odd days we held a sailor's holiday if the weather was fine, and aired our clothing and bedding on deck, so that the ship looked like an old-clothes shop rolling over the North Atlantic Ocean? That sometimes, in calmer weather, the bubbles around the bows reflected a perfect image of the ship sailing, in every detail?

But all these things are part of the poetry of the sea, something of the song of the oceans, and I cannot easily imagine that there is anyone alive who does not know them by heart, and can only feel the deepest sorrow for anyone who does not know what it is to be truly a part of the universe and pure, naked lovely Nature in all its wildness and grandeur.

Most days there was fair weather, with a clean salt tang, taut straining sails and clear blue water falling away in the sunlight. For Terry it was his first-ever taste and feel of the charm of the sea and often he would be seen hanging his head over the stern to watch the water swirl by the rudder—that crystal clear, translucent water of deep sparkling blue that can be found only under the stern of a sailing ship well out at sea.

Pat sometimes climbed to the lower stay tangs on the mast, where he sat with the wind all about him around the mast and could feel the jerky motion and stiff pull of the sails when every rope and stay was working and alive and full of life. Or lying on the bow of the starboard ama, Terry would watch the dark waves flash by and see the wedges of our bows saw their way through the seas, tossing them aside gently.

At the wheel sometimes, with the Aries laid off for an hour, the kick and pull of each wave and puff of wind kept us enthralled. Always changing, always alive. Then the helmsman was complete monarch of all he surveyed, from horizon to horizon, over the sea and across the moving sky; he could ease her, push her, put her up for this wave, and off for that one. Sailors sometimes talk of how they hate wheel-steering by hand, but on an ideal day with a stiff breeze and a lively sea, not even I could help sitting up and feeling every little kick of the wheel.

One by one the days passed; we had got into regular and comfortable weather in the westerlies, and into that routine of sea life that is broken only by storms, sightings of ships, and landfalls.

In the mornings she went easy, as the seas were easy, and aft we left a long bubbling wake, but after the sun came up the wind awoke from his doze and soon we were setting up cockscombs from both the ama sterns. Sometimes, not often, it rained. Then large splashes, in the rare calms, dropped on our faces and woke us from our doze on deck. At first we dreamed that we dreamed of them, and nodded off again, or tried to. They became more and more insistent, and we would curse softly and seek shelter in the after cabin or the galley. A frenzied argument with the ensuing squall would follow, and then the wind would relent and all be steady again for hour after hour.

My first appearance on deck in the morning was generally an occasion of repressed grumpiness mitigated by a keen interest in my immediate surroundings and everything concerning the boat's sailing. I would glance around and aloft to determine the present and future state of the sea. I would question Terry regarding the course and the speed he guessed we had made during the morning watch; then a cigarette smoked in the lee of the after-cabin hatch and smoked with deep inhalations, a perfunctory application of a little fresh water to face and salt water to teeth— all these things were necessary before I could feel myself to be the human equal to Terry, who had kept watch while I slept. His inevitable superiority was felt each morning, for about three minutes, until I was fully awake; then I was skipper again.

After the testing gale, the remaining passages of the transatlantic voyage in gale-force winds were a bit anticlimatic. I have no doubt that the average person would have felt, in the gale of the second of August, that he was having the shit shaken out of him, as *Outward Leg* rafted and rolled, then screeched forward, all her three hulls cutting through the seas ahead like sharp knives through soft cheese as we raced on a broad reach with a southwesterly wind. By now, however, all our crew were thoroughly accustomed to the motion and the speed, and anything less than six knots was thought of as almost hove to.

Some may wonder how we could be on a broad reach, sailing due east, with the wind in the southwest. But *Outward Leg* is so fast on any kind of reach that she continually puts the wind ahead of her, a bit like the wind you feel when riding a motorcycle on a calm day. This is one of the problems still to be solved: how to adjust the wind vane automatically so that it takes into account the wind shift caused by the vessel's foward speed. I'm working on that one now and may have a good answer before much longer.

During the leg from Newport to the Azores, three whales were sighted. Pat and Terry saw only one. The one they saw leaped out of the sea, all hundred and fifty tons of him—he was a bowhead—just as they finished sewing the last of the torn mainsail seams. He was only fifty yards or so away, and came right out clear of the water directly ahead of the boat. It was an exciting but, at the same time, worrying sight. He was there, and in the twinkling of an eye, with an almighty splash, he was gone, leaving behind him a mere trace of phosphorescence in the green Atlantic water. He didn't seem to be at all curious about us; he was too intent on chasing something else. But the curious one—well, we'll come to that later.

All the passage long, a boil had been developing on Pat's stomach. He had tried penicillin tablets and injections, but it persisted in bothering him right up until our arrival at Horta. This curtailed his activity somewhat, and we wound up in the situation where I, as the prospective patient, advised and watched the prospective nurse treat himself. But it was all in good humor, of course.

Meanwhile, Terry came up with better and better meals in all weathers. It amazed me now he took to seafaring, with no previous experience. I guess it must be his Norwegian blood. He shows no sign of fear, even in the strongest blows, but just plods on doing his job or keeping his watch. He was a bit slow at first to get the hang of the ropes and rigging, and the idea of apparent wind, but he progresses daily. By the time the voyage is over he should make anyone a good crew for a passage practically anywhere. Both Pat and Terry are Reaganites, so, me being an old-fashioned British Whig, politics were a forbidden subject while on passage (or anywhere else, come to that). Terry's biggest asset is his ability to make friends with just about anyone and keep them entertained. This is very handy indeed when we arrive in a port and a dozen sailors turn up at the boat for a chat. It means I can get over the necessary greetings and then leave them to Terry, who can tell them all they need to know about the boat and the voyage.

Broadside on to heavy seas is unpleasant in any sailing vessel, but in *Outward Leg* it was not unbearable. She slid down a few seas sideways, and of course the variation in wind speed, as she rose to the tops of seas and then descended into the troughs, made her forward movement a bit jerky, but there is, as far as I can tell, no way of avoiding that and at the same time holding the course. These seas were well over twenty feet, and rearing over the top of the masthead at times.

We streamed a fishing troll every morning and evening on the transatlantic leg, but caught nothing. Six times the lure, a chrome spoon, was taken and six times the nylon line, breaking strain eighty pounds, was snapped. They must have been big, hungry buggers. The main problem with catching fish was, of course, our speed.

Another problem, in any vessel, is getting the wind vane to steer in light winds. In *Outward Leg,* when running directly before the wind, I discovered a method that worked most of the time but still needed a helping hand about every thirty minutes: Put the wind vane so it faces almost directly forward, as if you were going to beat at twenty degrees off the wind. Then, when the spool on the wheel is hard over, engage the wheel. I've no idea how it works, but it does, and will keep the boat on course until the Aries gets a headache and decides it needs human contact.

Three days out of Horta, we found—an easterly wind. This is about as frequent an occurrence as me being decked out by Pierre Cardin and, I can tell you, I cursed. I out-Chaucered Chaucer. I cursed in seven different languages, but to myself, as American humor is different from mine and the lads wouldn't have understood anyway. In any case, Pat was newly married and I didn't want to put certain ideas into his head but, my God, I cursed. We were only ten days out from Newport, and if the wind had held up in the west at gale force we could have completed the whole two thousand miles in just over thirteen days. As it was, beating this way and that, with first Flores, then Faial, islands in sight, it took another two and a half days to get into the port of Horta. But fifteen days wasn't bad, not for a one-legged crock, a seminovice and a monohuller.

I can't say that I felt anything especially different upon our fetching Horta, except that the harbor was far more crowded now than it had been the last time I was there, in *Barbara* in 1969. Then we had been the only yacht in the place, and the whole town, from the mayor down, had turned up at the jetty to stare in wonder at our twenty-eight-day passage from Bermuda. Now there were—I counted them—sixty-four yachts from eight different countries, either at anchor, at moorings, or alongside the now extended jetties. The crew were both excited, because to them the Azores was part of "Uurop," while to me it was only a sort of halfway house between Newport and England, where the brewery company berth was waiting. The distance sailed was 2,063 miles.

Don't misunderstand me. I'm not complaining about the increase in yacht presence in Horta. On the contrary, it is a very good thing. It means that now there are good facilities there, and all sorts of very necessary gear—even butane gas and long-life milk—can be obtained; the people are much more aware of sailors' needs and services are fifty times better, and the youngsters seem much brighter, much more well informed, than their parents did years ago. Now, still, there are no harbor fees. Only a one-dollar entry fee is charged by the navy. But a new marina, to hold a hundred yachts, is being built inside the harbor, and then the fees will be much, much more. Which is fair enough, I suppose. Someone has to pay for all the work.

The first thing that Pat did in Horta was to take the ship's papers along to the harbormaster. He was soon back with no problems. Then he went to the post office to pick up mail. There a thunderbolt struck him. A cable said his mother had sustained a heart attack and was seriously ill. Would I mind if he left us? Of course I did, but I said certainly not, and the next day Pat was off by plane back home. I was sorry to lose him. He had been good company and a good mate.

I was quite prepared, now, to make the leg to England with only Terry on board, as we both could handle the working sail single-handed without leaving the cockpit, but fate intervened. Martin Shaw, twenty-eight, turned up, having arrived from Florida in the sloop *Southern Comfort*, bound for South Africa by way of Gibraltar.

Martin had an unusual story to tell. He had been part owner of the forty-six-foot ketch monohull *Jullanar of Essex*, which he had helped to build. She was a concrete vessel and, together with five companions, Martin had sailed from Maldon, Essex, England, in 1981, bound out on a circumnavigation of the world. They had sailed down the length of the Atlantic Ocean and rounded from the Cape of Good Hope, but disaster struck in the Indian Ocean. *Jullanar* had been making her way north to the Seychelles Islands in bad weather, with overcast skies. There was no chance, for two days or so, of celestial sights, and the Indian Ocean currents are notorious for both strength and sudden changes of direction. One night they found themselves slammed down onto the reef of the coral island of Astove. There a valiant attempt had been made by the male crewmen to kedge the vessel off the reef by dragging her right over it to the calm water beyond, but the dinghy, with Martin and two anchors in it, had capsized, and he had been very lucky to survive the risk of being dragged to his death by the anchor chain.

Once ashore from the stranded vessel, Martin and his companions searched the island and found seven locals living there. They stayed with the locals for two and a half months until they were picked up by a Seychelles-based supply vessel. Meanwhile, they salvaged what they could from the wreck of *Jullanar,* for sale in the main island of Mahé.

From Mahé, Martin had hitched working lifts on a Colin Archer ketch to the West Indies and Fort Lauderdale, and now, at Horta, he was working his way to Gibraltar, there to try to earn his way delivering boats across the ocean. I admired his pluck. It was obvious that his present skipper thought the world of him, and that his crewmates liked him. I took him on as soon as he asked for a berth in *Outward Leg* and soon knew that I had encountered one of those very rare diamonds—a born sailor.

Before he had left England, Martin had been an engineer, so his mechanical bent is employed to the full in *Outward Leg,* putting all the little odds and ends that were not quite right when she sailed from San Diego. As soon as Martin started work on board I knew that the old synchronistic destiny was at work again. What better mate than he to help me see *Outward Leg* safely over and through Europe and back again to the oceans? I found that he and I had dogged each other's footsteps from the Windward Islands north, and all the time we had both been making for the same port of call: Horta, the steppingstone for England.

We were soon at it, Martin, Terry and I, checking out all the gear and buying the needed fresh stores for the twelve-hundred-mile passage to Falmouth in Cornwall, at the southwestern tip of England. It wasn't easy with the sparse cash I had, and by the time we had finished—getting the butane bottles filled (honestly filled this time) and buying fresh grub—I was down to twenty dollars. From Falmouth up the Channel I would have to draw on a London bank account, where lay my carefully hoarded naval pension for five months past—all £300 of it

But before we left Horta—in fact, soon after we arrived—I went to call on my friends at the Café Sport. Peter, the present owner, remembered me from his teens; his father, Dom Enrique, and I were great friends and used to go horseback riding round the island. There are few horses now in Horta but Peter arranged with his niece, a schoolteacher, to drive us right round the island in her car, so that we could enjoy the sight of miles of hydrangeas on the hedges, the mists around the peak of the central volcano, and the stark, terrible beauty of the ravaged land where the earthquake of 1952 almost destroyed a third of the island of Faial.

In the Azores, it seems, while a few racing trimarans call from time to time, a cruising trimaran is an unusual sight. This, I believe, is because up to now their weight-carrying ability has been severely re-

stricted, and so people have been nervous about crossing oceans in vessels where the ability to tote enough food, water and fuel, has been in
doubt.

In Horta I was shown two "tales of the sea." One was a small sloop
arrested for carrying the drug *ganja* from Ghana for delivery to Horta.
The villain's Ghanaian friends had shopped him to the Portuguese police, but he had escaped from custody and was now hiding out on the
island. The other was a small steel sloop, which had been sighted adrift
a hundred miles or so southwest of Faial a few weeks previously. Inside
it was found the decomposing body of her lone skipper-owner who had
simply run out of wind, fresh water and food on his way over to Faial
from Bermuda. His log indicated that he had been at sea for sixty days.
After his death (pray God it was gentle!) the boat had remained afloat,
her sails tattered by various gales and storms, for almost four months,
while all the while she drifted in the ocean currents closer and closer
to Faial, her dead skipper's destination. Which goes to show two things,
I feel, without wishing to be disrespectful to the dead: Most of our boats
are far tougher than we are, and it is risky to sail the oceans in small,
heavy boats, with not enough food and water on board to absolutely
ensure a completed passage. It confirms what I have been trying to prove:
that not only are swift passages necessary, they are also possible for all,
without undue risks.

We sailed from Horta on the eleventh of August, after a stay of only
five days. I would have liked to stay longer, but I'd very little money
with me, and to get it transferred there would take more than was in
Lloyd's Bank, Falmouth, and so that is where I headed. Besides, I'd
promised the brewery company I'd reach London at high tide on the
thirty-first.

The first twelve hours were spent beating against a northerly wind
so as to get out of the irons between the islands of Faial and Pico. Then
the wind suddenly shifted to southwest during the night, and we kept
it there for practically all the leg to Falmouth. It was a classical passage—1,254 miles in ten and a third days; and that was with three days
of weak winds. Most of the way we were on a quartering run with either
the roller headsail up forward, or the genniker.

On the eighth day out from Horta a gale overtook us from the south-
southwest, with winds up to thirty-five knots. We shortened down a
bit, but not much. I wanted a fast passage as it was now the sixteenth
of August and I had to take into account the possibility of fog or calm
in the Channel, or strong headwinds. That twenty-four hours we covered 167 miles; the next it was 176

The most-remembered untoward incident on the Azores-Falmouth leg was the courting of the boat by an enormous whale. He was gigantic. The first I knew of it was when I heard a loud blast quite close on the port side. I turned my head, and there, only five feet away from the boat in the late forenoon sunshine, was an enormous head with two tiny eyes gazing longingly at the side of the port ama. As I stared, fascinated and aghast at the same time (one flip of his tail and we were goners), he dived and slid right under the boat obliquely and surfaced alongside the starboard ama bow. Each time he surfaced he blew water all over the boat and there was an almost overwhelming fishy tang in the air all around. He carried on his antics, while Martin, as astonished and worried as I, discussed what we should do to discourage the whale. To my mind, it was perfectly obvious that this great innocent of the deep, looking at the white underside of our hulls, thought that here was a female of the species and perhaps her two offspring, and that here was a ready-made family to ease his loneliness. Hardly stopping to think about it, we started the engine. Then Terry banged on the steering wheel for half an hour. The idea was that if this great fond lump had any sense at all, he would figure out that *Outward Leg* was not a prospective mate. Finally, after two hours of, quite frankly, sickening worry while the whale played around the boat, all eighty feet and two hundred tons of him at least, he seemed to get the message and dropped back astern. But it seemed he wasn't quite convinced and he trailed us, forlornly, for another two hours, continually blowing his waterspout about a hundred yards astern. Then, with a tremendous burst of speed, he flashed for one last time under the boat. I reckon he must have been making a good thirty knots and he left behind him a trail of bubbles, very wide, like that a torpedo would leave, only much, much bigger.

We had discussed heaving to, but finally decided that if we did that, the whale might take it as a sign of encouragement, thinking it was a female waiting for him to mount her, and then it would be Davy Jones's locker for all of us, unless we were extremely lucky.

On the nineteenth of August we were becalmed and motored for three whole days at economic speed, until at last on the evening of the twenty-first I sighted the light of the Lizard. It was the first British Isles lighthouse I had sighted for just over twenty years. The Manacles soon passed to port.

At 0200 we tied up alongside the town jetty in Falmouth. We had completed 3,379 miles since Newport; almost 14,000 miles since San Diego. I had made my nineteenth passage of the Atlantic Ocean under sail in a craft less than forty feet long. Terry had made his first. Martin had made his way, under sail, home at last. It was the same for us all.

I felt more weary than elated, after several hours piloting the coast from the Lizard to Falmouth. Yet there was some elation in me. I now *knew* that a heavily loaded trimaran can cross the ocean swiftly and safely. And that means that cargo-carrying long-distance multihull sailing vessels are a distinct probability in the coming years. Then three men will be able to shift a thousand tons a very long way for a fraction of what it now costs.

31

Home—and Dry

Now as I was a-walking down Radcliffe Highway,
A flash-looking packet I chanced for to see,
Of the port that she hailed from I cannot say much,
But by the cut of her jib I first took her for Dutch.
Singing too-ra-la-addie, too-ra-la-addie,
Singing too-ra-la-addie, aye, too-ra-laye-ay!

Her flag was three colours, her masthead was low,
She was round at the corners and bluff at the bow,
From larboard to starboard and so sailed she,
She was sailing at large, she was running free.

She was bowling along with her wind running free,
She clewed up her courses and waited for me,
I fired my bow-chaser, the signal she knew,
She backed her maintopsail and for me she hove to.

I hailed her in English, she answered me clear,
"I'm from the *Black Arrow*, bound to the *Shakespeare*,"
So I wore ship and with a "What do you know?"
I passed her my hawser and took her in tow.

I tipped her my flipper and took her in tow
And yard-arm to yard-arm away we did go,
She then took me up to her lily-white room,
And there all the evening we drank and we spooned.

Soon the evening did pass, boys, I lashed up and stowed,
I gave her five shillings 'fore I left her abode,
But it weren't quite enough, boys, she wanted some more,
She cursed me and called me a son of a whore.

She blazed like a frigate and one me she let fire,
And nothing could stem, boys, that Irish tart's fire,

272

She kicked me and cursed me and stove in my jaw,
And I beat a retreat through her open back door.

I've fought with the Russians, the Prussians also,
I've fought with the Dutch and with Johnny Crapo,
But of all the fine fights that I ever did see,
She beat all the sights of the heathen Chinee.

Now all you young sailors take warning I say,
Take it easy my boys, when you're down that Highway,
Steer clear of them flash gals, on the Highway they dwell,
Or they'll take up your flipper—and you're soon bound to hell!

"Radcliffe Highway." From the terms used ("Johnny Crapo"
meant Frenchman), this originated in the early nineteenth
century. It was a forebitter but became a capstan shanty as the
melody changed through the years. It was very popular in the
windjammers of the mid-1800s. Radcliffe Highway was in
London, just outside the Surrey docks.

In the misty early morning, four hours after our arrival at Falmouth, I
was woken by a voice hollering, "Hey, *Outward Leg!*"

Bleary-eyed, I shoved my head up from my companionway. I was
still too sleep-soaked to say anything.

There was a middle-aged man standing on the jetty, looking down
at me. He wore one of those adjustable caps with long peaks, which are
favored by farmers in Wisconsin and such places. He also wore thin-
rimmed spectacles and a lumber jacket.

"?" I managed a stare of inquiry. Mornings are never my best time.

"Tristan Jones?" he inquired back. I thought he had a Cornish drawl.

"Mum," I replied.

"Waal, as a felluh Amurrican ah jest want to welcome you to li'l ol'
England!" he sang out.

"Gee, thanks, buddy!" I mumbled. Then I hopped back down the
steps, fell back into my berth, and stared at the deckhead for a minute
or so. Then I laughed my head off, softly, until sleep overtook me again.

That was my welcome back to Britain. It could hardly have been
better. It certainly couldn't have been funnier. Later I found that the
American gentleman, bless him, was cruising a yacht he'd bought in
England, and had recently read of some of *Outward Leg's* exploits in the
U.S. journal *Sports Illustrated.*

Falmouth has quite a few things going for it; its safe harbor, a fine
arrival point in the United Kingdom and an ideal departure point for

boats headed south and west; its quaint streets, good beer, fish and chips—genuine and wrapped in newspaper, with lots of vinegar—and Mr. Philip Fox, the local Lloyd's agent, a most hospitable Quaker gentleman. The bookstores are well stocked, too.

Against Falmouth are, for a cripple, its traffic-choked main street, narrow pavements, and public telephones up flights of steps that would be more suitable for an Olympics decathlon gold-medal winner to reach. With the number of yachts visiting the place from abroad and from other regions of the country, it is a mystery to me why there isn't a telephone installed at the public landing jetty. The first thing most sailors who have crossed the ocean, or even the narrow seas, want to do is telephone their relatives or friends (sometimes, I suppose, they are both at the same time) and tell them that they are safe and well.

In my case, after climbing a steep lane, crossing the main street at risk to life and limb, and clambering up about thirty steps beside the town church, I arrived breathless and hot, just in time to overhear a startlingly arrayed young female chirp away for half an hour into the device about someone called Stevie Wonder, whoever that is. By the time I'd called various people to let them know that *Outward Leg* was safe, home and dry (and spent about ten pounds doing it), I was only too ready and willing to stumble back down to the jetty and the boat and take refuge. There I stayed, until Philip Fox turned up and took the crew and me for lunch at the Norway Inn, a pretty little pub inland. He also arranged to write a letter on my behalf to the Bulgarian ambassador in London, a friend of his. That should come in useful on the next leg of the voyage.

I had telephoned my good friend Wally Herbert, the polar explorer, at his cottage in Devon, but Wally was tied up for a day or two. Could I call at Dartmouth, near his home? It would save him from driving for several hours. It was on our way up-Channel, too. After Terry had visited the local castle, just like a tourist, with a camera draped around his neck, we took off. People from republics, and especially Americans, are, it seems, always fascinated—you could say almost in love with—all the old litter of the feudal system that they struggled so hard to get rid of in past times. There was no fort, no castle, no country mansion, all the way along the English shore, that Terry did not stare at until the last morsel of the structure faded away astern out of sight. Even in thick fogs he stayed glued to the glasses, gazing at some ghostly pile almost completely hidden in the swirling mists.

The Channel winds outside Falmouth had gone on strike. There must have been too many Frenchmen out on holiday, so we motored up to Dartmouth, where the Royal Naval Sailing Association had arranged a berth for me just below the Royal Naval College. Despite the fact that we were guests at this place, and that the college pays Dartmouth Harbour Board £1,500 a year for berthing and slipping rights, we were charged by the harbor board for our berth. There was no one except the boatman to protest to—the whole college was on leave—and he told me, "The harbor bottom and the foreshore belongs to the Duke of Cornwall, so he can charge whatever he likes."

I told Terry he didn't need to go tramping over castles to find the relics of the feudal system. All he had to do was see the harbor master's launch chug alongside, like a paddling vulture, every vessel that so much as poked her bows into any water within a few miles of Dartmouth. When you're down to a few quid in all the world and this kind of thing happens, this highway brigandage, it's very easy to feel complete sympathy for striking miners and dockers. For me it would be easy, anyway.

After coughing up my contribution to the Prince of Wales's family education fund, as the weather was fine, we decided to go for a spin inland up the River Dart. It was pleasant, after so much ocean, to see peaceful moorings (even though we knew they were exorbitantly expensive) and Hereford cows grazing in the green, green fields. Cheeky cub scouts in canoes shouted out to us, on seeing Old Glory fluttering astern, "Eh, mate, you're going the wrong way. America's down there!" They pointed downstream.

It took us only an hour or so to arrive in Totnes, a sleepy little town at the headwaters of the Dart—or at least at the ocean boat's headwaters. I thought it would be nice for Martin to take a photo of *Outward Leg* from the village green. I backed the boat up to the town jetty; Martin, his camera slung around his neck, jumped for the jetty . . . missed and in he went, straight into the river. Terry scrambled to rescue him from deck. Martin, spluttering and trying his best to be very British and laugh the whole thing off, wetly crawled over the stern.

Ashore the townsmen and tourists were all looking on, at first with curiosity, it seemed—it can't be every day that a full-blown ocean-sailing vessel visits Totnes—and then, as Martin fell in, with consternation, then amusement. By the time the mate dragged himself, sopping wet, over the stern they were mostly laughing.

Martin now looked very sorry for himself. His camera was ruined.

I thumbed at the flag fluttering astern. "It's all right, mate," said I, "they'll think we're American!"

That made us all feel much better.

We made our way back downstream with the tide, and tied up again at the college berth, astern of the new Royal Navy tail-training yacht *Samuel Pepys*. I recalled the time when I saw the original *Samuel Pepys*, which had been captured from the Nazi navy at the end of World War II, in Bermuda in 1948, when ocean-crossing small craft were rare indeed.

That evening Wally Herbert, who in 1970, along with his mate, Alan Gill, was the first man ever to walk across the Arctic, came on board with his wife. There we discussed my plans for the near future, and Wally set to arranging to visit us in London. He also offered to replace Martin's camera with one of his own. I accepted.

Outward Leg sailed out of Dartmouth in the blackness of midnight so I could get the maximum value for the outrageous harbor fees by outstaring the two or three winking buoys in the offing and carried on up the Channel. There was not enough wind to blow out a candle, and by dawn a thick fog smothered everything but the noise of large ships rumbling past in the offing. It's one of the world's busiest shipping lanes, and not the ideal place to be in a thick fog. Although Terry had been in the misty fogs off the Grand Banks, he had experienced nothing like a thick Channel pea-souper. He woke me from my snooze in the early dawn, almost scared out of his wits. It was the first time I had ever seen him anything but calm, cool and collected. There, only yards away, dead ahead, in the gray wall all around us, were two bright lights and a green one over them. I dived for the wheel and swung it over hard to port. We missed the fishing trawler by a foot or so. It was the closest call I'd ever had in a fog.

I'd kept a careful dead reckoning all night so that we should not miss Portland Bill on our way into Weymouth. I had no log, only a very guess-y way of reckoning our speed, and the Channel tidal streams are playful, to say the least. As it was we were swept well past the Bill, and to the south of it, in the fog, but we made our way into port from the sound of the bell buoys. I managed, somehow, to pick up the harbor entrance in visibility of about ten yards. Of course, as soon as we got ourselves into the narrow harbor, the fog lifted and the sun came out, so the early-morning risers in the other craft moored alongside could not have any idea of our achievement of feeling our way in such conditions, like a blind man in a dark train, from Dartmouth to Weymouth. And all this in mid-August!

The crew expressed some criticism of this kind of weather, but I said that anything that keeps the French away from Britain is welcome, to me anyway.

The harbor master at Weymouth had arranged an alongside berth for me, tied up to the sail-training vessel *Sir Winston Churchill.* It was not easy clambering over her sides and decks to get ashore, but it was better than having, otherwise, to clamber slippery ladders as the tide receded. In Weymouth we were charged double the rate for monohullers and this despite the fact that *Outward Leg* is not as broad in the beam as some of the older sailing vessels in port, which were paying only half the rate per foot.

There is a danger here that unless the berthing fees are closely looked into, people will be paying a tax on being handicapped. The multihull vessel is without doubt the best, most convenient form of small craft for the handicapped and for elderly people.

Other than the hardly hidden resentment against multihulls entering the port, Weymouth is a good stopover. The Royal Dorset Yacht Club made us welcome and there are hot showers there. Shopping for food and other bits and pieces is convenient, for the yacht berths are right in the middle of town. In fact, you could say that the visiting yachts—up to three hundred of them—*are* the middle of town. Travel is easy, because a railway train wends its way right along the street jetty and connects with the main railway system.

Martin and I were having a pint in the yacht-club bar (downstairs for visitors, upstairs for members). A big man, jolly and bedecked with gold rings, along with his wife, engaged us in general conversation. He told us about his first voyage to France, which he'd just completed in his new thirty-footer (equipped with radar!). Suddenly he leaned over and said to me, in a confidential tone, "Do you know who you remind me of?"

"Who's that, mate?" I murmured in reply. I felt tired.

"Tristan Jones."

"Who the hell is that?" I asked, brightening up. Martin was grinning like a Cheshire cat.

"This Welsh bloke—" and he went on to praise "this Welsh bloke" in the most glowing terms in a thick Birmingham accent, while I lied and maintained stoutly that I'd never heard of him. Then Brummie's wife chimed in; "'E's never been int'rested in boats before 'e read that Welsh bloke, what's 'is name, an' now 'e can't keep away from 'em!" After about twenty minutes of this, Martin let the cat out of the bag. The Brummie wouldn't believe him until I showed him my RNSA card.

Then the big man and his wife almost collapsed with astonishment, while Martin and I called out cherry good-nights to all, and I wended my hobbly way over *Sir Winston Churchill,* back to *Outward Leg.* That was all the acclaim, all the acknowledgment, I need.

The next day was more fog. But we had to push on up the Channel so that I could keep my word to the brewery company and arrive at high tide on the thirty-first in London. The prize was precious to me— a free berth for two weeks! Somehow we made our way in the shifting tidal streams thirty-one miles to where the Needles rocks, on the western end of the Isle of Wight, sprang out of the fog slap-bang on our nose, only three hundred yards away. From there on it was buoy to buoy up the Solent, with the fog, now that navigation was easier, of course, lifting. I had intended to go direct to the RNSA mooring at Cowes. Money was in very short supply on board and it was Bank Holiday so everything, including the banks, was closed. Everything except the pubs and restaurants, that is. Instead, we headed for the River Hamble, a yachting center on the Hampshire coast.

No sooner had we passed the first buoy at the mouth of the river than a fast motor launch pulled alongside. In it was an elderly gentleman with what used to be called an Oxford accent. He hailed us:

"I say, where are you going, old chap?"

"Up the River Hamble. I thought I might find a spot to lay alongside for an hour or so, for lunch—or we'll go to anchor—"

The elderly head shook automatically. "Quite out of the question, old chap. You're far too *wide!*"

I thought I'd appeal to his humanity. "We've just come from the States and this is my first visit in a boat for twenty years—"

The English head shook again, the English lips pursed as only English lips can. The blue English eyes stared down at the bottom of the fast launch. "Can't help that," he said, and repeated, "You're far too *wide!*"

"Can we buy fuel here?" I asked him.

The head perked up. The eyes gleamed. A nation of shopkeepers, Napoleon called them. "Oh, yes, old chap, by all means. Just head for the sign. You may have to wait for your turn, of course—but that's all right—"

And so we did. We were "too wide" to berth alongside for an hour to rest and lunch in peace and quiet. We were "too wide" to anchor in the trot—but we were not too wide to go alongside to spend money on fuel, or to manuever our "too wide" vessel in the channel by the fuel dock for an hour while we waited to go alongside.

This is the kind of thing that makes visiting yachtsmen from abroad absolutely furious. This hypocritical attitude that you are not "allowed" because of some obviously cock-and-bull reason—until you show that you intend to spend money. Why not be honest, as the majority of marina owners are in the States, and say, "If you ain't spending, get the hell out!"

As it turned out, we motored the whole way up the River Hamble, right to the headwaters bridge, turned round, ate lunch under way, steered carefully, slowly, disturbed no one, except those who obviously enjoyed watching a most unusual oceangoing vessel pass by, fueled up to the tune of fifteen quid, and passed several vessels wider than *Outward Leg.*

On the way we renamed the river "Humble." In an hour and a half, with a good westerly breeze, we had crossed the Solent, passed by all the waterfront restaurants and yacht clubs of West Cowes, and their "helicopter-set" clientele sitting outside, and passed by the ferry, to the RNSA mooring buoys in front of the hovercraft depot in East Cowes. There we spent the Bank Holiday evening, resting and reading while around us yet another fog twirled its tendrils.

Under the pressure of my promise to the brewery company, the prize a free berth, we took off again next day, on the tide, into a thinning fog. On the way out of Cowes we were chased, then hailed, by a police boat. I wondered what we had done to break the law, but it was instead a pleasant surprise. The sergeant wanted to come on board *Outward Leg* and chat with us for a few miles, until his mates caught up with us again. He seemed amazed that no one knew of our coming, but I told him that suited me very well. As the fog cleared, we sat in the cockpit and yarned over cups of hot tea until it was time for him to leave us, and for us to hoist sail in the rising westerly breeze.

At midnight we entered Brighton marina. The haven is a completely artificial one, and a great engineering feat, but as it is built out on the sandbanks, it means that there is a heavy swell at the entrance. For us it's not too bad, but smaller craft must find it very uncomfortable getting in and out of Brighton.

As we slid through the narrow port entrance, between the steady green and red lights, I thought of the last time I had been in Brighton, in *Cresswell.* Then I had tied up to the end of the pier, gone across the road with old Nelson, my dog, and bought five pounds of spuds at Woolworth's. All without being charged a penny for berthing or entering—I'd come from Holland direct—and without being challenged by any nosy Parkers. Of course, there was no marina in those days. "Marina" was the kind of name, then, used by the sort of ladies who walked the streets of Kensington with their little dogs in the late afternoon. I suppose it means about the same kind of thing now, too.

I was surprised and delighted to see, berthed in Brighton marina, H.M.S. *Cavalier,* an old C-class destroyer from World War II. I had served (and by God, *served* is the word!) in her sister ship *Cavendish.* I was somehow touched to know that the destroyer lads are not forgotten. I would have liked to go aboard her, but although she was only a hundred yards away over the water, she was much, much farther around the piers, and as my stump was red raw I had to give it a miss. Staring at *Cavalier* brought back a veritable Niagara of memories to me, and I wondered where all my old mates were, those who were still alive.

Euan Cameron, my editor from The Bodley Head, came to see us in Brighton and, after affording us a much-needed lunch, sailed with us as far as Folkestone, where we awaited the turn of the tide. Folkestone is very handy for that. It's an easy anchorage, protected from the west, but the big ferries charging in and out on their way to and from France kick up quite a maelstrom, and we had to be careful they missed us. In the misty rain, Folkestone looked depressing, but I suppose that's how it should look to anyone bound from France, and serve them right, too.

The next leg was up the coast, quite close to the white cliffs, past Dover in a howling gale (I had to keep my record with the brewery company, remember) on a dead run, round the Foreland, to anchor off Westgate, just west of Margate (where else?) in twenty feet of very soupy Thames esturial water. I remember how many times I had been to anchor here before, almost in this very spot, with the church bearing due south, in the old *Second Apprentice* almost half a century ago. Around the English Channel and up the Thames it's a case of hopping from haven to haven, to await the turn of the tide, and ride with it. A bit like resting on the floors of a department store in between rides on the escalator.

A journalist and a photographer joined us at Westgate from a harbor launch, which in the fresh southwest wind and chop almost stove in our sides. They got in the way and ate our food and drank our tea all the way to the Isle of Sheppey, where we anchored to await a flood tide, and then to St. Katharine's Dock, hard by Tower Bridge, London.

There was no fuss, no palaver, no lurking photographers, no one to welcome us as *Outward Leg* slid in through the lock gates and so to her berth at 4:30 P.M. on August 31. I was told later that the brewery-company people had showed up at noon but by 3 P.M. had become discouraged. After all, it *was* Friday and with the weekend coming up—who could blame them? I had told them *six weeks* and four thousand miles earlier that we would arrive at high tide on the thirty-first of August. Not one of them had the wits to stroll to the lock gates and see the state of the tide—anyway, they had far more important things to do than wait for some irascible old crock to drift upriver in a funny-looking boat. After all, it was the weekend—so it looks like no free berth.

By the reckoning, *Outward Leg* had sailed 14,800 miles from San Diego and I'd already decided where I would plant my little tree in London. We tied up and I reached for the atlas for the map of Europe—but that's another story.

Epilogue

When first I sailed to London,
I went upon a spree,
My hard earned cash I spent it fast,
Got drunk as drunk could be.
Before my money was all gone,
Or spent with some old whore,
I was fully inclined, made up my mind,
To go to sea no more! No more, no more, no more!
There goes Jack Spratt, poor sailor boy,
Who'll go to sea no more!

Come all you bully sailormen and listen to my song,
I hope that you will listen while I tell you what went wrong,
Take my advice, don't drink strong rum,
Nor go sleeping with a whore,
But just get spliced, that's my advice, and go to sea no more!

From "Go to Sea No More." Also known as "Shanghai
Brown." A forebitter (nonworking song), late nineteenth
century. The name of the port was changed at will.

Acknowledgments

Companies, societies and individuals who have aided Operation Star and the voyage of *Outward Leg* to 10 September 1984.

Companies

H. & S. Bluewater Multihulls, Inc., California, vessel's hull and part rig.

Brookes and Adams, Ltd., Birmingham, England, deck and rigging parts.

Davey and Co., London, lamps.

Yanmar Diesel Engine Co. Ltd., Japan, who sold us the finest propulsion unit I have ever known in a small craft, their 3 GMC "Saildrive" model. It gave no problems at all between San Diego and London.

Aries Marine Vane Gears, Ltd., Cowes, England, discount on wind-vane gear.

Eden Foods, twenty-four meals.

Edward and Son, USA, twelve meals.

Fantastic Foods, USA, twelve meals.

Urika Foods, Canada, one hundred and twenty meals.

Pacific Marine Supplies, San Diego, California, discount on hardware.

Tai-ping Foundation, Weatherfax weather-forecast machine.

R.E.C. Inc., California, electric light fittings.

Walder and Cie, France, main boom preventer.

Yachting Tableware, Inc., New Jersey, galley ware.

Individuals and Societies

Ralph Cadman, San Diego, sign writing.

John Ciscowsky, carpenter's labor, San Diego.

Rich Garner, carpenter's labor, San Diego.

Leo Surtees, yacht designer, many hours of hard labor.

Anne Lisa Gerbault, Switzerland, chronometer.

Glen Elia, Philadelphia, therapist's advice.

Richard Curtis, New York, literary agent.

Russel Gurnee, Puerto Rico, financial loan to aid transatlantic leg.

Jesús Montoya, Santa Marta, Colombia, anchor.

Henry Wagner, Sailor's Bookshelf, New Jersey, help and promotion.

Joe Gribbins, editor, *Nautical Quarterly*, New York, advice and labor.

Café Sport, Horta, Azores, help, encouragement, and transport.
Ivan Buenza González, crew member, November 1983–June 1984, *loyalty*.
Terry Johansen, New York, crew member, July 1984–, hard work and long hours.
Martin Shaw, Essex, England, crew member, August 1984–, hard work.
Wally Herbert, explorer, England, moral support and help with berths.
Bernard Moitessier, Pacific Ocean, moral support and digestive advice.
Larry and Lin Pardy, ornamental leg and moral support.
Charles Groesbeek, Colorado, small loan to help in Colombia.
Abner Stein, literary agent, London, patience and diligence.
Euan Cameron, editor, The Bodley Head, London, help with communications.
Peter Drew, developer, St. Katherine's Dock, London, discount on berth.
J. D. Sleightholme, editor, *Yachting Monthly*, London, amusing letters.
Richard North, journalist, London, added notoriety, reminiscences.
Major Peter Thompson, Royal Marines, moral support.
Lt.-Col. Peter Thomas, Royal Marines (Rtd.), help with moorings and berths.
Lt.-Col. John Blashford-Snell, Royal Engineers, Operation Raleigh, moral support.
British brewery company (which shall be nameless), three T-shirts, three cases of beer
  and the unfruitful prospect of a London berth, which led me to fetch London on
  time.
Mr. Philip Fox, Falmouth, warm hospitality, a good meal and help with Bulgarian of-
  ficials.
Many readers throughout the world who wrote encouraging letters.
Marie Roy, Explorer's Club, New York, help and advice.
Peter Coles, Adlard Coles and Son, Publishers, England, promotion.
The owner, Deven Black, and staff of the New Star pub, New York, for taking messages
  and general assistance.
Malcolm Jones, owner, Yacht Club, St. Katharine's Dock, London, help with messages
  and phone calls.